THE ECONOMICS OF HEALTH CARE

The Authors

Alistair McGuire is a Research Fellow at the Social-Legal Centre, Pembroke College, Oxford. He has worked in the areas of regional and energy economics as well as in the area of health care economics, and has acted as a consultant for the World Health Organization. He is co-editor with Gavin Mooney of *Resource Allocation and Medical Ethics in Health Care* (Oxford University Press, 1987).

John Henderson is a Research Fellow at the Health Economics Research Unit, Department of Community Medicine, University of Aberdeen. His research interests include the economics of health and prevention, and investments appraisal in the NHS. He is co-author with David Cohen of *Health, Prevention and Economics* (Oxford University Press, forthcoming).

Gavin Mooney is Professor of Health Economics at the Institute of Social Medicine, University of Copenhagen. He was Director of the Health Economics Research Unit, University of Aberdeen, from 1977 to 1985. He has worked as an Economic Adviser in the Department of the Environment (1969–72) and the Department of Health and Social Security (1972–4), and has acted as a consultant to the World Health Organization, the DHSS and the University of Limburg. His publications include *The Valuation of Human Life* (Macmillan, 1977) and, with E. M. Russell and R. D. Weir, *Choices for Health Care* (Macmillan, 1986).

THE ECONOMICS OF HEALTH CARE

An Introductory text

Alistair McGuire, John Henderson
and Gavin Mooney

Routledge & Kegan Paul
London and New York

First published in 1988 by
Routledge & Kegan Paul Ltd
11 New Fetter Lane, London EC4P 4EE

Published in the USA by
Routledge & Kegan Paul Inc.
in association with Methuen Inc.
29 West 35th Street, New York, NY 10001

Set in Times Roman
by Hope Services, Abingdon
and Printed in Great Britain
by Richard Clay Ltd
Bungay, Suffolk

Library of Congress Cataloging in Publication Data
McGuire, Alastair.
The economics of health care.
Bibliography: p.
Includes index.
1. Medical economics. 2. Medical care—Cost
effectiveness. I. Henderson, John, 1957–
II. Mooney, Gavin H. III. Title. [DNLM: 1. Delivery
of Health Care—economics. W 74 M478e]
RA410.M39   1987   338.4'73621   87–13105

British Library CIP Data also available
ISBN 0–7102–0989–4 (c)
      0–7102–1300–X (p)

Contents

Contents

Preface

This textbook on the economics of health care is founded upon the lecture course which the authors have given for a number of years at the University of Aberdeen. As Kuhn (1962, p. 1) has stated in the introduction to a book with a somewhat different intention, the aim of all textbooks is 'persuasive and pedagogic; a concept of science drawn from them is no more likely to fit the enterprise that produced them than an image of a national culture drawn from a tourist brochure or a language text'. In the difficult transformation from a series of lectures into a text we hope we remain persuasive in our argument that the action of choice over consumption patterns in the health care sector is modified to a sufficient degree that it warrants explicit attention.

As a pedagogic aid the book was written primarily as an introduction to health care economics for undergraduate and postgraduate economics students. However, we have attempted to structure the text in such a manner that a motivated reader interested in the topic will also gain an understanding of some of the more specialist literature. To this end we have started with the more approachable (and to some degree more practical) subject matter and built up to the more complex literature. Although the text is not presented in sections it is none the less true that the first three chapters may be considered as an introduction to the subject; chapters 4 to 6 cover economic evaluation in the health care sector; chapters 7 to 9 examine the literature on the demand for health care; chapters 10 to 12 consider supply issues. The non-economist should be able to cover and experience a positive rate of return on chapters 1 to 6 and 12, even if this requires a little perseverance.

Overall responsibility for the text was taken by Ali McGuire. However, we have collaborated closely in reading, redrafting and criticising each other's material during the entire period of writing. Therefore responsibility for the final product is shared equally.

We have amassed a number of debts in writing this book. Our first acknowledgment must go to Roy Weir who has given tremendous support (as well as showing great restraint on occasion) to the economists who have 'occupied' his Department of Community Medicine for some time now.

A number of friends and colleagues read and commented on various drafts of the text or parts thereof. In particular we wish to thank John Cairns and David Pearce, who provided very helpful advice and criticism. In addition our thanks go to our colleagues in the Health Economics Research Unit who performed a similar task, especially Brian Yule, Linda Oldroyd and Anne Ludbrook, and to the students in Aberdeen who have taken our health economics course. We are also grateful to Rochelle Coutts, Annelise Nielsen and Isabel Tudhope for their patience in typing the various drafts of the book which appeared before them. We must also thank Anita Alban and Anne Keen who provided persistent encouragement throughout.

We have failed to resolve (at least) one technical problem: we have not yet found a gender-neutral pronoun which does not distract the reader's attention. Therefore we have relied upon the second-best, male alternative – he.

Finally we would like to thank the following for permission to use copyright material: Thomas McKeown for Figure 2.1; Michael Jones-Lee for Tables 5.2 and 5.3; the *British Medical Association* for Figures 7.1 and 7.2; and Pergamon Press for the use of material in chapters 10 and 11.

1

The economics of health care: an overview

1.1 Introduction

Economic analysis, like the study of the relationship between health and health care, may be pursued at a number of different levels. This book is predominantly concerned with the micro-economic analysis of health care. This introduction attempts to explain the coverage of the text, as well as outlining some definitional concerns.

It may immediately be asked what has economics to do with health care in any case? Is not health such a fundamental concern that absolute priority should be given to maintaining and improving it? However, resources are scarce and choices over patterns of allocating resources, therefore, must be made, ideally with recourse to the principle of minimising opportunity costs. Some of these choices inevitably relate to the resources allocated to health care. As health care may be viewed as one of the many inputs into the production of health, such choices will also affect the health of the population. Such choices are problematical, not only because the relationship between health care and health status is not exact but, additionally, there is no widely agreed definition of health.

Often health is defined simply as the lack of illness, but unless illness is itself defined, this is not helpful. There are many different ways of defining illness and each may be related to the different actors supplying the definition. For example, the medical model of illness, as proffered by the medical profession, defines illness in terms of physical and mental disorders. The presence or absence of disease and the stage of its invasiveness dominate such definitions which are pathologically based. Other definitions, however, may be more functionally based. It is possible to define illness in terms of its effects upon the way in which individuals function in their daily lives. For example, emphasis would be placed upon the amount of pain suffered or the degree to which individuals are restricted in undertaking normal activities.

The difficulty in defining health is reflected in the relationship between health care and health status. Thus the maintenance of health may be seen to involve, for many, not just the treatment of disease but also the prevention of disease. On another level it may be argued that the maintenance of health is also linked to the social environment. In this respect health may be linked to, for example, unemployment and wealth.

The broadest definitions of health would appear to accept that anything and everything can affect health status. This immediately presents the economist with the problem of defining the parameters of economic analysis relating to health. To the political economist the widest possible approach would be the only acceptable one. Economic issues, for him, must be set against the socio-political background and are analysed only to support social and political policy initiatives. Economics would have no meaning without detailed consideration of the complexities of the real world.

Economics as a social science has moved quite a way from political economy and has tended to concern itself with abstraction, model building and hypothesis testing. Obviously, political economy underlies modern economic analysis as the model building is inevitably based upon explanations of economic behaviour and may lead on to predictions, which in turn may lead to the advocacy of particular economic policies. However, modern economic analysis remains founded upon abstraction and upon a distinction between normative and positive positions, even if such a distinction is sometimes less than clear. An aim of this text is to consider the application of the normal analytical simplifications and abstractions of economics to the health care sector. Given this, it may then be asked: Why the interest in health care? Why not concentrate upon health *per se*? And at what level of aggregation are we operating? Let us address the first two questions. Health has value in use but not value in exchange. A full explanation of this statement is given in chapter 3, but essentially this means that health cannot be traded and, therefore, markets in health do not exist. Health *care* is tradeable. The important distinction is that health cannot be purchased directly while health care can. Certainly the consumption activities of an individual help to produce health, but there is no market in which health itself may be traded directly. Now while a large number of marketable commodities affect health, health care is consumed specifically and singularly because of its relationship with health. Health care is only consumed on the presumption that it has investment benefits in health status. The demand for health care is, therefore, a derived demand based upon the consumer's desire for health which in turn is desirable for the full enjoyment of all other production and consumption activities. It is thus not surprising that society holds health care in an especial esteem.

Moreover there is the added complication that, given the choice, the overwhelming majority of people would not wish to participate in the consumption of most forms of health care. The actual process is not one that is willingly engaged in under normal circumstances. In the consumption of most health care, for rationality to hold, the consumer must be ill and most individuals would prefer not to be. This simple fact has significant consequences for the economic analysis of health care. Of course in considering preventive health care the consumer may not be ill at the time of purchase. However, preventive health care retains some of the characteristics of its curative counterpart, for example, the demand for it remains a derived demand based upon its expected investment benefits with regard to health.

The importance of highlighting health care in this way is that it serves, as Evans (1984) points out, to distinguish it from other commodities. Generally the consumption of other commodities is not primarily related to health status. While the consumption of a vast range of commodities may have important health effects, they are primarily consumed for other reasons. While there are, as we shall see, economic arguments that have been forwarded suggesting that health care is somewhat different from other commodities, it should certainly be appreciated that it is only consumed because of its effects upon health status.

That health is not tradeable is a good starting point for the analysis of health care as an economic commodity. This is not to say that economics cannot contribute to the analysis of consumption or indeed production choices as they affect health. Notable examples of such contributions are the analysis of unemployment as it relates to health and the consideration of health issues in the literature on the economics of pollution. However, the majority of studies in health economics are in practice concerned with health care economics. Given that the industrialised countries, at least, have all seen the establishment of a set of specialised institutions concerned with the production and distribution of health care, this is perhaps not surprising.

Such arguments are also partly responsible for dictating the level of aggregation which dominates most of the economic analysis in this text. Since economics is concerned with choice then it is of interest to examine choice in circumstances where the consumer is ill. Economics assumes normally that the choices which are most consistent with maximising utility are those made under conditions of full information. However, once an illness is contracted it is unlikely that the consumer is going to be willing, even if he is physically able, to start collecting the necessary information to allow an optimising choice to be made. Moreover such informational requirements are likely to be considerable – which is after all the reason for training doctors. The trained doctor not only holds the information required by the consumer but also supplies the treatment. Such considerations obviously affect the basic choices over the form and amount of health care consumed. A large part of the economic analysis of health care discussed in the text is concerned with the implications for choice under such circumstances. In particular, therefore, we shall be concerned with consumer behaviour and the behaviour of producers.

That illness is unpredictable is a fact of life. Added to this is the fact that for a wide range of illnesses the consumer may have little knowledge about treatment and consequently the cost of treatment. Even though health care is a heterogeneous commodity this is generally the case. Therefore, it is not surprising that insurance is sought to cover at least some of the risk of cost bearing. This of course introduces another market into the analysis: the market for health care insurance. Thus health care insurance is demanded because of the risk of incurring health care costs, with health care consumed because of its expected positive effects upon health status. To the extent that insurance is about the pooling and spreading of risks across a number of individuals, then the analysis of health care insurance inevitably moves away from an analysis of individual consumers. Furthermore the form of the insurance system will affect the form in which health care services are supplied, as well as the individual consumer's choices over consumption. Therefore the introduction of the analysis of health care insurance broadens the economic analysis of health care, introducing such questions as whether health care should be privately or publicly financed.

Such considerations cannot be discussed purely on efficiency grounds, however, as distributional aspects are also important. Thus another aspect of the economic analysis of health care has to be the issue of equity as it relates to the distribution of this commodity. Such considerations must be dealt with at both the micro- and macroeconomic level. With regard to the latter, distributional issues will affect the structure and nature of aggregate health care provision. On the other hand, the introduction of equity considerations into an individual's utility function raises questions relating to the assumptions made about individual behaviour.

It will be appreciated then that the text is devoted largely to microeconomic analysis. That this forms the dominant part is attributable to the fact that, once the distinctive relationship between health care and health status is recognised and accepted as a starting point for the economic analysis of health care, analysis of decision-making with respect to health care must begin with a re-examination of the process of choice. As we shall see, choice is affected in such a fundamental manner that pure market solutions to resource allocation problems in this sector become untenable. As such a major concern of the text is with the opportunities available to individual consumers and producers in the decision-making process. It is these opportunities which largely determine variations in behaviour and the institutional responses to market failings which are so important in the health care sector.

1.2 Outline of the text

To some extent the reader will by now have an idea of what to expect by way of content. The structure of the book is discussed below. The fact that health itself cannot be, and much of health care in most countries is not, traded in normal markets is widely recognised. The special nature of the purchase and supply of doctors' services is probably as old as medicine itself, or at least as old as the Hippocratic Oath. This peculiar trading relationship is, we feel, the most distinctive aspect of health economics as a branch of economics and is, therefore, the main theme of this text.

To give some background to our economic analysis chapter 2 discusses the nature of health, the causes of ill-health and their relationship to health care. The measurement of health improvements is also discussed. Taking such measurement as a starting point, chapter 3 analyses health care as an economic commodity. As a basis for this, the chapter begins by considering the axioms of consumer choice under conditions of risk and then proceeds by examining the difficulties in this framework when analysing health care. Not surprisingly then these two chapters are largely concerned with definitional matters.

Chapters 4 to 6 discuss the distribution and evaluation of health care. Although distribution was earlier suggested to be integral to the economic analysis of health care, such issues often receive much less attention than those of production and exchange. Therefore, detailed discussion of distributional considerations is undertaken in chapter 4, where questions of equity are outlined in the context of its relationship to utility maximisation. Other criteria for distribution are also discussed with regard to the most distinctive economic contribution to the evaluation and planning of health care, that is cost-benefit analysis. Why and how it should be used in planning health care are dealt with, at a theoretical level, in chapter 5. Chapter 6 discusses the uses and difficulties which arise in the practice of cost-benefit analysis. These two chapters should be read in conjunction.

Chapters 7, 8 and 9 look at the demand for health and the utilisation of health care. The first of these chapters is concerned particularly with the implications of applying the standard consumer theory to the demand for health. The second emphasises the influence of the supplier in the consumer's choice of consumption patterns. Chapter 9 considers the insurance market and how the supplier's role affects the empirical analysis of consumption.

The implications of the powerful position of the supplier of health care are debated with respect to the choice of production plans in chapters 10 to 12 where the supply side of the health care sector is discussed. The framework used is the industrial economics paradigm which explores structure, conduct and performance relationships. Chapter 10 gives a theoretical overview of the supply of health care, while chapter 11 analyses the hospital sector in detail. Chapter 12 considers some existing health care sectors.

1.3 Analytical framework

As a branch of economics, health economics draws upon a wide cross-section of economic theory. Readers will become aware that the text draws upon the cost-benefit literature, welfare economics and public finance, consumer theory and industrial economics. That health economics is a relative newcomer to the economists' baggage is apparent through an examination of the age of the references on health and health care economics, few of which go back beyond the 1960s. The subject may indeed be grouped with the other 'new' applied economics literature, such as environmental economics and urban economics, which also developed in the post-war period.

Of course the economic analysis of health care is only as solid as the economic theory upon which it draws. In recent years there has been increasing questioning of the foundations of particular aspects of economic theory. For example there is a growing literature on the alternatives to expected utility theory as a means of exploring risk and uncertainty (see Schoemaker, 1982 and Sugden, 1986 for a review), as well as increasing criticism of the pervasiveness of autonomy and rationality in matters of choice (see Sen, 1982 or Simon, 1959). Throughout the text we have attempted to make the reader aware of the restrictions that traditional (neoclassical) economics may place upon analysis of the health care sector. As an alternative, and given that much of the economics of health care is concerned with the institutional responses to market failings, we have sought refuge in the analysis of transactions suggested by Williamson (1975). This is not new, given that one of his former students has already (successfully, we believe) applied this approach to the hospital sector (see Harris, 1977) and the importance of these institutional responses has

7

already been outlined (with considerable insight) by Evans (1984).

These then are the origins of the text and, given that the economic analysis of health care has many avenues to explore this can only be a starting point. We have tried to indicate the main problems to be addressed and some of the conclusions reached to date. The text is primarily aimed at economics undergraduates who are interested in the economics of health care. It should also be useful to postgraduates who wish an introduction to the subject. However, we have attempted to make the text accessible to those who have had little or no formal training in economics. To this end it is structured such that the more complex literature is dealt with in the later chapters. This is not to say that the earlier chapters are any less formal than the later ones; merely that they contain the parts of economic theory which should be more accessible to the lay person. Thus the non-specialist should have few problems of understanding chapters 1 to 6 and also chapter 12. However, chapters 7 to 11 require prior knowledge of microeconomics.

2

Health and health care

2.1 Introduction

Measuring health and the effects of medical interventions upon health are not new. In Mesopotamia around 2000 BC there was in force a law – the code of Hammurabi – governing the payments to be made to, or forfeits to be suffered by, a medical practitioner (Singer and Underwood, 1962, p. 12):

If a physician has treated a nobleman for a severe wound and has cured him or opened an eye-abscess of a nobleman and has cured it, he shall take ten shekels of silver.

If he has treated a nobleman for a severe wound and has caused him to die, or opened an eye-abscess of a nobleman and has caused the loss of the eye, the physician's hands shall be cut off.

If a physician has treated the severe wound of a slave of a poor man and has caused his death, he shall render slave for slave.

If a physician has cured a shattered limb, or has cured a diseased bowel, the patient shall give the doctor five shekels of silver.

It was clearly believed, then, that the saving or destroying of eyesight was the outcome of the surgeon's ability to intervene skilfully.

It has also been appreciated since ancient times that 'Seventy years is the span of our life; eighty if our strength holds' (Psalm 90, verse 10, *New English Bible*, 1970). Life expectancy is today commonly used to describe the health of a population – see Table 2.1, which shows that the life expectancy at birth of males in many

Table 2.1 Life expectancy

OECD countries	Life expectancy at birth (1980)	
	Females	*Males*
Australia	78.0	70.9
Austria	76.1	69.0
Belgium	75.5	69.8
Canada	79.0	71.0
Denmark	77.6	71.4
Finland	77.6	69.2
France	78.3'	70.1
Germany	76.5	69.7
Greece	77.8	73.2
Iceland	80.5	73.6
Ireland	75.0	69.5
Italy	77.4	70.7
Japan	79.2	73.7
Luxembourg	75.1	68.0
Netherlands	79.2	72.5
New Zealand	76.4	69.7
Norway	79.0	72.2
Portugal	75.0	67.0
Spain	78.0	71.5
Sweden	78.9	72.6
Switzerland	79.1	72.4
Turkey	62.3	58.3
United Kingdom	75.9	70.2
United States	76.7	69.6

Source: OECD, 1985.

industrialised countries is around seventy years while for females it is nearer to eighty.

As well as life expectancy, a second fundamental aspect of health is the quality of life. Both are clearly important, and while formal measures that combine the two have been developed only recently, they will undoubtedly prove to be a major advance in evaluation and analysis of health care.

In this chapter we examine the links between economics and the measurement of health and health care, the reasons why health has improved over past centuries, the causes of ill-health today, and what the impact of health care upon health is (section 2.2).

Thereafter the ways in which health improvements can be quantified and valued are discussed (section 2.3). Conclusions are summarised in section 2.4.

2.2 Sources of health improvement

Health care consumes a large proportion of every industrialised country's resources – from 6.2 per cent of GDP in the UK to 10.8 per cent in the USA (OECD, 1985). The extent to which health care improves health is, however, an area where popular belief and scientific evidence diverge. Economic analysis of health care requires scientific knowledge of the technical relationships between inputs and outputs in the improvement of health. Hence health economists must concern themselves with questions of effectiveness – the ability of a drug, treatment or other measure to improve health – as a background to examining efficiency. This chapter aims to provide that background.

An early source of information about health in many countries is parish records of deaths. Such records have long been used for purposes such as monitoring the progress of disease. For example, during the Great Plague in London in 1665 changes in the weekly number of deaths were used to assess the spread of the plague from parish to parish, to attribute to the plague the excess number of deaths over those expected, and also to estimate the success of medical and social measures to control it.

England and Wales were the first countries to register cause of death, beginning in 1838. Combined with data from the decennial census of population, these registrations allowed trends in mortality from particular causes to be monitored. McKeown (1979) has used such data to examine why health has improved. While these data enabled him to measure the decline in death rates since 1841 he argues that the enormous (three-fold) growth in population in England and Wales between 1700 and 1851 shows that the decline in death rates began well before the mid-nineteenth century. His analysis indicates that the main reason for the fall in mortality is the reduction in diseases borne by air, water and food (see Table 2.2). But why did deaths from the infectious diseases decline? McKeown suggests three main reasons. First, better nutrition made people healthier and better able to fight disease with their

Table 2.2 Sources of reduction of mortality, 1848–54 to 1971: England and Wales

		Percentage of reduction
Conditions attributable to micro-organisms		
1 Airborne Disease:		
1.1 Tuberculosis (respiratory)	17.5	
1.2 Bronchitis, pneumonia, influenza	9.9	
1.3 Whooping cough	2.6	
1.4 Measles	2.1	
1.5 Scarlet fever and diphtheria	6.2	
1.6 Smallpox	1.6	
1.7 Infections of ear, pharynx, larynx	0.4	
TOTAL		40
2 Water and food-borne diseases		21
3 Other conditions		13
TOTAL		74
Conditions not attributable to micro-organisms		26
All diseases		100

Source: McKeown (1979).

bodies' own defence mechanisms. The improved nutrition was made possible by increases in food availability *per caput* owing to increased agricultural production from the end of the seventeenth century and by falling birth rates from the nineteenth. Second, better hygiene caused the decline of water- and food-borne diseases, following measures such as improved water supplies and sewage disposal in the nineteenth century, and sterilisation, bottling and safe transport of milk, for example, which reduced diseases such as gastro-enteritis and thus infant mortality, in the early twentieth century. Third, some immunisation and therapeutic measures may have contributed, although not by nearly as much as nutrition and hygiene (see Figure 2.1).

There are some immediate parallels to be drawn here with attempts to improve health in developing countries today. Mc-Keown's analysis suggests that better nutrition, clean water, hygiene, sanitation and family planning may have at least as important a role to play as any medical interventions, and that, of the last, primary health care such as immunisation may be more important than secondary health care, such as hospital in-patient services, in improving the health of the population, as measured in terms of life expectancy.

McKeown's analysis leads him to the conclusion that traditional medical services place too much emphasis on investigation and treatment of illness and too little on prevention and care of the sick (McKeown, 1976, p. 178):

> The immediate determinant of the traditional range of interests is the patient's demand for acute care and the physician's wish to provide it. But the approach rests also on a conceptual model, on the belief that health depends primarily on personal intervention, based on understanding of the structure and function of the body and of the disease processes which affect it.
>
> This concept is not in accord with past experience. The improvement of health during the past three centuries was due essentially to provision of food, protection from hazards, and limitation of numbers; medical science and services made an important contribution to the control of hazards but only a limited one through immunisation and therapy.

A theoretical assessment of the determinants of human health suggests

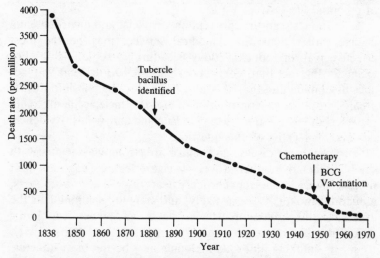

Figure 2.1 Respiratory tuberculosis: mean annual death-rates (standardised to 1901 population): England and Wales
Source: McKeown (1979).

13

that the same influences are likely to be effective in future; but there is this difference, that in developed countries personal behaviour (in relation to diet, exercise, tobacco, alcohol, drugs etc) is now even more important than provision of food and control of hazards.

While McKeown here stresses that such influences are likely to be effective, deciding whether they ought to be promoted involves consideration also of whether they would be efficient. This distinction will be returned to shortly.

Today in the industrialised world the main causes of death are heart disease, stroke, cancer and road accidents. Table 2.3 shows the main causes of death for the USA for men and women and for blacks and whites. For most causes, the death rates are highest for black men followed by white men, followed by black women and are lowest for white women. The differences between blacks and whites may be related to differing income levels.

Expressing the figures in terms of years of potential life lost gives greater emphasis to those causes of death that are most common amongst the younger age groups – i.e. accidents. Tables 2.4 and 2.5 show the causes of the most years of life lost in England and Wales, and the USA, and Figure 2.2 shows these for Canada, where motor vehicle accidents are the single biggest cause of years of potential life lost.

As in the last century, prevention via social and environmental change rather than direct medical services may be the most effective way of reducing today's leading causes of death. For example, the fact that teenagers are allowed to drive at younger ages in Canada and the USA may be, partly, responsible for the greater proportional contribution of motor vehicle accidents to life years lost in these countries than in England and Wales. Evidence, however, is lacking on this question.

Coronary heart disease and cancer are strongly associated with smoking: heavy smokers (over 40 cigarettes per day) are four times as likely to die from coronary heart disease as non-smokers, moderate smokers twice as likely, and stopping smoking cuts the excess risk; 40 per cent of all cancer deaths and 90 per cent of lung cancer deaths are due to cigarette smoking (McCarthy, 1982). Reducing smoking and road accidents may be the most effective ways of reducing life years lost. Although these measures may not be the most efficient, nor most efficiently brought about by medical services.

14

Table 2.3 Age-adjusted death rates for selected causes of death, according to sex: United States, 1980

Male	White	Black
All causes	745.3	1,112.8
Diseases of heart	277.5	327.3
Cerebrovascular diseases	41.9	77.5
Malignant neoplasms:	160.5	229.9
Respiratory system	58.0	82.0
Digestive system	39.8	62.1
Pneumonia and influenza	16.2	28.0
Chronic liver disease and cirrhosis	15.7	30.6
Diabetes mellitus	9.5	17.7
Accidents and adverse effects	62.3	82.0
Motor vehicle accidents	34.8	32.9
Suicide	18.9	11.4
Homicide and legal intervention	10.9	71.9

Female	White	Black
All causes	411.1	631.1
Diseases of heart	134.6	201.1
Cerebrovascular diseases	35.2	61.7
Malignant neoplasms:	107.7	129.7
Respiratory system	18.2	19.5
Digestive system	25.4	35.4
Breast	22.8	23.3
Pneumonia and influenza	9.4	12.7
Chronic liver disease and cirrhosis	7.0	14.4
Diabetes mellitus	8.7	22.1
Accidents and adverse effects	21.4	25.1
Motor vehicle accidents	12.3	8.4
Suicide	5.7	2.4
Homicide and legal intervention	3.2	13.7

Source: National Center for Health Statistics (1983).

Health services are used to a great extent for conditions that are rarely fatal. For example 13 per cent of hospital admissions in England are maternity admissions (OPCS, 1985), and much of a general medical practitioner's workload concerns common conditions such as coughs, colds and other respiratory infections (OPCS/RCGP/DHSS, 1986).

Thus there is much more to improving health than utilisation of

15

Table 2.4 Estimated years of potential life lost before age 85, England and Wales, 1984

Years of potential life lost – thousands – top 10 causes

Males		Females	
Ischaemic heart disease	1,302	Ischaemic heart disease	567
Cancer of trachea, bronchus and lung	398	Cerebrovascular disease	288
Cancer of colon	324	Cancer of breast	239
Cerebrovascular disease	286	Cancer of colon	224
Motor vehicle traffic accidents	170	Cancer of genitourinary organs	173
Other heart disease and hypertension	136	Cancer of trachea, bronchus and lung	151
Cancer of genitourinary organs	129	Other heart disease and hypertension	122
Bronchitis, emphysema and asthma	122	Congenital anomalies	89
Other respiratory diseases	113	Pneumonia	60
Congenital anomalies	112	Other respiratory diseases	58

Source: OPCS (1986).

Table 2.5 Estimated years of potential life lost before age 65, United States, 1984

Cause	Years of potential life lost by persons dying in 1984 (thousands)
All causes	11,761
Unintentional injuries	2,308
Malignant neoplasms	1,803
Diseases of the heart	1,563
Suicide, homicide	1,247
Congenital anomalies	684
Prematurity	470
Sudden infant death syndrome	314
Cerebrovascular diseases	266
Chronic liver diseases and cirrhosis	233
Pneumonia and influenza	163
Chronic obstructive pulmonary diseases	123
Diabetes mellitus	119

Source: MMWR (1986).

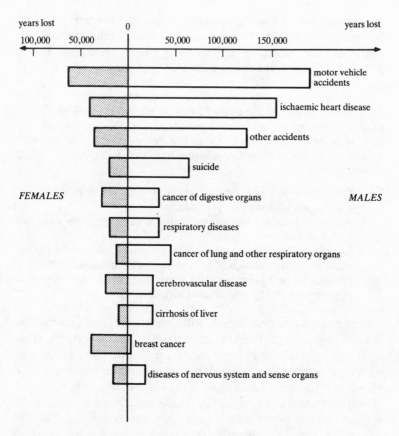

Figure 2.2 Distribution of potential years of life lost between 1 and 70 by major causes, by sex, Canada 1974
Source: Romeder and McWhinnie (1977).

health services. And there is much more to utilising health services than increasing life expectancy.

A related question concerns the effect of any medical intervention, or health service provision upon health. McKeown made his analysis from historical records and argued that health services have had a small impact upon health. A potentially more reliable way of finding out is through scientific comparisons and experiments.

Epidemiology was originally the study of epidemics (hence its name). Now, however, epidemiologists specialise in finding the determinants of ill-health, methods of prevention or amelioration, and in measuring the 'effectiveness' of medical interventions and health service provision in improving health. Alderson (1983, p. xiii) has described the three aims of epidemiology thus:

To describe the distribution and size of disease problems in human populations; to identify aetiological factors in the pathogenesis of disease; to provide the data essential for the management, evaluation and planning of services for the prevention, control and treatment of disease. In order to fulfil these aims, three rather different classes of epidemiological study may be mounted:

(1) Descriptive studies concerned with observing the distribution and progression of disease in populations;
(2) Analytical studies concerned with investigating hypotheses suggested by the descriptive studies;
(3) Experimental or intervention studies concerned with measuring the effect on the population of manipulating environmental influences thought to be harmful, or by introducing in a controlled way preventive, curative and ameliorative services.

Epidemiology is concerned with measuring the quantity of health 'output' of particular interventions or health services. It is, therefore, distinct from, but necessarily related to, efficiency, which is concerned with relating the value of inputs to the quantity of outputs (technical efficiency), or the value of inputs to the value of outputs (social efficiency). Thus studies of efficiency often build upon the results of epidemiological study. Other aspects of health economics also are intrinsically related to epidemiology. For example, studies of the supply of health care, and of health, need measures of output, and modelling the demand for health and health care needs information on how health may be acquired and how it is affected by consumer decisions. Hence for the purposes of pursuing economic analysis in health and health care studies it is necessary to have some basic knowledge of epidemiology, especially of intervention studies and trials.

Epidemiological study of the effectiveness of medical interventions and health service provision uses different methods of comparison, with different levels of reliability. One of the simplest is the 'before and after' study that measures health before the intervention and then again afterwards. The trouble with such studies is that the results may be biased, so that the effectiveness of the intervention may be exaggerated, or understated, because the effect is due to some other factor, such as the body's natural ability to heal itself, a placebo effect, a 'Hawthorne' effect,[1] a natural trend, or other changes that have taken place between the dates when health was measured.

Adding a control group, which is not subjected to the same intervention to compare with those who are, can remove some sources of bias. However, if the controls are selected then it may be impossible to estimate the effects of the intervention with confidence, because the selection process itself may have introduced bias. In particular, if the control group selected themselves, for example, by opting out of the treatment, while people who take more care of their health opted for the treatment, there may be a disproportionate number of less healthy people in the control group.

The best method of selecting controls is by randomly allocating people between the intervention group and the control group. While the problem of the 'Hawthorne' effect may remain unless the subjects themselves and those measuring the effectiveness are unaware of which group any given subject has been allocated to, the process of randomisation does remove most problems of bias. It is then possible to obtain a probabilistic basis for statistical inference about the effectiveness of the intervention, since the probability of the results having happened purely by chance can be calculated.

Randomisation may be considered unethical, however, if there are already reasons to believe that the treatment is better than an alternative, and hence doctors or patients or society may refuse to consent to such an experiment. It is important to be aware of the inferior reliability of non-randomised studies, though, and that the best evidence of the effectiveness of a medical treatment comes from randomised controlled trials (RCTs). Cochrane (1972) lists many treatments that were thought to be beneficial, but which have been shown to be ineffective by RCTs (Cochrane, op. cit., p. 29):

If anyone had any doubts about the need for doing RCTs to evaluate therapy, recent publications using this technique have given ample warning of how dangerous it is to assume that well-established therapies which have not been tested are always effective. Possibly the most striking result is Dr Mather's RCT in Bristol in which hospital treatment

19

(including a variable time in a coronary care unit) was compared with treatment at home for acute ischaemic heart disease (Mather et al., 1971). The results . . . do not suggest that there is any medical gain in admission to hospital with coronary care units compared with treatment at home . . . Dr Elwood (Elwood *et al.*, 1967) . . . has demonstrated very beautifully how ill-founded was the general view of the value of iron in non-pregnant women with haemoglobin levels between 9g and 12g per 100 ml in curing the classical symptoms of anaemia, while Dr Waters (1970) has undermined the widespread belief in the value of ergotamine tartrate in the treatment of newly diagnosed cases of migraine.

Cochrane's book provoked acclaim and discussion when it was published in 1972, but it would take a long time to evaluate all currently dubious therapies using RCTs. In 1983 Hampton, a professor of cardiology, made a similar plea for clinicians to base their practices upon the results of RCTs and consideration of the alternative uses of resources (Hampton, 1983, p. 1237):

"The active management of myocardial infarction" [heart disease] makes a good example (Petch, 1983), though similar topics could doubtless be found in any medical specialty. In theory restoring the blood supply to heart muscle after occlusion of a coronary artery is a highly desirable aim, and there are several ways in which this might be achieved. In practice what we need to know is whether any of the possible treatments saves life or reduces morbidity. Just because one centre has performed coronary artery bypass operations on a small number of highly selected patients with acute infarction (Phillips *et al.*, 1982), and has achieved the remarkably low hospital mortality of 3.8% does not mean that everyone else should attempt to do the same. Those who claim that such results are possible should conduct a randomised trial to compare early operation with conservative management, and until this has been done healthy scepticism is the appropriate attitude.

Modern high technology medical care is clearly as subject to the law of diminishing marginal returns as any other productive process. The health improvements that it brings about are not generally as dramatic as those of some of the public health and primary care measures in previous centuries in industrialised countries, or in parts of the third world today. Thus the efficient use of health care resources increasingly relies upon the measurement of the outcomes of health services.

2.3 The measurement of health improvements

Assessing the effectiveness of health care clearly requires *inter alia* the measurement of health improvement – the difference in health with and without some intervention. This section examines first the quantification of health improvements and second their valuation.

It was suggested earlier that there are two fundamental aspects to health – duration of life and quality of life. Duration of life is fairly readily quantified by measures such as life expectancy. However, quality of life is less easily measured. The World Health Organisation (1961) has defined health as: 'A state of complete physical, mental and social well-being, and not merely the absence of disease or infirmity.' If this is health, then few of us will ever be healthy! While this may not be the most practical definition of health that could be devised, it does nevertheless contain some useful pointers – that health includes the absence of disease and infirmity, but also takes account of subjective feelings.

The first stage in measuring health is to describe different possible states of health in terms of how they affect people, for example whether and to what degree mobility is restricted and/or physical activity is impaired and/or social activity is constrained. One such set of descriptions is shown in Table 2.6.

Such states of health may then be graded according to how good or how bad they are felt to be. The grading may be *ordinal* – that is, a simple ranking from best to worst, where being ranked, say, 4th is not necessarily twice as bad as being ranked 2nd. Alternatively the grading may be *cardinal* on an *interval* scale – like temperature, for example – 64°F (18°C) cannot be said to be twice as hot as 32°F (0°C) – but intervals between the numbers may be compared cardinally – the difference between 100°C and 75°C can be said to be the same as the difference between 50°C and 25°C. Alternatively the grading may be cardinal on a *ratio* scale – like height and weight, for example – where it is meaningful to make comparisons such as 'twice as' or 'half as'.

In the literature on health measurement it is becoming increasingly common to rate states of health on interval scales. After describing the possible states the next stage in this process is to fix two reference states against which the other states may be rated.

Table 2.6 Preference ratings (weights) for function levels, PKU consultants and graduate students*

Mobility	Physical activity	Social activity	Preference rating Consultants'	Students'
Travelled freely (No symptom/problem complex)	Walked freely	Performed major and other activities	1.000	1.000
Travelled freely (Symptom/problem complex present)	Walked freely	Performed major and other activities	0.845	0.804
Travelled freely	Walked freely	Performed major but limited in other activities	0.805	0.689
Travelled freely	Walked freely	Performed self-care but not major activity	0.580	0.646
Travelled with difficulty	Walked freely	Performed major activity with limitations	0.610	0.536
Confined to house	Walked freely	Performed self-care but not major activity	0.435	0.594
Confined to house	Walked freely	Required assistance with self-care	0.273	0.505
Confined to house	In bed or chair	Performed self-care but not major activity	0.290	0.534
Confined to house	In bed or chair	Required assistance with self-care	0.186	0.436
In hospital	Walked freely	Performed self-care but not major activity	0.293	0.528
In hospital	Walked freely	Required assistance with self-care	0.165	0.440
In hospital	Walked with limitations	Performed self-care but not major activity	0.205	0.440
In hospital	In bed or chair	Performed self-care but not major activity	0.152	0.428
In hospital	In bed or chair	Required assistance with self-care	0.083	0.343
Death	Death	Death	0.000	0.000

Source: Bush, Chen and Patrick (1973).

* This table describes 15 different levels of health status reflecting possible states of impairment caused by PKU, and the consultants' and students' ratings of these health status levels.

(In measuring temperature the two reference states for the celsius scale are the freezing point and boiling point of fresh water at sea level.) In health measurement the two reference states are commonly 'good health' (= 1) and 'death' (= 0). In Table 2.6 these are the reference states against which the intermediate states – or 'health status levels' – have been rated. In this particular set the states are designed to reflect possible health status levels caused by the inherited disease phenylketonuria (PKU). The authors of this study asked both PKU consultants and graduate medical students to rate the different states on the 0–1 scale, and their (differing) ratings are shown in the final two columns of Table 2.6.

They then established the health status level that those suffering from PKU would experience at different stages of life, if they were alive, and then combined the ratings of health status with the mortality rate experienced at different ages to produce a lifetime profile of PKU health status levels on the 0–1 scale. The results (using the consultants' ratings) are shown in Figure 2.3. Also shown in this figure is the effect of treating newborn infants affected by PKU with a special diet to prevent the effects of the disease. The restricted diet reduces the child's health status for a few years, but thereafter health status is approximately normal. Thus Bush, Chen and Patrick (1973) estimated that the early treatment of classic PKU would on average improve health by 47.3 'function-years', or, as they are more often referred to now, 'quality-adjusted life-years' (QALYs).

Asking 'experts' to rate health status levels against the reference states of good health and death is one way of producing an index of health status. An alternative is to ask non-experts. Kind, Rosser and Williams (1982) developed a classification of 29 health states involving varying degrees of disability and distress. They then got a variety of subjects – doctors, medical nurses, medical patients, psychiatric nurses, psychiatric patients and healthy volunteers – to rate the states, by means of several different psychometric techniques. The median scores of the 70 subjects interviewed are shown in Table 2.7. Two of the states – unconscious, and bedfast with severe distress – are rated by these subjects as being worse than death. These authors report that age, religion and social class were not associated with differences in the way the states were valued but experiences of illness were.

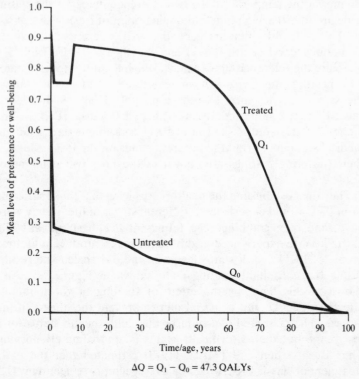

$$\Delta Q = Q_1 - Q_0 = 47.3 \text{ QALYs}$$

Figure 2.3 Effect on health status of treating newborn infants for phenylketonuria
Source: Bush, Chen and Patrick (1973).

Torrance and his colleagues in Ontario have developed two particular techniques to elicit valuations from various subjects, including members of the general public. These are the 'time trade-off' method and the 'standard gamble' (Torrance, 1986). In the former the subject whose values are being sought is asked to make a trade-off between the chronic health condition of interest for t years and good health for a shorter period, x years. Both periods are assumed to be followed immediately by death. The period x is varied in length until the subject is indifferent between the two. At the point of indifference the valuation (h) of the health condition is calculated as $h = x/t$. This trade-off is illustrated in diagrammatic form in Figure 2.4, along with trade-offs for health conditions worse than death and temporary health conditions.

In the standard gamble the subject is asked to make a trade-off between the certainty of having for *t* years the chronic health condition of interest, or a gamble with good health for *t* years as one alternative and death as the other. The probabilities of the

Table 2.7 Valuation matrix for 70 respondents

		\multicolumn{4}{c}{1 = Healthy 0 = Dead (Median Scores)}
		\multicolumn{4}{c}{*Distress Rating*}
Disability Rating		*A* *None*	*B* *Mild*	*C* *Moderate*	*D* *Severe*
I	No disability	1.000	0.995	0.990	0.967
II	Slight social disability	0.990	0.986	0.973	0.932
III	Severe social disability or slight impairment of performance at work, or both, able to do all housework except heavy tasks	0.980	0.972	0.956	0.912
IV	Choice of work or performance at work severely limited, housewives and old people able to do only light housework but able to go out shopping	0.964	0.956	0.942	0.870
V	Unable to undertake any paid employment, unable to continue any education, old people confined to home except for escorted outings and short walks and unable to shop, housewives able to perform only a few simple tasks	0.946	0.935	0.900	0.700
VI	Confined to chair or wheelchair or able to move only with support	0.875	0.845	0.680	0.000
VII	Confined to bed	0.677	0.564	0.000	−1.486
VIII	Unconscious	−1.028	*	*	*

* Not applicable

Source: Kind, Rosser and Williams (1982).

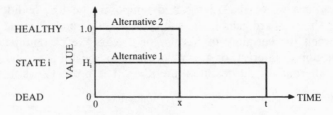

Time trade-off for a chronic health state preferred to death

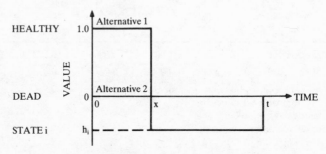

Time trade-off for a chronic health state considered worse than death

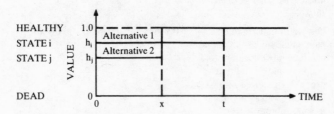

Time trade-off for a temporary health state

Figure 2.4 The time trade-off
Source: Torrance (1986).

gamble resulting in health or death are varied until the subject is indifferent between the gamble and the chronic health condition with certainty. At the point of indifference the valuation of the health condition is calculated as being the same as the probability (p) of health in the gamble. This trade-off is also illustrated

26

(Figure 2.5) along with trade-offs for health conditions worse than death and temporary health conditions.

Torrance and his colleagues have used such techniques in eliciting preferences for health states from various subjects. For

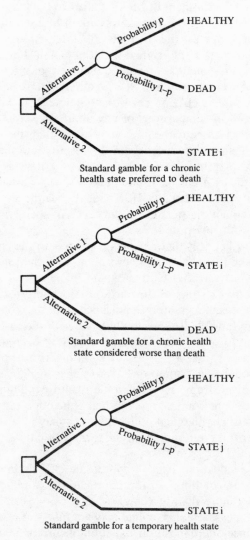

Standard gamble for a chronic
health state preferred to death

Standard gamble for a chronic health
state considered worse than death

Standard gamble for a temporary health state

Figure 2.5 The standard gamble
Source: Torrance (1986).

27

example, Sackett and Torrance (1978) measured the preferences for different levels of quality of life of a stratified random sample of the general public of Hamilton, Ontario, using the time trade-off technique. They found that women equated one year with a mastectomy for treatment of breast cancer to 0.48 years with full health: 0.48 QALYs. Such measures could be used in economic appraisal to express the benefits of interventions in terms equivalent to years of life gained with full health. For example, a screening programme that prevented the need for mastectomy for treatment of breast cancer and with no other adverse effects would bring a gain of 0.52 QALYs per woman per year. Ideally QALYs might be used in comparisons of any alternative uses for health care resources thereby helping to ensure that the maximum amount of health is produced from the resources available.

However, in principle there are various criticisms of health measurement, as it has been undertaken to date, which make it inappropriate and premature for 'global' health care decision-making, although the practical significance of such criticisms has yet to be thoroughly tested.

The first criticism is that people's responses to the choices that they are asked to make in interviews about hypothetical situations may not reflect the choices they would make in real life. Their preferences may change as they acquire more information, or as the choices assume greater significance and the consequences appear more tangible when actually faced with the real decision.

Second, most of the measurements that have been undertaken reflect the move from a position of good health to worse health states (although see Thompson, 1986). They do not reflect the value of moving from, say, a chronic health condition to good health or from one condition to another. If health is subject to the law of diminishing marginal utility then this may be an important source of error if the results from the former situations were to be applied to the latter situations.

Third, the valuations elicited will be affected by the expected duration of the condition – suffering a chronic condition for two years may be more than twice as bad as for one year. A related point is that measurements to date may not take sufficient account of the influence of prognosis on valuation of current health status.

These three criticisms are illustrated by Table 2.8, where it is shown that dialysis patients rated dialysis not as bad as did the

Table 2.8 Relation of health status to health state utility

| Duration | Health state | Mean daily health state utility | | % difference | Probability that the difference is due to chance |
		General population	Dialysis patients		
3 Months	Hospital dialysis	0.62	0.81	31	0.01
8 Years	Hospital dialysis	0.56	0.59	5	NS
8 Years	Home dialysis	0.65	0.72	11	NS
Life	Hospital dialysis	0.32	0.52	62	0.01
Life	Home dialysis	0.39	0.56	44	0.06

Source: Sackett and Torrance (1982)

general public, rated the difference between home and hospital dialysis differently from the general public, and both groups' rating declined as the period of duration asked about was increased.

A fourth criticism is that, as Torrance points out, the valuations given may change with the way the question is asked. Differences have been found between the values placed on a given condition when using the time trade-off and the standard gamble. (In principle the time trade-off should be adjusted for the individual's time preference rate, and the standard gamble for risk aversion/preference – see chapter 5.)

A final criticism is that QALYs may not measure the full benefits to be derived from health care. Other benefits may relate to the value of health care to the relatives of patients, to the value of information that doctors and others can provide, and to the relief of the burden of decision-making concerning the appropriateness of types of health care. These are, however, subjects that will be returned to in subsequent chapters.

Having quantified health improvements in terms of the increase in quality of life and its duration in terms of years of life, the next step is to try to value the health improvements in money terms. One method of eliciting such values is to ask individuals, directly, how much they would be willing to pay to obtain a particular health improvement, or avoid a health deterioration. Thompson (1986) reports how this was tried with a group of 247 people, aged between 21 and 66, suffering from chronic rheumatoid arthritis.

They were asked to imagine that a (complete) cure for their condition was available, but only through private purchase. Ninety-six per cent of the subjects responded, and their willingness to pay for the hypothetical cure was 22 per cent of their family's (household) income. Willingness to pay as a proportion of income was positively correlated with their degree of impairment in activities of daily living, and negatively correlated with age. While this direct approach is open to the criticism of being too hypothetical, the answers obtained in this case do not seem unreasonable. Other methods of valuing health improvements are discussed in chapter 5.

2.4 Conclusions

Assessing health and the effects of health care have been practised for millennia. Historical data suggest that public health measures produced dramatic improvements in health in previous centuries. Today many important diseases may be as amenable to prevention as treatment. Modern treatments (and prevention) need to be subjected to scientific evaluation to determine their effectiveness. The outcomes in terms of health improvements may be measured in several different ways – two methods that have been widely tested being the time trade-off and the standard gamble. Such testing has established the feasibility of these methods, but they are in principle subject to some reservations concerning their accuracy and comprehensiveness. Their use, for example, in economic appraisal is discussed further in subsequent chapters.

3

Health care as an economic commodity

3.1 Introduction

In this chapter, the focus is on the nature of the economic commodity with which we are primarily concerned in this book, i.e. health care. The chapter builds on the more epidemiological, demographic and medical concerns of the last chapter.

The emphasis here is on a description and definition of health care and its characteristics as an economic commodity. In this book, while being concerned with the economics of health care (as reflected in the title), we cannot completely ignore other commodities which are health-inducing (or health-damaging) especially as some of the former represent close substitutes for health care. (This is established more firmly in chapter 7 on the demand for health care and its relationship to the demand for health.) But we have chosen to make the focus health *care*.

This is a chapter which sets the economic scene and which identifies key features or characteristics of health care which are relevant to the ensuing chapters. Indeed the prime purpose of this chapter is to provide the basis to allow our analysis of the implications of these characteristics to be pursued.

In the next section, the process of scene-setting is begun by outlining in economic terms the important relationship between health and health care which we see as revolving around the whole question of the interpretation of the concept of value. Thereafter we set out the main principles of expected utility theory, that is the theory that lies at the heart of the neoclassical paradigm of conventional economics. (For a more detailed discussion of expected utility theory and its variants, see Schoemaker, 1982.) It is not that we expect that health care will fit neatly into that paradigm nor that health care is unique in not doing so. We have no desire to set up a straw man. Rather we want in section 3.4 to consider the extent to which the neoclassical paradigm is relevant to health care. Different commodities, in our view, 'fit' to greater or lesser extents. In pursuing this matter our aim is not to establish that health care is 'different' from other commodities. The issue is rather: where on the spectrum of potential relevance and usefulness of expected utility theory does health care lie?

This turns out to be a rather difficult question to answer, not least because with health care we are not dealing with a single, homogeneous commodity but with many. What may be true of intensive therapy in a coronary care unit, may not hold for an initial visit to a general practitioner for the treatment of some infection in the upper respiratory tract. Further, the individual patient and the individual doctor can themselves directly influence the nature of the commodity itself.

3.2 Health and health care as commodities

Our prime concern is with health care rather than health. From an economic perspective, we would argue that this has to be the case since the focus of economics is on the demand, supply and distribution of commodities and it is health care, rather than health *per se*, that is the commodity. Health itself is not tradeable in the sense that it cannot, strictly, be bought or sold in a market: it can be no more than a characteristic of a commodity. Thus health is a characteristic of health care, seat belts, fire extinguishers, wholemeal bread, etc.; but health is not exchangeable.

This is an important conclusion to reach. It also merits some explanation. Indeed it relates to the central question in economics, as addressed by Mill, as to what constitutes value. Mill (1909, p. 436) writes:

> The word value, when used without adjunct, always means, in political economy, value in exchange. . . . Political economy has nothing to do with the comparative estimation of different uses in the judgement of a philosopher or a moralist. The use of a thing, in political economy, means

its capacity to satisfy a desire or serve a purpose. . . . Value in use . . . is the extreme limit of value in exchange. The exchange value of a thing may fall short, to any amount, of its value in use; but that it can ever exceed the value in use implies a contradiction; it supposes that persons will give, to possess a thing, more than the utmost value which they themselves put upon it as a means of gratifying their inclinations.

Translating this into terms of health and health care, health can only have value in use and not in exchange. Further it can normally only be attributed with the appropriate amount of utility by the consumer, i.e. the recipient of, for example, changes in health status. Health itself is not tradeable.

It is thus argued that health is not a commodity but health care is. In turn, given economists' prime concern with value in exchange, the main subject matter of this book is not health but health care as the commodity which is primarily characterised by health.

It does not follow that economic analysis can ignore health. For example, as Williams (1977, p. 302) indicates, defining health is an important feature of health economics: 'To the innocent beginner in health economics it hardly seems necessary to give a moment's thought to what turns out to be a highly controversial topic among the cognoscenti, viz what is "health" anyway?' In economic analysis it may be necessary to work with many different definitions, the most important of which will relate more to social functioning and cultural attitudes to ill-health than to bio-medical considerations such as levels of blood pressure. Clearly measuring health, as indicated in the previous chapter, is also an important aspect of health economics. But it is health care, the tradeable commodity, upon which this book concentrates.

From the supply point of view, health care produces primarily health but also other 'outputs' (of which more below). From the demand standpoint, people want to improve their health status, so they demand health care (as one way of achieving this). The reason they want better health is presumably because of the desire to enjoy life, in all its consumption and production aspects, to a fuller extent than would be the case with less health.

The apparently simple relationship of wanting health and demanding health care becomes more complex, largely because of problems of lack of information. Translating a want for health into the consumption of treatment involves *inter alia* a demand for information about various aspects of existing health status, of improved health status, of treatment availability, of effectiveness, etc. It follows that the demand for health care involves uncertainty which makes the informational characteristics, and not just the treatment characteristics, important. As Arrow (1963) has argued, the medical profession specialises in the supply of information and this information influences what health treatments are then demanded and utilised.

The uncertainty generated by ignorance about health status, availability and effectiveness of treatment, etc. makes decision-making about the consumption of treatment difficult, especially as there may be substantial anxiety about making a wrong decision which could have serious adverse (ill-health) outcomes. Consequently, the consumption of health care – especially for life-threatening conditions – may also include the characteristic of being able to pass the burden of decision-making to the clinician. In other words, the demand for health care may include a demand to avoid having to make difficult decisions and bear the responsibility of such decision-making. These informational and decision-making features are central to the issue of the 'agency relationship' whereby the doctor acts as an agent on behalf of and in the interests of the patient (of which more in chapter 8).

Thus we move from the individual's want for improved health status to a situation where, in the context of the consumption of health care, that want is but one feature of a more complex process which leads to the utilisation of health care. Indeed it suggests that the view in conventional neoclassical economics of a sovereign consumer lying behind the demand curve may not always be appropriate in the market for health care. In so far as this is true then the normal assumption of a complete separation of decision-making and decision-makers on the supply and the demand sides of the market may not hold. In other words the distribution of 'property rights' in decision-making in health care may be different from that implied in the standard consumer sovereignty of neoclassical markets.

By property rights is meant 'The sanctioned behavioural relations among men that arise from the existence of things and pertain to their use. . . . The prevailing system of property rights in the community can be described . . . as the set of economic and social relations defining the position of each individual with

34

respect to the utilisation of scarce resources' (Furubotn and Pejovich, 1972, p. 1139). Conventionally neoclassical economics assumes that property rights over consumption decisions are vested in the consumer, i.e. the notion of the rational consumer exercising his sovereignty. As Mishan states (1971, p. 172): 'economists are generally agreed – either as a canon of faith, as a political tenet, or an act of expediency – to accept the dictum that each person knows his own interest best'. In health care, at least for some situations, there may be substantial limitations on how far such a dictum can be considered valid.

There is another feature of health care which also raises questions about the extent of the relevance of expected utility theory and thereby neoclassical economics to the commodity health care. This is the issue of interdependencies of utility functions, or more specifically equity, which appears in so many health care systems to be an important objective. While it is possible to incorporate equity into the neoclassical paradigm through the introduction of externalities, there are reasons to believe that this is not the most valid way to consider it. We will discuss this in more detail in section 3.4.2 below and in the next chapter.

The key concern in this book is thus health care. In this chapter it is primarily the consumer's perspective of that commodity that is discussed while the supply perspective is given more consideration in chapter 10.

3.3 Basic principles of expected utility theory

The basic principles of expected utility theory, which lie at the centre of neoclassical demand theory, involve a rational economic person faced with choice under uncertainty over which he, as the consumer, is sovereign. Such rationality, as traditionally conceived, is based on the following axioms:

(i) the axiom of completeness: the consumer is able to order all available combinations of goods according to his preferences;
(ii) the axiom of transitivity: if A is preferred to B and B is preferred to C, then A is preferred to C, with A, B and C normally conceived as being bundles of commodities;

(iii)   the axiom of selection: the consumer aims for his most preferred state.

Risk is introduced by suggesting that there are various possible states of the world, all of which are known with certainty, and to which it is possible to attach probabilities of occurrence.[1] Utility is derived from the final consequences of the states of the world and the probabilities then attached to the utilities. The products of these probabilities and utilities are then summed to give the overall expected utility.

Using the formulation of Hey (1979):

$$U(C_j) = \sum_{i=1}^{I} P_i U(A_{ij})$$

where $U(C_j)$ is the expected utility associated with the choice, C, for individual j.

A_{ij} is the consequence if the individual chooses C_j and the state of the world, i, occurs

$U(A_{ij})$ is the utility associated with A_{ij}

P_i is the probability that the state of the world, i, occurs

I   is the number of possible states of the world such that $i = 1, 2, \ldots$ I.

There are several assumptions and implications in this statement which it is worthwhile spelling out in some detail. Essentially, taking a world of certainty first, it is assumed that the consumer is involved in a number of acts, the property rights over which are vested in that individual:

(a)   judging the cost of consumption which will normally include the price of the commodity but also other costs (e.g. time costs);
(b)   bearing the cost in full at the point of consumption, i.e. there are no subsidies and insurance is not present;
(c)   judging the benefit – the fully informed, rational, sovereign consumer determines the utility gains associated with consumption on the basic premise that no one is better placed than he is to determine what these utility gains are;

(d) obtaining benefit – the consumer receives the utility gains directly from the consumption;

(e) decision-making – on the basis of (a) to (d) the fully knowledgeable, rational, sovereign consumer chooses whether, and if so how much, of what to consume. Normally there are no utility gains or losses associated with decision-making *per se* except that failure to be able to undertake decision-making may sometimes be viewed as involving a loss of utility, i.e. there is utility in freedom of choice (see, for example, Hahn, 1982).

Introducing risk in principle changes little, particularly as risk is conventionally defined as the probability that various possible states of the world will occur. All the states of the world are known with certainty, all the consequences of the states of the world, should they occur, are known with certainty, and all the sets of choices the individual faces with respect to the states of the world and their consequences are known with certainty. It is also the case that the probabilities are known with certainty albeit often as judged subjectively by the individual. Uncertainty in expected utility theory is thus defined in rather constrained terms – i.e. it is commonly taken to be synonymous with risk.

It is assumed in expected utility theory that the individual consumer is sovereign and can assess the utility associated with all the relevant sets of final consequences. In doing so it is only the final consequences that are utility-bearing, a fact which follows directly because of the consequentialist utilitarianism of expected utility theory and neoclassical economics. Thus (see von Neumann and Morgenstern, 1944) not only is the individual assumed to be sufficiently able, willing and knowledgeable (in terms of choices, states of the world, final consequences, probabilities and utility assessment) to make the relevant choices; in his goal of maximising utility, he is asumed to derive utility only from the consequences or outcomes of actions or processes and not from the actions or processes themselves. The 'domain of preferences', as Hahn (1982, p. 190) calls it, is thus normally taken to be narrowly defined by welfare economists, the consequences usually being restricted to 'the commodity space' (op. cit., p. 190). Hence the expression derived by Margolis (1982, p. 68) of 'goods' utility which he adopts in order to draw attention to this essentially narrow view of the source of utility.

On risk and the relevant probabilities in expected utility theory, one condition is that all the probabilities together sum to unity. Further it is normally assumed that individuals are risk averse with the result that the utility function is concave throughout. (Risk aversion means that the individual prefers a certain event, s, to a probable event, z, with probability p of occurrence, even although s = p.z. Concavity means that under a willingness to pay criterion, for example, individuals would be willing to pay more, *ceteris paribus*, for a given change in probability of a desirable state of the world occurring, the higher the initial probability, i.e. a change in the probability of an illness from 0.02 to 0.019 would be valued more highly than if the change were from 0.005 to 0.004.)

That is the basis of expected utility theory which is the cornerstone of neoclassical demand analysis. It is clear that there are many commodities that fit, at best, imperfectly into this paradigm. In the next section we discuss these imperfections in the specific context of the commodity health care and its relevant characteristics.

3.4 The nature of health care

3.4.1 Health care and information

In the consumption of health care, much of the consumer's sovereignty assumed by expected utility theory is lost or eroded. There is, in health care, often a different distribution of property rights in decision-making than is conventionally assumed in economic analysis. Certainly the individual consumer still obtains the utility but, to varying degrees, consumer sovereignty is diminished with regard to judging and bearing costs, judging benefits and decision-making. It is possible to argue that, given the importance of external benefits in health care (of which more below), that even the obtaining of utility is diminished for the patient. Further, the utility of health care consumption may come, not just in the form of the outcome utility associated with health status changes (i.e. the consequences of states of the world as emphasised by expected utility theory), but also in different forms of process utility associated with information and decision-making *per se*.

The final consequences of the states of the world that the consumer is interested in relate, of course, to improved health. To obtain this, he may demand information, for example, on his current health status, treatments available and their effectiveness. In his uncertain state, and given the uncertain outcomes, the patient may in turn demand that the doctor acts as a decision-making agent (and not just decision-aiding). The patient may do this because of a fear of getting it wrong and then having to bear the burden of knowing he made a wrong choice.

The extent to which these health-bearing, information-bearing and decision-delegating characteristics of health care are present will vary depending on a number of factors including the specific health care commodity being examined, and perhaps the personalities of the doctor and the patient involved. Most people have relatively good knowledge of toothache, the treatments available and their effectiveness. The information content in health care for toothache is thus relatively low; so also is the decision-delegating characteristic. Getting it wrong in this context is of relatively no great consequence. Substitute breast cancer for toothache and the position changes.

Further, it cannot be assumed that these three sets of characteristics are uninfluenced by the personalities of the individual doctor and the individual patient. Some doctors will be more ready to accept the decision-making role than others; some patients will want to retain their autonomy in terms of their capacity to make decisions, others more ready to abrogate the responsibility for decision-making to the doctor (even if the consumer must remain the main utility gainer). And the doctor's attitude to giving information, and the patient's to receiving it, are unlikely to be independent of their respective views on the distribution of property rights over decision-making.

This particular dimension of heterogeneity relating to the personalities of the doctor and patient is one which is perhaps not given enough attention. It makes for difficulties in the 'agency relationship' since the nature of that relationship is itself a potential source of utility to the patient and is 'customised' to a very considerable extent, i.e. it is individual to each patient.

The provision by the supplier to the consumer of information on existing health status, availability and effectiveness of treatments, places the doctor in the position of not only acting as supplier but also markedly influencing directly the utility function of the consumer. The normal Marshallian separation of supply and demand is no longer maintained and the phenomenon of 'supplier induced demand' has to be recognised, i.e. the possibility of a shift in the consumer's demand curve as a result of some intervention by the doctor. The autonomy of the consumer may be further reduced by the effects of ill health on the consumer's decision-making capabilities.

Health care is clearly a heterogeneous commodity; it is also an intermediate commodity in the sense that it is not consumed for itself. The fact that it is both heterogeneous and intermediate in practice may reduce the extent to which heterogeneity matters. This is because while there are clear differences between a simple headache and a brain tumour, it is not always so clear at all stages of the consumption process that these are the diagnoses, nor that the headache might not be a symptom of some more dreadful condition. This 'what it might be' syndrome is a direct function of the consumer's poor information and while it is possible to exaggerate its importance it does seem likely that individuals will tend to over-perceive small risks of seriously adverse outcomes and that, in turn, this will tend to reduce the degree of heterogeneity in the commodity health care.

An added complication about information lies in the need to distinguish information from knowledge. While information may be supplied by the doctor, and health services more generally, it will not always be converted into knowledge – information that is understood and retained for at least some period of time – by the patient. Consequently, supplying information may not result in increased knowledge. This will be especially so for the more unusual health events and because of the irregular nature of much health care utilisation. Where the information is seen as having particularly serious implications for the patient's ill-health it may be difficult for the patient to process the information in a sufficiently objective way to convert it into reasonable knowledge. In some instances, too, it may be that the doctor will experience difficulties in conveying information of a kind that is particularly upsetting to the patient. No one, not even a doctor, likes to be the bearer of bad tidings. Consequently the patient who does demand knowledge may not be supplied with the information to allow him to pursue this demand.

For this and other reasons, the nature of the commodity health care can be perceived differently on the two sides of 'the market' reflecting, as discussed above, the distinction between what is wanted (primarily but not exclusively health) and what is supplied (health care). For example, the commodity provided by doctors for the health care of women with breast cancer (largely treatments to improve the quantity of life) may be different from that wanted by the women, for example, both quality and quantity of life, together with information and thereby knowledge (Adamsen and Alban, 1984). Again, in ante-natal care, a study in Barcelona (Artells, 1981) showed that obstetricians supplied, almost exclusively, treatment aimed at minimising risk of adverse outcomes for the newborn, while the women wanted additionally information and reassurance.

Clearly the demand and supply perspectives can and do differ and for a number of reasons. Yet they tend to come together through the exercise of the 'agency relationship'. More detail of this relationship is provided in chapter 8. For the present it is necessary to appreciate that in principle the agency relationship reflects a recognition on the part of both parties – the patient and the doctor – of the asymmetry of information which exists between them. The patient accepts first, his own ignorance, second, the doctor's superior knowledge and, third, the likely utility gains to be obtained by having the doctor directly influence the arguments and the weights thereon in his (the patient's) utility function. In other words, the patient accepts that the doctor knows more about the final consequences of the states of the patient's world (in terms of health status) than the patient does himself. Part of the reason for the existence of this information 'impactedness', as Williamson (1973, p. 341) indicates, is the high cost (for the patient) of achieving information parity. However, to attain a perfect agency relationship – one in which the outcome is precisely what it would have been had the patient been able to make his own choices from a fully knowledgeable position, i.e. the one assumed by expected utility theory – is extremely difficult and perhaps even impossible. It involves an understanding of health status, health care and the individual's utility function; and indeed not just those features of that function directly relevant to his health. This is because there is a need not only to judge benefit, which will be at least in part in health terms, but also to judge cost which could involve many aspects of the individual's utility function. For example, a decision on whether to admit a woman to a local maternity hospital or a distant specialist maternity hospital requires not only a weighing up of the relative risks to mother and baby but the costs as perceived by the woman of being in the two locations.

It is also clear from the discussion above that it is not just the 'states of the world' in terms of health status that are relevant in the patient's utility function. Information and the extent of patient autonomy also matter. Yet the inclusion of these factors is not considered often enough in the literature on the agency relationship. This involves a difficult issue. Essentially it is about the agent's forming (i) a prior judgement about the amount, and perhaps also type, of information and knowledge which the patient wants, and then supplying that information; and (ii) in the light of that and other aspects of the patient's personality, determining how far to go in acting as the patient's agent, i.e. deciding what the patient's preferences are in respect of the distribution of property rights over decision-making in his treatment (and events surrounding it) between the patient and the doctor.

Hence the agency relationship is not just about getting the outcome 'right' in terms of what the patient would do if he were informed and prudent. It is about seeking to achieve this in a manner conducive with both the patient's preferences for obtaining information and his retaining an optimum level of decision making. That makes the 'perfect' agency relationship even more difficult to achieve. At the same time it would seem to make it more apposite than is the case when it is constrained to considering only those benefits which are related directly to health status.

A particularly good example of the problems associated with the agency relationship is provided in the discussion by Berwick and Weinstein (1985) of diagnostic tests. They suggest that clinical decision-making is normally couched in terms of the 'expected value of clinical information'. Yet in their study of ultrasound, they found that such a view was all too narrow. They estimated that only 74 per cent of the average woman's willingness to pay for ultrasound was related to the value of the information for decision-making purposes and that this was split 63 per cent on the medical decision-making and 37 per cent on the patient's decision-making.

In other words less than 50 per cent of the patient's willingness to pay was for informational content that could possibly affect the clinical management of the patient. From this it is clear that the informational characteristic of health care is not only important: the nature of that information from the point of view of the patient's utility may extend well beyond that which is strictly relevant to medical decision-making.

Given the above, it would appear that health care, like various other commodities, does not fit neatly into expected utility theory. In the case of health care this is primarily for two, closely associated, reasons both related to information. First, health care *per se* is to a large extent information. Consequently the individual, in the specific context of the axiom of completeness (see p. 35 above), may not be able to rank a set of goods, of which one is health care, according to his pre-information preferences. Second, this is especially the case as he may need to consume certain characteristics of health care – information – before being able to have preferences in which he has sufficient faith upon which to make decisions.

In terms of selection the individual consumer of health care is short of the necessary information to form a judgement about the most preferred health state at which to aim. (This is a potentially major criticism of the 'rationalist' school of thought on the demand for health – most closely associated with Grossman (1972a, 1972b); see chapter 7.)

It is not suggested that these characteristics are absent from other commodities. However, it is submitted that they generally have less importance elsewhere. This key issue about the 'difference' of health care is neatly summarised by the following quote from Weisbrod (1978, p. 52) in a comment on Pauly's support for competition in health care (Pauly, 1978). Weisbrod states:

The key reason that I am less sanguine than Pauly about consumers of health care being well informed involves the difficulty consumers have in specifying the 'counter-factual.' What a buyer wants to know is the difference between his state of well-being with and without the commodity being considered. For ordinary goods, the buyer has little difficulty in evaluating the counter-factual – that is, what the situation will be if the good is not obtained. Not so for the bulk of health care (and legal representation, to cite another example). . . . The noteworthy point is not simply that it is difficult for the consumer to judge quality before the purchase (as it also is in the used car case), but that it is difficult even after the purchase.

Thus, while we do not want to argue for health care's 'uniqueness', this question of being unable both *ex ante* and *ex post* to judge quality does tend to push it towards the end of the spectrum of commodities where expected utility theory is potentially less valid.

3.4.2 Health care, information and insurance

Insurance is discussed in detail in chapter 10. However, given its relevance to information problems and uncertainty it is apposite to consider certain aspects of it here.

Health status is uncertain in the sense that it is unpredictable. Health care is then consumed irregularly. As individuals it is not possible to state precisely and with certainty what our health status will be in ten years' time, next year, or even next week. Various actions can be taken as a response to the uncertainty regarding future health status.

The probability of future ill-health may be reduced through adopting a particular pattern of consumption now – jogging, eating a good diet, refraining from smoking, moderating drinking, etc. – although the extent of the contribution of these to improved health status in future is also uncertain. Such actions, in so far as they are effective, will reduce both ill-health and thereby the cost of health care in the future. Thus the individual can be involved in the production side as well as the consumption side. (See chapter 7 on Grossman (1972a, 1972b) for more detail.)

Other actions may be taken now to reduce the financial loss to be suffered if health status falls. Saving can mitigate the impact of loss of earnings as a result of not being able to work, or to allow the costs of health care to be more readily met. Again action can be delayed until illness arises and then health care can be purchased when it is required out of current income and wealth holdings or future income through borrowing.

The other major alternative to these actions is insurance whereby some of the costs of ill-health can be pooled across a group of individuals. Insurance in practice will inevitably be 'actuarially unfair'. (Actuarially fair insurance involves the payment of a premium of m to cover a 1 in x chance of an insured event costing mx occurring.) It is 'unfair' partly because of the need for insurance companies to 'load' premiums to cover administrative costs. Actuarially unfair insurance can exist, however, because individuals are commonly risk averse when faced with the relevant uncertain outcomes and/or because they simply misperceive the probabilities and/or their losses if the uncertain outcomes do occur.

In practice it is important to note that it is only those aspects for which money is able to compensate that can be deemed truly insurable. There is here an important consideration in the chain of health, health care and health insurance. Health insurance like health care is tradeable while, as indicated in section 3.2 above, health is not. But further, ill-health *per se* cannot be insured against except in so far as it is possible to compensate an individual financially for a loss of health status. There are limits to the extent that this is possible. Thus, for example, individuals cannot insure themselves for the loss of utility associated with losing their life since they cannot be financially compensated for their own death.

Insurance arises largely as a result of the unpredictability of ill-health, rather than the unpredictability of the effectiveness of health care, or because of the irregularity of consumption. Thus insurance normally covers the financial costs of care regardless of its effectiveness – except in circumstances where ineffectiveness is a function of negligence. In effect this means that uncertainty regarding the effectiveness of treatment is not normally covered by insurance.

In Arrow's classic article on uncertainty and the welfare economics of health care (Arrow, 1963, p. 959) he concentrated in his discussion of insurance on the costs of medical care, suggesting that these 'act as a random deduction from . . . income, and it is the expected value of the utility of income after medical costs that we are concerned with' although he does add that if illness is a source of dissatisfaction 'it should enter into the utility function as a separate variable'. The formulation by Evans (1984, pp. 30, 31) of ill-health loss is also relevant:

Only if care of a specific and well defined amount were instantly and perfectly efficacious in relieving illness could one represent the consequences of illness for well being by the dollar cost of care. In general, the money equivalent loss . . . of an illness will exceed any consequent [change in] health spending by some amount which allows for pain and suffering, anxiety, lost wages and/or leisure, and a risk premium for uncertainty of outcome.

What is also particularly germane to note is that the commodity health insurance may be more amenable to treatment by expected utility theory than is health care *per se*. That, perhaps, is in one sense surprising given what appears to be the relatively close and logical links between health, health care and health insurance. However, in another sense it is not, once it is recognised that to a very large extent health insurance is a misnomer since the risks that are normally insured against are the costs of health *care*. In other words it is not ill-health insurance but income maintenance that is the issue.

The commodity health insurance fits expected utility theory better, therefore, since the real world is quite a good approximation, given that it is frequently the costs of health care which constitute the coverage. Hence health insurance is more amenable to the neoclassical paradigm than is health care.

3.4.3 Process utility in health care

One important feature of expected utility theory is its reliance on consequentialist utilitarianism, i.e. the notion that it is the outcomes or consequences of the states of the world that alone bear utility. While that can be challenged in the case of a number of commodities, it seems particularly germane to question it in health care where 'process utility' may be present and in two forms, one related to decision-making and risk-bearing and the other to equity. This section discusses the relevance of both forms of process utility and, consequently, the strengths of expected (outcome) utility theory in analysing health care.

As already suggested, health care decision-making involves risk-bearing. There are outcomes in terms of health status which are potentially very adverse: in the extreme death or reduction in life-years.

Making decisions where such adverse outcomes are possible may involve disutility in itself. Additional to the 'outcome' disutility associated with the adverse health outcomes, there is a 'process' disutility associated with having to make (or having made) decisions where the adverse outcome is possible (or has occurred).

There may be gains to the consumer from that characteristic of the commodity health care which, through the agency role, allows the patient to 'offload' responsibility for difficult decision-making on to the doctor. This is what Harris (1977, p. 473) has described as the clinician's 'moral burden of ultimate responsibility for the outcome of the case' where the patient may willingly default on the act of decision-making. In so far as expected utility theory is based on consequences or outcomes, this process utility would not normally be incorporated into the relevant utility function.

Turning to equity, it is clear that, in many health care systems, considerable weight is attached to distributive goals. Quite why is less than clear. Tobin (1970) suggests that traditionally, in so far as economists have been concerned with equity, it has been in the general sense that problems of distribution are best resolved at the most general level, for example, through taxation of income and wealth. However, he proposes that economists' willingness to accept inequality is 'tempered by a persistent and durable strain of . . . specific egalitarianism . . . the view that certain specific scarce commodities should be distributed less unequally than the ability to pay for them' (op. cit., p. 448). In these he includes health care. Given the importance attached to equity in health care a separate chapter (chapter 4) is devoted to it. However, at this point it is necessary briefly to try to establish the possible reasons for the concern with equity in health care as a form of 'specific egalitarianism' and some of the problems this creates for neoclassical economic analysis.

There are at least three possible explanations for equity, any one of which is likely to create some difficulties in the market for health care. First there is the concept of a caring externality (or as Culyer (1976, p. 88) has described it 'the humanitarian spillover') which suggests that individuals care about the health status, or consumption of health care, of others. Second, there is Sen's notion of commitment whereby, perhaps because of some Kantian sense of duty, individuals are 'committed' to the provision of equitable health care (Sen, 1977). This is very similar to Titmuss' 'gift relationship', of which more in the next chapter. Third, there

47

is Margolis' related concept of participation whereby individuals obtain utility through participating in group activities – such as health care provision – where they are equal members of the group and utility is obtained through the process of participating.

The extent to which equity enters as an argument in individuals' utility functions and subsequently in social welfare functions appears to vary between countries. Yet it seems to be present in most health care systems, indeed even in such individualistically based systems as those of the United States.

Of course it is possible to incorporate externalities into neoclassical analysis but the basic 'selfish' goods utility function which includes only the goods available to *homo economicus* would have no room for any 'caring externality'. Even if the utility function is extended to include interdependencies of utility, these are normally considered solely in terms of final consequences of the states of the world, i.e. outcomes. There are thus problems in incorporating process utility derived from others' opportunity to use health services, and in the notion of 'participation utility' as another explanation for equity. Certainly neoclassical analysis in its standard form cannot live with Sen's commitment which explicitly runs counter to the axiom of selection (i.e. the goal of maximising individual utility). It is also incapable of incorporating Titmuss' Kantian moral imperative explanation of equity.

Thus one problem of expected utility theory, in its application to health care at least, lies in its emphasis on outcome utility to the exclusion of process utility. This is a direct result of the fact that expected utility theory is based on consequentialist utilitarianism and, as such, on the utilities associated with the final consequences of states of the world, these normally being conceived in terms of bundles of goods.

In health care there appear to be some potentially important arguments missing from such a utility function, which may be incorporated in the concept of 'process' utility and are related to issues of utility in choice and in participation.

The first of these is perhaps best exemplified in terms of the utility of *freedom* of choice. Harsanyi (1982, p. 61) suggests that free personal choice ought to attract some value (V) in any utility function. He states: 'Suppose we have to choose between two alternative strategies S^* and S^{**} likely to yield the outcome utilities W^* and W^{**}, with $W^* > W^{**}$, then classical utilitarianism would select strategy S* as the *only* morally permissible strategy. But . . . we must recognise S** as being an equally permissible strategy, provided that W** + V > W*.'

Again Hahn (1982) argues that his utility may be adversely affected if he is taxed to provide funds for a particular good cause rather than if he were left free to choose to provide the same funds to the same good cause. In both cases, it is suggested that utility lies in the decision-making process and not just the outcomes.

In health care we may have the reverse of this idea of utility in being able to choose. There may be utility because the patient is able to default on decision-making and pass the burden of responsibility to the clinician. There is a cost in making difficult choices: the consumption of health care has the characteristic of allowing the patient to pass this cost to the doctor, resulting in a redistribution of property rights over the consumption decision and a loss of relevance of the conventional concept of demand.

Second, and largely separate from this choice question, there is the issue of participating in group activities which may or may not affect the distribution of goods across different individuals. Thus there may be, as Margolis (1982) has suggested (more detail follows in chapter 4), a form of utility to be derived from 'participation altruism', the idea of a citizen doing his fair share for society, the utility here being derived from the process of participating, i.e. from the act itself.

Both of these forms of process utility, which are excluded from expected (outcome) utility theory, seem particularly important in health care. Both are somewhat similar to Williamson's 'atmosphere'. He states (Williamson, 1975, p. 39): 'The standard economic model . . . assumes that individuals regard transactions in a strictly neutral, instrumental manner . . . it may be more accurate . . . to regard the exchange process itself as an object of value.' It is of interest to note that as an example of atmosphere Williamson draws attention to Titmuss' arguments on the commercialisation of blood and its effects on altruistic donation, a discussion to which we return in the next chapter.

One of the difficulties about many economists (but not necessarily economics) is that they are on the whole unwilling to accept potentially loose concepts such as atmosphere, especially when they are difficult to quantify. Arrow defines an economist as one who 'by training thinks of himself as the guardian of rationality, the ascriber of rationality to others, and the prescriber of rationality to the social world' (1974b, p. 16).

Such rationality is the rationality of consequentialist utilitarianism where transactions bear no utility, positive or negative, in themselves. That appears too narrow in health care both at the doctor/patient level and at the level of societal distribution. It is then of interest to note that Williamson (1975, p. 256) conjectures 'that transactions which affect conceptions of self-esteem and/or perceptions of collective well-being are those for which attitudinal considerations [i.e. essentially atmosphere] are especially important'.

Indeed there are other features of Williamson's discussion of markets and hierarchies that are relevant to health care – especially bounded rationality and information impactedness. The former was originally defined by Simon (1961, p. xxiv) as human behaviour that is '*intendedly* rational, but only *limitedly* so' which is an accurate description of the position that most health care consumers are in.

Bounded rationality exists to allow individuals to cope better with the problems arising from a combination of complexity and uncertainty and can exist either in computational or language form. The computational problems are both great and apparent in health care decision-making; the language problems equally so, given Williamson's description of these as a situation in which 'participants to a transaction . . . lack the ability to communicate successfully about the nature of the transaction' (op. cit., p. 255). However, in this matter the important point is made by Simon (1957, p. 199): 'it is only because individual human beings are limited in knowledge, foresight, skill and time that organizations are useful instruments for the achievement of human purpose.' Health care organisations certainly fit that description. The informational needs, computational and language requirements of the unbounded rationality of expected utility theory seem all too demanding in the consumption of health care.

Information impactedness was mentioned above (p. 41). It refers to a situation in which there is major asymmetry of information between the parties to a transaction, the costs of reaching parity for the poorly informed party are very great, and the parties tend to behave opportunistically. This seems, again, a very accurate description of the situation in health care, except that opportunistic behaviour seldom becomes a reality (at least in part because of the existence of ethical codes, of which more in chapter 8).

These features of Williamson's thesis on the appropriateness of hierarchies *vis-à-vis* markets for performing various types of economic transactions are raised here as possible alternatives or adjuncts to expected utility theory. In later chapters their fuller relevance in health care will be highlighted.

What is perhaps of most significance in this, in the context of health care, is that it allows greater propensity for various characteristics of the individuals involved in the decision-making process to influence the expected utility gain or loss. Given the presence of the doctor on both 'sides' of the health care market, the imperfect agency relationship, and Williamson's framework, it is easier to understand why decisions regarding apparently the same choices may be made differently across different patients/ doctors.

As Tversky and Kahneman (1981) state: 'The framing of acts and outcomes [note the inclusion of both] can also reflect the acceptance or rejection of responsibility for particular consequences. . . . When framing influences the experience of consequences, the adoption of a decision frame is an ethically significant act.' There seems little doubt that, in the context of medical decision-making under uncertainty, 'framing influences the experience of consequences'.

3.5 Conclusions

This chapter has indicated that health care is a commodity which, from the consumption standpoint, has a number of interesting and important features. These create some problems if expected utility theory and traditional economic demand principles are to be applied in analysing health care.[2]

This is not to suggest that health care is in some sense uniquely different from other commodities. Rather, in terms of a spectrum which stretches from commodities where expected utility theory fits very well to those where it fits badly, health care is at the latter end.

The complexity arising from the changing nature of wants/ demands is central to this, i.e. the want for health becoming a demand for treatment leading to a demand for information and in turn to a demand for avoiding difficult decisions, but to varying extents for different health care commodities, patients and doctors. At the same time, of course, other commodities share some of the informational characteristics of health care. However, few share the risk-bearing/avoidance characteristic to the same extent.

Further few other commodities share the need for the consumer to rely on an agent to define the final consequences associated with the states of the world, which are central to the whole concept of expected utility theory. Consequently the consumer has problems with, as Weisbrod (1978) has described it, the 'counterfactual'. Certainly *ex ante* and frequently *ex post*, the consumer cannot judge what the effectiveness of health care consumption on his health status will be, or has been.

Expected utility theory also leads in health care to emphasis on consequences – essentially health status changes. Yet the processes involved in health care may also bear utility. These may matter in two ways and at two levels: the process utility associated with decision-making itself, i.e. the ability to pass difficult decisions to the clinician; and, second, the process utility associated with equity (which is discussed in more detail in chapter 4).

Again it is not argued that health care is unique in having utility associated with the decision-making procedures, just far from typical. It is also clear that 'health care' cannot be placed at a single point on a spectrum of these characteristics, since health care is a heterogeneous commodity. While even apparently minor symptoms of ill-health carry risks of major complications, thus reducing the apparent heterogeneity, it is clear that the extent to which those 'atypical' characteristics are present will vary depending on what specific health care commodity is being discussed.

Nor is it suggested that the nature of 'exchange' in health care is homogeneous; indeed it is clear that the personalities of the two central parties involved – the doctor and the patient – markedly influence the nature of the exchange and in fact the nature of the commodity itself. Attitudes to patient autonomy, to giving and receiving information, to risk and to other factors will influence the exchange and this applies to the attitudes of both patient and doctor. It is this aspect of heterogeneity, together with the problems associated with the individual patient's lack of knowledge of the relevant states of the world and their consequences, which almost make health care uniquely different.

However, that point is not the central issue. Rather it is that health care has these particular characteristics which should influence how economics is used in analysing this commodity. We try to indicate this in more detail in later chapters.

4

Distribution

4.1 Introduction

In chapter 3 it was stated that distributional considerations are important in health care. *Why* this is the case is the key question addressed in this chapter.

Before that, however, the next section, 4.2, provides some evidence to show that distributional issues *are* a concern of various health care systems in terms of both policies to promote equity and attempts to monitor changes in the distribution of health and health care across different groups in society.

Section 4.3 addresses the central question of equity in health care, i.e. what it is that best explains departures on distributional grounds from the objective of welfare (very often narrowed to health) maximisation subject to some budget constraint – which tends normally to be seen as constituting the efficiency goal of health care. In section 4.4, the precise form of equity in health care is discussed and the conclusion reached that, from the evidence of practical policy, i.e. the revealed preferences of policy-makers, equal access is the dimension of the most appropriate definition. The key issues arising in the chapter are summarised there.

4.2 The presence of equity in health care

4.2.1 Introduction

One of the complicating factors regarding distributional considerations, issues of interdependence of utility and equity, is that they can be built on various different theories of justice. For example, Veatch (1981, p. 265) identifies four: entitlement theory (in which individuals are entitled to what they have acquired justly), utilitarianism (which in its classical form may be interpreted to be about efficiency and not strictly about equity at all), maximin (involving maximising the benefit to the least advantaged) and egality (which involves a strict view of equality, in health care perhaps defined as equal health).

For the purposes of this book, equity is defined as involving some conscious departure(s) from the pursuit of maximising welfare (subject to some budget constraint) in the interest of a more equal distribution of some health-related characteristic (e.g. health care utilisation). Combining the concepts of efficiency and equity has spawned a very large literature which it is not appropriate to review in detail here (although relevant aspects are discussed in the next section). However, the central problem in such a combination process has been identified by Weale (1983, p. 84) as being that the Pareto principle of economic efficiency is concerned with the utility of one set of individuals under one set of circumstances as compared with those same individuals in another set of circumstances. Equity is about comparing different individuals one to another across the same or different circumstances.

In essence concern with equity involves the wish to abandon a strict willingness to pay criterion since such willingness must inevitably be based on ability to pay, which in turn reflects the existing distribution of income and wealth. If ability to pay is for some individuals or groups judged to be in some way or other 'impaired' then for various reasons this may mean that society generally, or those unimpaired in this respect, may wish to ensure that the distribution of certain relevant commodities (in this case health care) is not based solely on willingness to pay. As both Tobin (1970) and Weitzman (1977) indicate, and as discussed in the previous chapter, this type of specific egalitarianism may well include health care.

The two areas in which there has been most concern for equity in health care are across socio-economic groups/classes and geographically. It is of interest to note that these may be interpreted as exemplifying two different basic types of equity respectively. First, vertical equity involves the unequal treatment of unequals, i.e. the idea that if individuals have different health conditions (e.g. a common cold and pneumonia) they should be treated differently. Second, horizontal equity is concerned with the equal treatment of equals: two individuals both with pneumonia should *ceteris paribus* be treated equally. While in principle there are no difficulties with these concepts, in practice there can be. Horizontal equity is perhaps the simpler to handle largely because recognising equality both of conditions and of treatments is easier. Vertical equity entails not only measuring inequalities in conditions (say the *extent* to which pneumonia is worse than a cold) raising the problems of the cardinal measurement of health status discussed in chapter 2, but also determining how unequal the treatment responses should be. This latter condition will be more or less problematical depending on the precise definition of equity, e.g. more problematical for equal health as a definition than equal access to health care. (We return to this point in the final section of this chapter.)

4.2.2 Some policies for equity

In health care, there are many examples of the presence of considerations of equity. For example, in the United Kingdom, it can be argued that the *raison d'être* for the National Health Service was equity. Beveridge, the father of the NHS, argued for a health service which would provide treatment 'to every citizen without exception, without remuneration limit and without an economic barrier at any point to delay recourse to it' (Beveridge, 1942, p. 162). Whatever the extent of success in practice of the NHS in achieving such an equitable health service, there is evidence nonetheless to suggest that it continues as a goal, or at least a concern, of the NHS (see below on the efforts of the Resource Allocation Working Party ('RAWP') to promote regional equity (DHSS, 1976) and the research published on health status differentials across social classes through time (DHSS, 1980)). Whether social class equity remains anything more than a concern has to be questioned given the UK government's attempt to suppress partially the distribution of the Report of the (government) Working Party on Inequalities in Health (the 'Black'

Report, DHSS, 1980). Certainly issues of social class equity remain very much a topic of debate. (See, for example, Le Grand and Rabin, 1986 below.)

Equity is frequently cited either explicitly or implicitly as a goal of public health care systems. For example, in Sweden as early as 1935, the Swedish National Board for Health stated: 'What one social group can buy for money society should provide for the others' (Dahlgren and Diderichsen, 1985, p. 34). In Canada the introduction of public health insurance in 1971 was explicitly stated to be motivated by a concern to make health care utilisation less dependent on income. There is evidence (Broyles *et al.*, 1983) that the policy has succeeded and that because of the relatively high morbidity of the poor, their utilisation rates now tend to be higher than those of the better off.

Such concerns are not restricted to those countries with a dominant public system. Frequently, whatever the financing system, the poor pay less for their health care (for example being exempt from paying the normal 20 per cent of the cost of services in France). In the United States both Medicaid and Medicare clearly have their roots in concerns with equity.

More efforts have been made recently in a number of countries to consider how resources for health care can be deployed more equitably across different regions. While the most notable of these has perhaps been in the public health care system of the UK, the concern with this issue is international. For example, in the United States efforts have been made to attract more doctors to undersupplied areas. Further, equity considerations were clearly a part of the argument for setting up in the USA the President's Commission for the Study of Ethical Problems in Medicine and Biomedical and Behavioral Research (1983) especially on securing access to health care. In the Netherlands attempts have been made to promote geographical equity by controlling capital developments (Maynard and Ludbrook, 1981) to alter the locational distribution of hospital services.

The avowed objective of the 'RAWP' (DHSS, 1976) formulae in the UK was to improve geographical (strictly regional) equity in terms of equal access (equivalent to equal opportunity to use) for equal need. In England, the central government allocates resources for health care provision to the 14 Regional Health Authorities. Prior to 1976, these funds were disbursed largely according to supply side considerations. The change in emphasis has meant that 'need' now dominates the process.

Of course defining need is problematical. (See the discussion on need in chapter 8.) The process adopted in RAWP involved taking the different populations in the different regions and adjusting these to take account of various factors which might influence health care need. These factors included, beyond the size of the population: the composition of the population (age and sex affect health care needs); morbidity; cross boundary flows from one region to another; medical education; and capital investment.

One of the major problems faced in such a formulation was determining the relative morbidity in different regions. Because of lack of reliable data on sickness, what were used instead were standardised mortality ratios. This statistic compares the number of deaths actually occurring in a region with those that would be expected if the national mortality rates by age and sex were applicable to the population of that region.

It is also the case that while this formulation marked a major step forward in moving from a supply-based to a needs-based determination of allocations – and the formulae are being used to move gradually to this basis of funding regionally – strictly speaking, it does not provide an 'access' basis of equity. Little attempt is made to take account of differential access in the different regions. Indeed this is in effect assumed to be constant. Consequently the formulae are effectively based on 'inputs for equal need' rather than access for equal need.

4.2.3 Monitoring equity

A further indication of concern with equity in health care is revealed in the various attempts that have been made to monitor the distribution of health status and health care over time. A few examples are noted here as evidence of such interest. (For more detail of more countries see the WHO publication on social inequalities in health, Illsley and Svensson, 1986.)

First, in the UK, the Black Report on inequalities in health across different social classes (DHSS, 1980) suggested that from the early 1930s to the early 1970s not only were there continuing disparities in health indicators (based largely on mortality) but in some instances these appeared to be widening over time. For example, Table 4.1 shows that male mortality differed markedly across different occupational classes at the start of the period and that the differences increased through time.

Table 4.1 Male mortality by occupational class, 1930–2 to 1970–2: standardised mortality ratios: Men aged 15–64

Occupational class	1930–2	1949–53	1959–63	1970–2
I Professional	90	86	76	77
II Managerial	94	92	81	81
III Skilled manual and non-manual	97	101	100	104
IV Partly skilled	102	104	103	114
V Unskilled	111	118	143	137

Source: 'The Black Report' (DHSS, 1980).

Second, Le Grand and Rabin (1986) have developed an alternative approach to such monitoring, partly as a result of problems in the Black analysis, specifically the changing of the size of groups being compared and the possibility of manipulation of the classification scheme (see Jones and Cameron, 1984). They have used the Gini coefficient, as an individually-based index, to measure changes in the variance of age-at-death through time.

What does this index mean? The authors themselves explain it in the following terms (op. cit., p. 120): 'Consider a population of four individuals, one of whom dies at birth, one who lives for twenty-five years, one who lives for fifty years and one who lives for seventy-five years.' From this they present the information given in Table 4.2. From this data set, they then produce the following diagram (Figure 4.1).

The Gini coefficient is equal to the difference between the area below the diagonal (equal distribution line) and above the actual distribution, divided by the total area under the diagonal, i.e. A/A+B. Thus the higher the Gini coefficient, the greater is the variance of age-at-death. Le Grand and Rabin take this to be a measure of inequality. Using this index their results for England and Wales are summarised in Table 4.3.

In the actual age-at-death (columns (i) to (iii)) there have been

59

Table 4.2 Derivation of Gini coefficient

Number of individuals	Percentage of population	Cumulative number of years of life	Cumulative percentage of total years of life
1	25	0	0
2	50	25	16.7
3	75	75	50
4	100	150	100

Source: Le Grand and Rabin (1986).

reductions in variation over time. Standardised for the age distribution at the start of the period (columns (iv) to (vi)), there is less of a trend but it is still marked. Perhaps most relevant however is the final set of 'cohort' figures which allows comparison of those

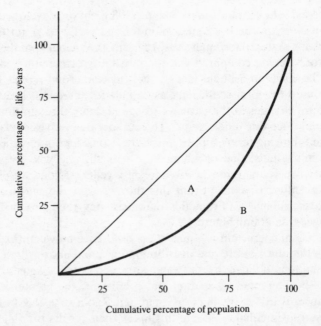

Figure 4.1 Derivation of Gini coefficient
Source: Le Grand and Rabin (1986).

Table 4.3 Inequality in age-at-death, all deaths, England and Wales, 1931–1983

| | Gini coefficients | | | | | | | | |
| | ACTUAL | | | STANDARDISED | | | COHORT | | |
Year	(i) Male	(ii) Female	(iii) Total	(iv) Male	(v) Female	(vi) Total	(vii) Male	(viii) Female	(ix) Total
1931	0.284	0.260	0.273	0.284	0.260	0.273	0.238	0.212	0.225
1951	0.160	0.143	0.153	0.184	0.176	0.182	0.146	0.127	0.138
1961	0.148	0.126	0.139	0.169	0.164	0.170	0.131	0.110	0.123
1971	0.137	0.116	0.129	0.161	0.160	0.163	0.123	0.104	0.116
1983	0.114	0.085	0.102	0.148	0.138	0.146	0.110	0.092	0.103

Source: Le Grand and Rabin (1986).

born in particular years (e.g. 1931 and 1983) by using the age-specific mortality rates in those years. Again there is this trend of reduction in variation through time.

Third, in terms of the use of health services generally, Le Grand (1978) concluded that equity was not being achieved. Later, however, Collins and Klein (1980, p. 1111), suggested that at least for primary health care 'the NHS has achieved equity in terms of access'.

In a country which has perhaps had the most long standing and comprehensive policy on social class in health and health care, Sweden, considerable disparities still exist aross different socio-economic groups. In Table 4.4, (with the exception of entre-preneurs) there is a clear, and quite steep, social class gradient in the prevalence of chronic illness.

Comparisons of equity in health and health care across different countries are difficult but can be revealing. For example, Maynard and Ludbrook (1981) compared regional inequalities in health care, using a RAWP-type formula, in England, France and the Netherlands. They found that England and the Netherlands showed approximately the same degree of inequality regionally, whereas France exhibited much greater variation (e.g. in France the worst region was funded to only two-thirds of what its allocation would have been if funds were to be allocated on a relative needs basis).

In Hurst's comparisons of England, Canada and the USA, he found greater variations regionally in the USA than in England or

Distribution

Canada (Hurst, 1985). By income group, interestingly, in all three countries extra hospital use by the poor was as great or greater than their extra morbidity. Also in Hurst's analysis it is tentatively suggested that payments for health care are either neutral or progressive in Canada and the UK, but distinctly regressive in the USA.

A note of caution is, however, justified in looking at such measurement and monitoring. As is true of many phenomena but, it seems, especially so of equity in health care (perhaps in part because of the ideological debate underlying considerations of equity) the monitoring of equity has to be examined critically with respect to precisely what it is that is being measured and why the monitoring is being conducted. For example, the evidence cited above from Collins and Klein (1980) that access to primary health care is equitably distributed in terms of social classes might appear to be contradictory to Le Grand's earlier evidence (Le Grand, 1978). Yet the former is concerned with primary health care: the latter with all health care. What is confusing here is that both are concerned with use of services, despite Collins and Klein's

Table 4.4 Index of those suffering from chronic illness in Sweden between the ages of 16 and 64 according to ULF* – 1980/81 (all employed persons = 100; standardised for age and sex)

	Chronic illness
Unskilled workers	111
Skilled workers	102
ALL MANUAL WORKERS	109
Junior salaried workers	99
Intermediate-level salaried workers	84
Executives	79
ALL SALARIED EMPLOYEES	89
Farmers	97
Entrepreneurs	114
ALL GAINFULLY EMPLOYED PERSONS	100

* Regular health interview conducted by the National Bureau for Statistics

description of their study in terms of access (which is the opportunity to use rather than use *per se*).

Overall, therefore, there is evidence of concern with and interest in equity in health care and not just in public health care systems (although it would seem more pronounced there). As indicated above this is manifested in two ways: first in policies in health care which attempt to promote equity, and second in various efforts to measure equity and monitor it over time.

4.3 Interdependent utility and equity

4.3.1 Introduction

It is legitimate to pose the question of whether or not economists should be at all interested with distributional concerns in health care and if so what the nature of their contribution to considerations of, for example, equity can be. This is especially the case as conventionally economics is, as indicated at the start of chapter 3, about self-interested egoistic man pursuing rational paths to the goal of efficiency.

Yet there is increasing concern among economists with this view. Collard (1978, p. 3) begins his book on *Altruism and Economy* by stating that his thesis is 'that human beings are not entirely selfish, even in their economic dealings'. He suggests however that 'self-interested "economic man" dominates the textbooks. Indeed rationality and self-interest are often taken as one and the same thing' (op. cit., p. 3). Despite this he maintains that it is possible to consider 'rational altruistic man' (ibid.).

It is a theme which has been considered by, *inter alia*, Lindsay (1969), Sen (1977), Arrow and Hahn (1971) and Margolis (1982). While raised, it is curious how little it is discussed specifically in the literature on the economics of health care despite the fact that there, as compared with most other markets, the extent to which 'every agent is actuated only by self interest', to quote Edgeworth (1881, p. 16), or 'economic man is concerned *only* with the bundle of goods and services he is to receive', to quote Collard (1978, p. 6), appears limited. How equity in health care can be handled conceptually by economics is the central theme of this section.

There are different ways of achieving this and while superficially

63

there may appear little to distinguish between them, important differences emerge. These revolve around certain key issues:

(i)   the extent to which equity can be dealt with through a 'caring externality';

(ii)   how far a utilitarian calculus can embrace equity, defined either as classical utilitarianism concerned solely with the final consequences of the states of the world or a moderated utilitarianism involving process utility as well as outcome utility;

(iii)   the need for and desirability of a Kantian moral imperative to explain equity; and

(iv)   the relevance of Rawls' theory of justice in the context of health care (Rawls, 1972).

4.3.2 Sympathy and commitment

Central to the debate on equity is the distinction which Sen (1977) draws between the concept of sympathy and that of commitment. Sympathising for another person means that as the other person's welfare increases (decreases) so does one's own, i.e. there is a positive (negative) externality. As Sen (op. cit., p. 95) states: 'behaviour based on sympathy is in an important sense egoistic, for one is oneself pleased at others' pleasure and pained at others' pain, and the pursuit of one's own utility may thus be helped by sympathetic action'. Not that the concept is new. Sympathy was discussed by, for example, Hume (1736), Smith (1776) and Edgeworth (1881) – indeed the latter proposed 'a coefficient of effective sympathy' as part of the individual's maximand (op. cit., p. 53).

Commitment is defined 'in terms of a person choosing an act that he believes will yield a lower level of personal welfare to him than an alternative that is also available to him' (Sen, op. cit., p. 95). Commitment thus violates the axiom of selection, i.e. the notion (see chapter 3) that the consumer aims for his most preferred state. This definition can be extended to include situations where a choice does increase an individual's anticipated personal welfare but where this is not the reason for the choice.

The existence of commitment creates many problems for the traditional stance of economics which is based primarily on the notion that personal choice and personal welfare have a common identity. Thus as Sen (op. cit., p. 97) states, 'the basic link between choice behaviour and welfare achievements in the traditional models is severed as soon as commitment is admitted as an ingredient of choice'.

Let us look, in the specific context of health care, at these two concepts in more detail, first sympathy and then commitment. Sympathy is most appropriately seen in terms of externalities. Culyer (1976), in his analysis of the NHS, identified as one of the key features that of the 'caring' externality. Initially he saw this in terms of individual's health. He suggested that people are not just affected by the risk of being infected by others' ill health but by the state of health of others. 'Individuals are affected by others' health status for the simple reason that most of them care' (Culyer, op. cit., p. 89). In this form it is thus positive in nature. However, given the discussion of health and health care in chapter 3 and the fact that it is only the latter which is the tradeable commodity, it is difficult to see how we can sensibly talk about equity in terms of redistribution of health. Certainly Sen's notion of sympathy is strong here: individuals sympathise with others' ill health.

Yet elsewhere Culyer (1980) argued for the dimension of equity being considered in terms of health care. This in principle changes the perspective markedly. It is rather difficult to see others' consumption of health care purely in terms of sympathy. It may be more helpful to change the perspective to that of health care as a merit good, i.e. a good which some 'élite' decides will be socially under-consumed if left to the willingness to pay of individual sovereign consumers.

Again while Lindsay (1969, p. 75) talks of 'the apparently universal desire and willingness to share' in the health care market and initially equates this with 'equal access', most of his analysis focuses on consumption rather than access. (The need for clarity in considering the objective of equity is discussed later in this chapter.)

The merit good view of health care consumption as the relevant dimension of equity, is more clearly seen when Lees' statement is examined, i.e. that 'the basic purpose of the NHS is to enforce equality of consumption of medical care' (Lees, 1962, p. 116). It is difficult to see how sympathy and merit goods (or essentially enforcement) can be genuinely reconciled. Indeed the argument has now become normative. It is this 'sympathy' view mixed with, in the latter instance, the merit goods nature of the commodity health care, which to date has tended to dominate discussion among economists of equity in health care.

4.3.3 Titmuss: the Kantian imperative

There is a second school of thought, of what is perhaps best described as a less egoistically-based motivation for behaviour, which may stimulate individuals to support equity as a social goal of health care. This is identified in the literature with Titmuss (1970), Sen (1977) and Margolis (1982).

In the case of Titmuss, one of the complications is that he would want to see altruism *per se* as an argument in his preferred social welfare function. This emphasises the normative nature of Titmuss' view of equity. He expresses regret that modern society provides little scope, outside family and friends, for 'giving' in morally practical terms. He further suggests that if altruistic behaviour is not practised sufficiently often then it may wither. This view is echoed by Singer (1973) who compares altruistic behaviour to sexual potency in that it may be strengthened by use. Arrow (1974a) adopts an alternative view, suggesting that the stock of altruism is a scarce resource and has an opportunity cost in use.

Titmuss argues that the 'true' nature of choices in social policy is not made sufficiently apparent by those who argue that economic markets can take care of health care. His concerns at this level are two and quite distinct. One is that of externalities, essentially the creation of a 'blood proletariat' serving large areas of the world. It is not, however, at this level that particular interest lies for the present. More important is the Kantian moral imperative lying behind, for example, Titmuss' view of blood donations in the UK. In other words, individuals have a duty to give. Such a view does not fit with egoistic selfish economic man. Nor does it fit with Culyer's caring externality.

In the case of Titmuss, his position may be best stated as a mix of what Collard (1978) has called the contagion thesis (i.e. altruism in one individual is in part a positive function of the amount of altruism around him) and a Kantian moral imperative. If all voluntary donors behaved in a non-Kantian way they would accept that their individual contributions would have a negligible impact on blood availability. The inconvenience costs of blood giving would almost certainly outweigh the benefits the individual could bestow by increasing the probability that an individual needing blood could obtain it. Thus no voluntary blood donating would occur.

However, if individuals act in a Kantian manner (see Collard, 1978) then they would give on the basis that it was their duty to give. If this is then linked to the contagion thesis, not only will the Kantian imperative directly affect the probability of blood's being available but indirectly by 'infecting' others to give. The key issue in Titmuss is, however, the Kantian imperative.

4.3.4 Sen's commitment

Sen (1977) does not consider health care explicitly. His concern is with the impact on economic analysis more generally through the introduction or acceptance of the concept of commitment. As indicated above the key distinction that Sen makes between sympathy (e.g. the caring externality) and commitment is that the conscious choice of the latter means either a reduction in anticipated utility, or if not, that it could have resulted in a reduction in utility had there not been an increase in utility as a result of some other characteristic of the choice. It is this feature of utility loss which is important to our discussion.

Sen offers no explicit explanation for individuals' choosing commitment. It is clearly a conscious choice otherwise it is not defined as commitment. This conscious choice element is crucial in another sense in that sympathy (externality) is already present in many economic models and even where it is not, can be built in without too great difficulties. But, as Sen (op. cit., p. 96) states 'commitment does involve, in a very real sense *counterpreferential choice*, destroying the crucial assumptions that a chosen alternative must be better than (or at least as good as) the others for the person choosing it, and this would certainly require that models be formulated in an essentially different way' (our emphasis added). Commitment is, for Sen (op. cit., p. 97), most characteristically seen in terms of 'the fact that it drives a wedge between personal choice and personal welfare'.

It is not clear (largely because of the lack of explanation of the phenomenon by Sen) whether or not Sen views this notion of commitment wholly positively or in part normatively. It is probably both, being descriptive of motives and normative in suggesting that it is how people should behave. Thus in applying it to health care it does no more than offer a normative explanation of what *may* be a useful description of the reasons for the concern over distributional matters which undoubtedly exists with regard to health care.

4.3.5 Margolis and participation

Margolis and Sen are not so very far apart, as indeed the former accepts (Margolis, 1982). It is possible, as a limited interpretation, to view Margolis as essentially a more detailed and rigorous formulation, but with important differences, of a process begun by Titmuss and pursued by Sen.

To understand Margolis it is necessary to examine two concepts of altruism, some aspects of which have already been raised in chapter 3. First, there is participation altruism: this arises because individuals gain utility from participating in social acts. This utility, it is to be noted, is in the participating, not in any utility from the consumption which the individual's contribution provides. (The utility is in giving to the charity not in vicariously getting utility from the spending by the charity.)

Second, there is outcome, or what Margolis calls 'goods' altruism. In this case the individual's altruism is directly a function of the fact that others are better off as a result of his having given. Others' pleasures contribute to the givers' pleasures; their pains to his pains. This second form of altruism is identical for all relevant purposes to Culyer's caring externality and Sen's sympathy. However, participation altruism and commitment, while having some common features, are not identical.

Margolis suggests that each individual has *two* utility functions, one concerned with utility selfishly, which is a conventional utility function in that the individual derives utility from the spending on his own private goals and the other (which is unconventional) concerned with utility derived by contributing to or participating in some group, i.e. a form of process utility.

This latter utility function needs some explanation. Margolis states (op. cit., p. 2): 'If individuals are observed to be acting in a manner that seems rational from a social but not an individual point of view then we can say that they are acting *as if* they had two different utility functions.' Further he suggests that allowing for two utility functions 'is not *necessarily* inconsistent with individual utility-maximising'. This differentiates participation altruism from Sen's notion of commitment.

This second utility function is not an 'outcome' utility function: it is born of the *process* of participation. The relevant utility to the individual is not in what is obtained by the group by way of increased group utility as a result of his contribution. It is the process of contributing, of participating, from which the second form of utility is derived. The individual then allocates his resources between these two utility functions in such a way as to maximise his utility. Thus there is no giving up of utility by the individual as is necessary in commitment as defined by Sen and it is possible to reconcile the concept with economic models based on self-centred egoistic man.

Thus in Margolis' analysis an individual can choose to devote his resources to 'selfish' ends and to 'group' ends. The division of his resources to these competing ends is determined by, what Margolis refers to as, the value ratio. This is defined as G'/S', which is the ratio of marginal group utility (G') to marginal selfish utility (S') as perceived by any individual. It is important to emphasise that the value ratio is defined in terms of the individual's *values*, not his resources. There is thus 'no necessary connection between the value ratio and (an individual's) own participation in the provision of goods either to himself or to society at large' (op. cit., p. 38). Also it should be noted that G' is the marginal utility to the group *as perceived by the individual* but is unaffected by his allocation (it is negligible *vis-à-vis* total group resources) to the group.

Thus for example, if individuals gave equal weight at the margin to group interest and to self-interest, then they would allocate additional resources to group interest if the value ratio $G'/S' > 1$ and would be in equilibrium when $G'/S' = 1$.

If all individuals in a group were equally self-interested (and, therefore, by definition equally group-interested) there would be a stable situation. However, if individuals within groups differ in the extent of their group interest, then the more self-interested may tend to do rather nicely, thank you.

It is to avoid the difficulties arising from the exploitation of the relatively unselfish that Margolis introduces the concept of 'participation altruism'. Essentially this assumes that relatively unselfish members have a propensity to limit their willingness to act in group-interest to the extent that they have done so. Thus the willingness to participate in group activities is subject to diminishing marginal utility.

The importane of the application of the Margolis model to health care is that it offers an explanation, which is reconcilable with rationality, as to why individuals may be concerned with the distribution of that commodity. Individuals are concerned with distribution to the extent that this allows them to exercise group utility.

What is significant in the similarities in standpoints between Sen and Titmuss on the one hand and Margolis on the other is that the former start from the position of questioning whether the self-interested egoist, that is economic man in neoclassical theory, is sustainable as a basis on which to build the principles of economic analysis. Moving to Margolis allows more of the self-interested egoist to re-emerge. (It is also the case – perhaps inevitably – that there is simultaneously a move away from a normative view to positivism.) To make such a statement is not intended to be anything other than morally neutral but technically it has advantages in allowing Margolis to develop his approach more rigorously.

4.3.6 Rawls' theory of justice

Several authors (see for example Culyer, 1976) have suggested that Rawls' theory of justice (Rawls, 1972) provides a solution to determining the role of justice in individuals' utility functions with reference to health care. But such a theory is not without its problems.

The particular features of Rawls' theory of justice as fairness that are relevant here are:

(i) it is based on 'maximin', i.e. it pursues the idea that the 'just' solution is to MAXimise the benefit of the least (MINimum) advantaged;

(ii) this is achieved on the basis that individuals, behind their veil of ignorance (regarding their position in society), are risk averse and consequently, essentially out of self interest, would want to improve their own lot most if they happened to be the worst off in society;

(iii) it is addressed to primary social goods, among which health care is not explicitly listed. These goods include: freedom of movement and choice of occupations; powers and prerogatives of office; income and wealth; a set of basic liberties; and the social bases of self-respect. It could be argued of course that *health* is included to some exent under the last three.

It would be possible to add health care to that list. Arrow (1974a) argues against doing so on two grounds. First, maximising the benefit to the least advantaged in health terms might impoverish a society. Second, it would form the interpersonal comparisons of utility that Rawls is keen to avoid, for example involving trade-offs between primary goods, e.g. in this instance health care and income and wealth. (For more discussion see Daniels, 1985, p. 44.) A preferred solution (see Daniels, op. cit.) might be to argue that if we want to adopt a Rawlsian stance, this can be done by including health care among his basic institutions involved in providing for fair equality of opportunity. If this choice is made, equality of opportunity (or equal access) for equal need is then the preferred equity objective.

4.4 Conclusions

The previous section gave a brief overview of the suggested means of analysing interdependent utility and consequently equity in economics. Some were specific to health care, others were general explanations. All have implications for the treatment of the distribution of health care. However, even if agreement could be reached about the behavioural motivations – and that has to be doubted given their nature and the limitations inherent in testing these empirically – there remain difficulties in defining and measuring equity in health care. Many of the measurement problems were rehearsed in section 4.2 and there is no need to repeat them here.

However, beyond the discussion above about the nature of the explanation for equity in health care, there is still left open the question of precisely what form it should or does take. Many suggestions have been made: equal expenditure *per caput* for equal need; equal access for equal need; equal utilisation; equal health (Mooney, 1983). The evidence would seem to suggest that equal access for equal need is most favoured, essentially the principle of equal opportunity.

One of the difficulties here is to decide how far to go, since equity (as discussed above and see West, 1981) often comes at a price in terms of a trade-off with efficiency, depending of course on how both equity and efficiency are defined. That is a more difficult question and one that it seems likely will vary from culture to culture depending on *inter alia* the extent of willingness (utility) associated with participation.

A Rawlsian interpretation might lend support to the notion of equity in terms of equal access. At an empirical level, the policy on equity of most health care systems is normally also defined in terms of access rather than health or health care utilisation. Thus Rawls and policy evidence seem to be more supportive of Titmuss, Sen and Margolis than of Culyer and Lees. Access is the relevant dimension of Titmuss' Kantian view and Sen's commitment. Participating in the group means, for Margolis, providing the service on grounds of process utility, not making any assumptions about the extent of its use or its effectiveness, although the extent to which individuals would be prepared to contribute would almost certainly be a function of both use and effectiveness.

Yet at the level of monitoring and measuring equity there is something of a conundrum. While policy is normally concerned with equality of access, measurement has been focused much more on health status and consumption or use. In many respects these are (at least theoretically) easier to measure, but that does not seem an adequate explanation. Perhaps there is a simple need for greater understanding of the differences which exist in terms of how equity may be defined in different dimensions.

Can we distinguish between the relevance of Titmuss/Sen and that of Margolis? At a simple level it can be clearly stated that the latter may be preferred to the former in the way that many economists might in any case choose Bentham before Kant.

More significantly perhaps it is to be noted that in health care we are not dealing with a homogeneous commodity, especially in this context regarding the equity characteristics of the commodity. In other words we would postulate that the extent of 'commitment' is likely to vary depending on the medical condition concerned, for example, whether it involved orthodontics or intensive hospital care. While perhaps not a strong argument, it appears more straightforward to build in variations in commitment in the form of the participation utility function in Margolis than in the Kantian moral imperative of Titmuss.

In his review of Collard's book on *Altruism and Economy* Jones-Lee (1980, p. 205) writes that the crucial question that needs to be posed regarding altruism is:

whether or not altruistically motivated preferences (or choices) *ought* to be treated just like selfish preferences in a social decision-making calculus, and in particular whether treating them in this way involves 'double-counting' of the interests of those individuals or groups that are the objects of altruism.

This question is especially pertinent to equity in health care. Perhaps, in so far as it is important to answer it, and given the capacity that Margolis gives to provide an answer, that is an added reason for preferring Margolis' approach.

Can Margolis' motivational perspective be supported by empirical evidence? In practice it is difficult to see how. Margolis (1982, p. 37) suggests that there is no normative content to his view and that 'the reasonableness of the principle . . . turns only on how well it accounts for the way people are observed to behave'. Sen (1977, p. 107) at the same time suggests that empirical evidence 'cannot be sought in the moral observation of actual choices, and must involve other sources of information, including introspection and discussion'. Perhaps that is unsatisfactory but it does seem to represent the 'state of the art' in this area at the present time. It also represents what would seem to be considerable advances in knowledge and insights on the not so distant past.

5

The cost-benefit approach in theory

5.1 Introduction

In the previous chapter the importance of distributional issues in health and health care was explored. Economic appraisal, or the cost-benefit approach, is concerned with increasing efficiency but, ultimately, efficiency cannot be divorced from issues of distribution and equity. Given its central importance, equity assumes a greater role in economic appraisal as applied to health and health care than in some other areas of application.

In chapter 3 the nature of health and health care was examined from an economic perspective and the implications of these matters discussed. Given the difficulties of achieving market mechanisms in health care (as discussed in chapter 11), especially in the acute sector, there is a need for the planned allocation of resources and hence for economic appraisal.

Economic appraisal clearly requires measures of the benefits of health care in order to plan the best uses for available resources. It must, therefore, build on the results of epidemiology and the measurement and valuation of health improvements, as described in chapter 2. This measurement and valuation of unmarketed outcomes is a major issue in the application of economic appraisal to health care.

Following this introductory section, this chapter is divided into four parts. The next part (section 5.2) sets out the underlying principles of the cost-benefit approach to allocating resources for health care, in particular distinguishing between technical efficiency, allocative efficiency, social efficiency and social welfare, and between technical judgements and value judgements in appraisal. Section 5.3 deals specifically with the valuation of human life. The process of economic appraisal in terms of its various stages, showing the special complexities that arise in the case of health care, is set out in section 5.4. Finally section 5.5. draws conclusions as to the usefulness of the cost-benefit approach in health and health care. This structure then provides the framework for chapter 6 which assesses applied studies of economic appraisal.

5.2 The principles of the cost-benefit approach

5.2.1 Efficiency and equity

It would not be appropriate to undertake here an extensive elaboration of the whole field of cost-benefit analysis. Rather the salient principles are briefly set out and the interested reader is referred to other more specialised texts for fuller arguments and details of the theory (Winch, 1971; Dasgupta and Pearce, 1972; Dasgupta, Marglin and Sen, 1972; Layard, 1972; Mishan, 1975; Nash, Pearce and Stanley, 1975; Sugden and Williams, 1978; Drummond, 1980; Drummond, 1981; Pearce and Nash, 1981; Sugden, 1981; Ng, 1983; Dreze and Stern, 1985).

In the absence of resource allocation using the cost-benefit approach, the resulting resource use could be 'inefficient' and/or 'inequitable' and we first discuss what is meant by these terms. Efficiency is a state where the costs of producing any given output are minimised and the utility of individuals' preferences is maximised. Efficiency can sometimes be attained in competitive markets. Private projects are undertaken if they produce profits, and not otherwise, or if a choice must be made between competing mutually exclusive projects then the most profitable one is undertaken. However, what is profitable to the person (or group) who gains the profits is not necessarily profitable to society as a whole. The cost-benefit approach adopts this societal perspective. In order to ensure consistency between the pursuit of maximum utility for society as a whole and the pursuit of maximum profitability, certain conditions must be satisfied. In essence these are that all effects relevant to the utility of all individuals must be correctly priced in markets and that perfect competition must prevail. If these conditions do not hold then the pursuit of maximum profitability may be inconsistent with the pursuit of maximum utility. If, for example, buyers are poorly informed about what they are purchasing, competition between sellers is not possible or not allowed, certain effects relevant to the utility of certain individuals or groups are not tradeable in markets, or market prices diverge from opportunity costs, then publicly directed control of resource allocation may allow more utility to be attained than would be achieved by private profit maximisation. In these senses the market may 'fail' to be efficient.

Undoubtedly such market 'failures' explain in part state intervention in health services. With such interventions, most of the markets in which health care might have been traded simply do not exist. Hence other procedures must be used for allocating resources, such as the cost-benefit approach. It is important to realise that market 'failures' are not just a feature of countries with a public health care system such as the UK but are common in countries with insurance-funded systems. Ignorance, prohibition of competition, externalities, prices that do not represent opportunity costs, and, therefore, the potential for inefficiency, are the norm, not the exception, in health services.

There is a need to distinguish between technical efficiency, allocative efficiency and social efficiency. Technical efficiency is where the costs of producing a given output are minimised, or where output is maximised for a given cost. Allocative efficiency exists where it is not possible to make any individual better off without making some other individual worse off. The existence of perfect markets can be shown to lead to both technical and allocative efficiency, given any initial distribution of endowments of resources. However, each different initial endowment will produce a different state of allocative efficiency – there is no uniquely allocatively efficient state. The choice between allocatively efficient states – or between endowments – must be made with reference to criteria other than efficiency.

Allocative efficiency is held by many economists to be important because the desirability of moving from allocatively inefficient to efficient states would, it is argued, command universal assent. That is, if it is possible to undertake some change so that at least one person is better off without making anyone worse off then this

76

must be a 'good thing' and consequently *ought* to be undertaken. This is a value judgement but, it is claimed, one from which few people would dissent. (For a critique of this claim see Sen, 1970, and Sugden, 1981.) These changes are 'Pareto improvements'. Public projects in which no one is made worse off are relatively rare, and in order to identify a larger range of projects that ought to be undertaken, the criterion of approval has been changed to that of *potential* Pareto improvement.

This is the corner-stone of the cost-benefit approach in that its aim is to identify projects that satisfy this criterion, as an aid to decision-making. A project would satisfy the potential Pareto improvement criterion if it *could* make at least one person better off and no one worse off, *if* the losers were to be compensated from the beneficiaries' gains. Thus the criterion is satisfied if the amount by which the beneficiaries gain exceeds the amount by which the losers lose. The aim is to maximise the total value of outputs produced, the achievement of which is social efficiency. This differs from allocative efficiency in that the latter implies no 'losers', whereas the pursuit of social efficiency implies that there can be 'losers'. If there is a potential Pareto improvement and additionally compensation from beneficiaries to losers is actually undertaken then social and allocative efficiency coincide.

Whether or not the losers *should* be compensated from the excess of gain over loss is, it has been argued, a separate issue requiring additional value judgements concerning society's views over the equity of distribution. The distinction is, however, false (Pearce and Nash, 1981; Sugden, 1981). The failure to compensate the losers requires the value judgement that they *ought not* to be compensated, and the permission of the gainers to receive the benefits requires the value judgement that they *ought* to gain. Thus value judgements concerning the distribution of welfare are in fact implicit if not explicit, and are not 'additional'. It is argued by some (Mishan, 1974) that the cost-benefit approach should simply try to identify potential Pareto improvements. However, from the point of view of aiding decision-making, analysis of distributional issues is also desirable. As was argued in the last chapter, to the extent that equity is more than just an externality, the case for this is even stronger when applying the cost-benefit approach to health and health care. Hence a broader classification of projects than just 'potentially capable of producing a Pareto improvement' (or 'socially efficient' for brevity) and 'incapable of producing a Pareto improvement' (or 'socially inefficient') is required. Rather the classification should also assess projects according to whether they are equitable.

The analysis of equity in conjunction with efficiency is still a controversial subject amongst economists. For example, Williams (1985, p. 326) has suggested that 'the objective of economic appraisal is to ensure that as much benefit as possible is obtained from the resources devoted to health care'. Culyer (1979, p. 45) has written that 'If the underlying rationale of the NHS is . . . concerned with the health status of individual members of the population, it is a natural extension to suppose that the general objective of the NHS might be summarised as being to maximise, given the budget allocated, the health of the population.' Ng (1983, p. 244) has argued that 'analysis based on efficiency alone is worth its face value with no need for a distributional proviso. In short, a dollar is a dollar.'

Certainly it is simpler to analyse only whether a project is socially efficient or inefficient. To use such analysis in decision-making, however, requires the additional value judgement that the gainers ought to gain and the losers lose. If this value judgement is accepted then all projects that fall into categories (i) and (iii) of Table 5.1 would be approved of, and those in (ii) and (iv) would be rejected. If it is not accepted then an additional criterion is required to judge whether projects are equitable or not. Using this additional criterion, projects in category (i) would be approved of and those in category (iv) would be rejected. Those in (ii) and (iii) would be indeterminate without an additional value judgement to specify how much equity gain would be worth an efficiency loss, or *vice versa*.

The value judgements trading-off the distributional and efficiency effects can be built into the social welfare function (SWF). Undertaking projects that fall into category (i) leads to the maximisation of social welfare if the SWF is defined in terms of both efficiency and equity. Undertaking projects that fall into categories (i) and (iii) leads to the maximisation of social welfare only if the SWF is defined solely in terms of social efficiency, which is a special case of the SWF. Thus the essential difference between social efficiency and social welfare lies in the incorporation of an equity criterion. Social efficiency takes no account of who gains which benefits or who bears which costs. Social welfare may take account of desert, need, rights, justice, fairness, and other criteria, in judging projects by their equity as well as their efficiency.

Table 5.1 Classification of projects

	Socially efficient	Socially inefficient
Equitable	(i)	(ii)
Inequitable	(iii)	(iv)

5.2.2 Measuring efficiency

Gains and losses, or benefits and costs, are usually measured with reference to the consumer's surplus. Such measurement assumes that consumers are 'sovereign'. As chapter 3 has explained, this assumption may not hold in relation to the consumption of health care. Consumer's surplus is usually measured by the compensating variation (CV). This is the maximum a consumer would be willing to pay for a benefit, or the minimum a consumer would be willing to receive to accept some loss. Thus the CV is measured with reference to the consumer's existing utility level.

An alternative measure is the equivalent variation (EV). This is the minimum a consumer would be willing to receive rather than forgo a benefit, or the maximum a consumer would be willing to pay rather than suffer some loss. Thus the EV is measured with reference to the consumer's new utility level.

Hence it follows that:

CV of a potential benefit = EV of a potential cost
CV of a potential cost   = EV of a potential benefit

The CV and EV will differ where there are 'income effects', that is where moving to a higher level of real income through the receipt of a benefit, or lower level through suffering a cost, changes the consumer's real income and hence the valuation of the goods gained or lost. Thus for normal goods EV > CV, and for inferior goods CV > EV.

In theory, for inferior goods these differences can give rise to the 'Scitovsky paradox' where a change is preferred *ex ante* (CV is greater than the cost of bringing about the change) but is dispreferred *ex post* (EV is less than the cost of bringing about the change). However, where income effects are negligible the Scitovsky effect will also be negligible. In practice it is rare that account is taken of income effects and most studies measure benefits and costs using measures of willingness to pay or be compensated – i.e. the CV. CVs can be measured as the area under the (real-income-compensated) demand curve – see Figure 5.1.

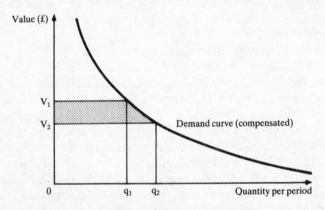

Figure 5.1 Measuring consumer's surplus

An increase in the quantity consumed, from q_1 to q_2, is valued as the shaded area, given that this demand curve shows the value to the demander of a marginal unit, at each quantity. While in theory real-income-compensated demand curves are *not* those which are measurable from actual price changes, in practice if the price changes are sufficiently small the income effects will be negligible, and the area under the uncompensated demand curve will normally serve as a sufficiently accurate measure.

5.2.3 Shadow pricing

Where there are external effects in consumption, or where there are constraints on what individuals may demand, observed valuations must be replaced by 'shadow prices'. For example, the social valuation of individual A's extra consumption of cigarettes may be less than A's CV if the cigarette smoke gets up B's nose. If involuntary unemployment is prevalent then the apparent valuation of leisure time may exceed individuals' true valuations if they are constrained to consume more leisure than they would prefer, given a choice. If no market exists then, obviously, the demand for a commodity cannot be observed at all. In such situations shadow prices are imputed to measure the CV that would have been present in the absence of market distortions.

A particular issue in this context is 'valuing life'. Many health care projects will affect some individuals' probabilities of death or life expectancy. Yet are there 'markets' where such risks are traded? And if there are, how distorted are these markets? The issue of valuing life has developed a considerable literature, and rather than being discussed here, section 5.3 deals with it specifically.

5.2.4 Time preference and discounting

The effects of a project may be spread over time and, hence, it is necessary to weight future *vis-à-vis* present effects. Individuals may have positive time preference rates which means that they will discount future costs and benefits. There are several reasons why this may be the case. A first is pure myopia or impatience. Pearce and Nash (1981) argue that myopia is irrational and, although individuals may determine their own time preference for consumption with reference to it, the myopia should be ignored in any social weighting of present *vis-à-vis* future consumption. A second reason is that there is always uncertainty in the future. If consumption of a good is deferred it may never be enjoyed at all because, for example, the individual may die during the period of deferment, or it may be enjoyed less if the individual's tastes change, as may occur in the event of illness. A third reason is that additional consumption at a later date may add less to utility than consumption now, given diminishing marginal utility of consumption, if the individual expects to be better off at the later date.

Another reason, apart from positive time preference, for

weighting future benefits less highly than present benefits, is that benefits available in the present may be invested to produce greater benefits in the future. For example, if the interest rate is 5 per cent, £100 available now may be invested for a year to produce £105 in 12 months time. Receiving £100 in 12 months time instead of now would mean forgoing the £5 interest. Therefore there is an opportunity cost to receiving benefits in the future instead of in the present.

There are thus two approaches to weighting future, as compared with present, benefits and costs. The former involves the social time preference (STP) rate and the latter the social opportunity cost of capital (SOC). The first approach is determined with direct reference to individuals' preferences regarding the future *vis-à-vis* the present, while the second with reference to the prevailing real rate of interest. If all markets were perfectly competitive then individuals' preferences would determine the prevailing rates of interest and the two approaches would give the same result. However, since markets are imperfect and since the STP approach may wish also to incorporate other value judgements – such as ignoring the element of individual myopia – then there will be differences between the STP and the SOC. These differences are more likely to be resolved in favour of the STP approach where economic appraisal is conducted with reference to a Social Welfare Function that incorporates judgements about equity, whereas if the objective is to maximise social efficiency then the SOC approach may be adopted.

The weighting of future costs and benefits is accomplished by means of a discount rate whereby CVs in different years are summed as follows:

$$\sum_{t=0}^{T} CV_t (1 + r)^{-t}$$

where $t = 0$ is the present, $t = 1$ is one year hence, and so forth, and r is the discount rate.

5.2.5 Risk and uncertainty

The effects of a project may not be certain. The value of CVs in such circumstances may diverge from where effects are certain. Risk is where the probability of an effect happening is less than certain, but the probability is known. For example, if an individual has a 50 per cent chance of gaining £100 and a 50 per cent chance of gaining £60 then the expected gain is £80. If the individual is averse to risk, then the certainty of gaining £80 will be preferred to the 50 per cent chance of £100 and £60. This will be the case if there is diminishing marginal utility of wealth. Hence some smaller sum – say £75 – may be preferred to the 50 per cent chance of £100 and £60. The proportionate difference between the expected sum – £80 in this case – and the smaller certain sum that is equally preferred, is a measure of the individual's *risk aversion*. In general, risky gains are less highly preferred than certain equivalents, and this must be taken into account in valuing CVs, which ideally should be valued at certainty equivalents.

Uncertainty is a more difficult problem. Uncertainty refers to where the possible effects are known, but their probabilities are not. In response to uncertainty individuals may adopt different strategies, for example, they may adopt a strategy that had the least bad worst outcome – the 'maximin' strategy. Again the value of the CV will be affected by the extent of uncertainty.

5.2.6 Direct valuation

An alternative to trying to estimate individuals' CVs *indirectly* is to do so *directly*. For example, individuals could be presented with two scenarios, one with a project, the other without, and asked directly how much they would be willing to pay for the project. One problem here is that if they themselves will not actually have to pay, they may have an incentive to under- or overstate their willingness to pay to try to influence the decision so that the outcome reflects their preferred option.[1]

5.2.7 Aggregation and equity

Specifying how equitable a project is poses major measurement problems as discussed in the previous chapter. Maximising social welfare involves taking account of the extent to which individuals are felt to merit a 'fair' share. If some individuals – e.g. the rich – derive utility from the utility gains of others – e.g. the poor – then there will be an external benefit to be included from the gains to the poor, over and above the poor's own assesment of their utility gain. One method of building in society's preferences for an equitable distribution of gains and losses is to attach weights (W_i) to individuals' CVs, according to the importance to be attached to particular individuals' gains/losses, before the aggregate CV is computed. Thus the social aggregate could be computed as:

$$\sum_{i=1}^{n} W_i CV_i$$

Effectively this weighting system treats equity as an externality. It may therefore be invalid if equity is a separate criterion. An additional weight would need to be incorporated if this was the case. In practice weights that have been proposed are often inversely related to the individual's marginal rate of taxation – by the argument that the marginal tax rate reflects society's preferences over the equity of income and wealth. However, since such a rate may reflect other objectives it may be a poor measure of equity – as evidenced by the fact that some low income groups sometimes face marginal tax rates exceeding 100 per cent. The use of income levels has also been widely advocated. In practice it is difficult enough to measure the true distribution of income and wealth, let alone the distribution of utility which is what would ideally be required.

5.3 The valuation of human life

While it would have been possible to incorporate the question of valuation of human life within the previous section – and indeed legitimate to do so – given the importance of the subject in health economics we have devoted this separate section to it.

There are three approaches to such valuation. First, there is the human capital approach which is the oldest and most easily applied. It equates the value of life of an individual with the present value of future lost output (as proxied normally by earnings and other labour costs). Some examples of this approach are provided in Jones-Lee (1976) and Mooney (1977).

The main comments to be made about the approach beyond its relative ease of application are:

(i)   it measures livelihood rather than life *per se*;

(ii) it is acceptable only under a GNP-based social welfare function;

(iii) health care objectives are not normally couched in terms solely of GNP;

(iv) no attempt is made to reflect willingness to pay either on the part of potential victims or society more generally. While individuals' earnings and income will affect their demand for safety (i.e. risk reduction) it is unlikely that there will be a simple 1:1 accounting relationship;

(v)   in health service planning, which is the primary emphasis here, valuing life or even livelihood would seem not to be the issue. What is to be valued in this context is not life-saving *per se* but more accurately relatively small reductions in risk of death;

(vi) finally, but relevantly, such an approach can give economic appraisal in health care a bad name, with an article in the prestigious *British Medical Journal* (Logan, Klein and Ashley, 1971, p. 521) claiming that 'cost-benefit analysis stops at 65'. (For a fuller critique of the approach see Mishan, 1971.)

A second approach is that of public behavioural or socially implied values obtained from teasing out the revealed preferences for safety in mortality-reducing endeavours of the public sector. It is based on the idea that for life-saving programmes the marginal cost per life saved (assuming like lives) should be the same if technical efficiency is to be pursued. If all lives were similar (and there were no other outputs from these programmes, such as reduced morbidity) this would ensure that the maximum lives possible would be saved from the 'life-saving budget'.

In so far as such marginal values differ then it has to be argued that the lives are not the same, that there are inefficiencies present or that other relevant aspects of output are present but not being counted. When implied values of past decisions suggest major departures from some mean public sector value for the type of life, then such decisions would be investigated to determine whether, relatively, these sectors were over- or underfunded. For decisions in the future, such mean public sector values could be used for benefit valuation purposes in appraising health service investments. The necessary conditions for the approach to be valid are discussed by Harrison (1974) and Mooney (1977).

Evidence suggests that similar lives are being implicitly valued very differently and that consequently there are potentially major inefficiencies in life-saving policy-making. However, such a conclusion can only be very tentative given that such analyses as have been conducted tend to assume that at best health status (and sometimes only mortality reduction) is the only output, and ignore equity and risk bearing considerations (as discussed in chapter 3). However, some work has been done on catastrophe avoidance which has a bearing on the issue of equity. For example Keeney (1982, p. 223) suggests that a 'reasonable preference would be that a small probability of a catastrophic loss of life is worse than a larger probability of a smaller loss of life, given the expected number of fatalities are the same for each case'. Linnerooth (1982), in a useful more general survey, addresses explicitly the question of equity in life-saving. More fundamentally this socially implied values approach is clearly based on the medico/administrative values in current decision-making.

In terms of conventional economic theory, the most defensible approach to valuing life is that of the willingness to pay for reductions in mortality risk on the part of potential victims (hereafter referred to as the WTP approach). The logic of this approach has been spelt out by Jones-Lee (1976):

> If cost benefit analysis is to be employed and the consumer's surplus adopted for those goods for which market information *is* available then consistency would seem to demand the development of procedures for eliciting some indication of the sums individuals would be prepared to forfeit to effect changes in the level of provision of those goods for which market information is not available.

The approach was first suggested by Dreze (1962) and has been more firmly established since in the work of Schelling (1968), Jones-Lee (1976) and Mishan (1971). For example, Jones-Lee assumes that an individual would be prepared to forfeit some of his present wealth to effect a reduction in the probability of death in the same period. Starting with wealth $\bar{w}$ and the individual's *own* assessment of the probability of death ($\bar{p}$), initial expected utility is given by:

$$E(u) = (1 - \bar{p}) \, L \, (\bar{w}) + \bar{p} D \, (\bar{w})$$

where L $(\bar{w})$ is the utility of wealth function conditional on survival during the period and D $(\bar{w})$ is the utility function conditional on death during the period.

Now if the individual has a chance of reducing his probability of death from $\bar{p}$ to p, as a maximum he will be prepared to give up some sum v, which can be established from the relationship:

$$(1 - p) \, L \, (\bar{w} - v) + p \, D \, (\bar{w} - v) = (1 - \bar{p}) \, L \, (\bar{w}) + \bar{p} D \, (\bar{w})$$ (For more detail, see Jones-Lee, 1976.)

Some examples of the values emerging from this approach are presented in Tables 5.2 and 5.3, the former being based on the study of individuals' behaviour when actually faced with mortality

Table 5.2 Estimates of the value of statistical life from revealed preference studies ($US 1983)

Authors	Data source	Estimated value of statistical life
Thaler and Rosen (1973)	Compensating wage differentials for workers in risky occupations (USA)	600,000
Melinek (1974)	Time/safety trade-off in use of pedestrian subways (UK)	520,000
Ghosh, Lees and Seal (1975)	Motorway speed/time/fuel trade-off (UK)	510,000
Veljanovski (1978)	Compensating wage differentials in industry (UK)	5,990,000
Viscusi (1978)	Compensating wage differentials for manual workers (USA)	3,410,000
Blomquist (1979)	Time/safety trade-off in use of car seat belts (USA)	560,000
Needleman (1980)	Compensating wage differentials for construction workers (UK)	170,000
Marin and Psacharopoulos (1982)	Compensating wage differentials for manual and non-manual workers (UK)	2,460,000

Source: Jones-Lee (1985).

87

Table 5.3 Estimates of the value of statistical life from questionnaire studies ($US 1983)

Authors	Data source	Estimated value of statistical life
Acton (1973)	Small non-random sample survey [$n = 93$] of willingness to pay for public provision of prevention of death from heart attack (USA)	72,000
Melinek, Woolley and Baldwin (1973)	Non-random sample survey [$n = 873$] of willingness to pay for domestic fire safety (UK)	330,000
Melinek (1974)	Non-random sample survey [$n = 873$] of willingness to pay for hypothetical safe cigarettes (UK)	170,000
Mulligan (1977)	Details of sample not yet available. Willingness to pay for decreased risk of nuclear power plant accidents (USA)	74,000 520,000 4,320,000*
Jones-Lee, Hammerton and Philips (1985)	Large random sample survey [$n = 1,150$] of willingness to pay for transport safety (UK)	2,370,000

* These three estimates involved annual risk reductions of 10^{-3}, 10^{-4} and 10^{-5} respectively.

Source: Jones-Lee (1985).

risk and the latter using a questionnaire approach to try to elicit how they would behave when faced with risk of death.

While the willingness to pay approach is the one which is defended and applied by the majority of economists there are some critics of this approach. Thus Broome (1978), for example, sparked off a lively debate over the valuation of human life. Essentially Broome suggests that the willingness to pay criterion is unsatisfactory as the losers (i.e. those whose deaths are associated with any project) cannot be compensated. The issue, according to Broome, rests upon the difference between *ex ante* and *ex post* valuations. Defendants of the willingness to pay approach have argued that Broome has misconstrued the argument in that it is the *risk* of death *ex ante* that is being evaluated and that the process of decision making is as important as the outcome when the decisions involve risk of death. Therefore, it is proper to allow individuals to attach their willingness to pay valuations to these risks. (See Buchanan and Faith, 1979; Jones-Lee, 1979; McGuire and Mooney, 1985; Ulph, 1982.)

5.4 The process of the cost-benefit approach

As indicated, economic appraisal in health care seeks to determine whether particular projects, involving the use of resources available for health care, are socially efficient and equitable. The problems involved in this process form the subject of this section. The process can usefully be divided into a series of stages, which form a helpful sequential classification for the purposes of exposition.

5.4.1 Specifying alternatives for appraisal

Since the objective of economic appraisal is to seek efficient and equitable uses of resources it is important that all potentially efficient and equitable options should be examined. However, since the potential uses of health care resources are virtually infinite, the options examined have to be selected as being those considered to offer the greatest potential. This again emphasises how economic appraisal builds on epidemiological evaluation and clinical trials.

For example, an economic appraisal of a heart transplant programme could examine the alternatives of:

- no programme
- a large programme
- a small programme
- a programme for young people only
- a programme for middle-aged people only
- for one city
- for twenty cities
- for every city
- a programme this year
- in five years

- phased over several years
- blood pressure reduction as an alternative
- a smoking reduction programme as an alternative

Which of these offers good potential clearly requires clinical and epidemiological knowledge and economic appraisal in the health care sector should therefore be multidisciplinary.

5.4.2 Specifying the appraisal objective

Ultimately the appraisal objective is to seek social efficiency and equity. However, where particular constraints are binding it may be sufficient, or necessary, to assess technical efficiency instead. Where there is a constraint on the resource budget, then seeking the most technically efficient – i.e. maximum benefit – way of spending it will be the objective. Where there is a fixed benefit or health effect to be achieved, the objective is to seek the most technically efficient – i.e. least cost – way. Questions of technical efficiency are addressed using *cost-effectiveness analysis* (CEA). A particular form of CEA that is becoming more widespread in health care is where the benefits/health effects are expressed in terms of 'quality-adjusted-life-years' (QALYs) gained (see chapter 2). This particular form of CEA is called *cost-utility analysis* (CUA). In CUA the health effects of a project are expressed on a 0–1 scale of quality adjusted life for each time period, and the tangible outcomes/resource consequences in monetary terms. The overall effects of projects are set in terms of 'cost per QALY gained' (see Table 5.4). Social efficiency is appraised using *cost-benefit analysis* (CBA) where all effects are ideally expressed in monetary terms.

The appraisal objective should also be set in terms of the criteria to be used in assessing equity, for example, variance in health care access costs, or even in health, or else the value judgement should be made explicit that the gainers, whoever they are found to be, ought to gain, and the losers, whoever they are, to lose.

Table 5.4 Comparison of costs per Quality-Adjusted-Life-Year (QALY) gained for various health care procedures

Procedure	Value of the extra costs per QALY
Pacemaker implantation for atrioventricular heart block	700
Hip replacement	750
Coronary artery bypass grafting (CAGB) for main vessel disease	1,040
Kidney transplantation	3,000
Heart transplantation	5,000
CABG for moderate angina with one vessel disease	12,000
Hospital haemodialysis	14,000

Source: Williams (1985).

5.4.3 Identifying all effects

This stage will rely on evidence from epidemiological studies showing what effects upon health there will be. Such effects will, of course, only be one part of the overall effects. Changes in resource used both within and outside the health care system need to be specified. Table 5.5 lists some possible costs and benefits of health service projects. Ideally the appraisal should at this stage identify all the beneficiaries and cost-bearers of each of the alternatives – those who gain, such as patients, their families, their friends and others – and those who lose, such as other patients who may be deprived of other therapies or care. It should identify the direct effects and the indirect effects – such as the immediate or long-term effects on health, and the effects on employment, consumption and so forth.

In the literature there is sometimes a confusion between what is a cost and what is a benefit – for example, Russell (1986) suggests that if less is spent on vacations and toys for children who are handicapped by measles complications then the reduced expenditure represents an economic *benefit*. (This is the sort of confusion

Table 5.5 Types of cost and benefit

Costs: examples	Benefits: examples
capital used	capital released for uses
land	land
buildings	buildings
vehicles	vehicles
revenue used	revenue released for other uses
labour	labour
supplies	supplies
support services	support services
more work for staff	less work for staff
fewer staff training	more staff training
possibilities	possibilities
patient/relatives/staff costs	patient/relatives/staff benefits
ignorance	information
dissatisfaction	satisfaction
decision-making burden	relief of decision-making
time lost	time saved
inconvenience	convenience
expense	less expense
unhealthier patients	healthier patients
less cure	more cure
(more pain, disability; worse prognosis, etc.)	(less pain, disability; better prognosis, etc.)
less care	more care
(more discomfort, boredom; worse environment, etc.)	(less discomfort, boredom; better environment, etc.)
lost output (outside health service)	increased output (outside health service)

that, amongst other things, makes people unsympathetic towards economic appraisal.) The reduction in spending is a better measure of the cost than the benefit. This sort of confusion may be avoided by strict and consistent use of the notion of opportunity cost rather than financial cost.

A benefit that has only recently been 'discovered' (or at least only recently featured in evaluations of the effects of health care projects) is the value of information to patients. For example Berwick and Weinstein (1985), in the study already mentioned in chapter 3, found that mothers-to-be valued being able to visualise the fetus they were carrying, from ultrasound scanning, even when the scan was of no clinical value to the woman's doctor. Strull, Lo and Charles (1984) indicated that patients being treated for high blood pressure valued being told of the future course of their condition. Only half, however, wished to be involved in making decisions about the management of their condition. Thus many patients may derive satisfaction from being able to pass such responsibility to their doctor. Omission of such benefits could bias the results of appraisal.

5.4.4 Measuring all identified effects

Again this stage will rely on evidence from epidemiological studies to indicate the magnitude of the health effects. Many effects outside the health service may be on resources that are not normally marketed – such as household labour, leisure time and so forth. Measures of these may require special development for particular appraisals. For all effects the relevant 'margin' needs to be specified – a common mistake is the use of averages: except in long-run competitive equilibrium (or replication of this position) marginal costs will be greater or less than average costs.

The problems of measuring health have already been discussed in chapter 2. Ideally the improvements in health should be quantified in terms of measures such as QALYs gained. Other outcomes such as reassurance to family and friends are more difficult to quantify.

Measuring QALYs involves many value as well as technical judgements. Value judgements are involved in deciding what aspects of health and quality of life ought to be included – e.g. physical, social, psychological functioning, diagnosis, prognosis, acquisition of information, relief of decision-making burden, etc. They are also present in deciding what measurement techniques should be used – e.g. the standard gamble or time trade-off (see chapter 2) may produce different results. They are also involved in deciding whose preferences ought to be measured – e.g. patients, patients' relatives, doctors, may have different perceptions of the seriousness of any given health state. Yet again there are value judgements in deciding what weight should be given to the expressed preferences of any particular group when views differ.

For example, should the preferences of patients currently in the health state of interest be given greatest weight, by the argument that they have the most appropriate knowledge about it? Or should the preferences of the general public, who may at a future date experience the health state, be given the greatest weight by the argument that this is the most 'democratic' set of preferences? (Sackett and Torrance, 1978).

Besides these judgements there are the technical difficulties of devising reliable measurement methods, of capturing all the relevant aspects of the health state in the methods selected, of framing questions to avoid influencing the answers and of selecting samples to avoid bias. Clearly the issue of measuring health is complex and value-laden.

5.4.5 Valuing all measured effects

In CEA and CUA the health effects and other intangible outcomes of projects may not be valued in money terms, but may be taken no further than measures of effectiveness such as QALYs gained. However, for CBA it is necessary to take the step of putting a money value on the QALYs (or other measures) so that their value can be compared directly with that of the costs.

For some goods or services that are traded in competitive markets the CV may be derived from the demand curve (in the absence of appreciable income effects). For example, the value to the consumer of reducing the price of aspirin tablets might readily be inferred from the prevailing price and demand elasticity. However, such examples are rare in health care and the usual case is where prices are distorted or effects are unmarketed. Some of the problems of deriving CVs in this context are discussed here.

Jointness is a common problem in valuing health service capital. Hospital buildings can accommodate a range of service provision and the marginal cost or benefit from altering the use of a building in many cases will be unrelated to construction costs, but related instead to alternative uses forgone or permitted.

Monopolistic or monopsonistic pricing may be endemic in health service labour markets. For example, the supply of doctors in most countries is limited through doctors' representative or governing bodies. By acting as a cartel doctors may be able to price their labour more highly than in a competitive market. Thus it may be necessary to derive shadow prices to value the true opportunity cost of such labour.

In many countries the health service may be a virtual monopsonist in the purchase of nursing labour (Altman, 1970; Yett, 1970), thereby being able to drive down the price of nursing labour below its competitive level. Again this suggests shadow pricing.

Macroeconomic disequilibrium may cause involuntary unemployment. Where the labour required for a project has perfectly elastic supply and comes from the pool of unemployed labour, then the appropriate shadow price is not the labour wage, but the value of the leisure time forgone, which at the margin may be zero. This will not be the case if the unemployed labour does not possess the appropriate skills required for the project. The supply of skilled labour may be inelastic even where there is unemployment – at least in the short run – owing to the length of training required. For example, in the UK the minimum training period for nurses is two years and for junior doctors eight years. In the case of inelastic supply, the opportunity cost is the alternative labour output forgone elsewhere in the health service. Time off work by patients may, however, be costless to society if the work output can be replaced by someone who would otherwise be unemployed and whose shadow price of leisure is zero at the margin. Time inputs may be difficult to value, if the forgone alternative is leisure activities. There have been several studies of the value put on leisure time, and after reviewing these, the UK Department of Transport concluded that 25 per cent of the national gross average wage was a suitable proxy measure of the shadow price of leisure (Harrison, 1974) – recently increased to 43 per cent.

The valuation of reduced risk of death has been discussed in section 5.3, and there have now been several studies using the WTP approach – see Tables 5.2 and 5.3. Two methods that have been utilised to assess WTP are direct survey and indirect inference. A recent study, by Jones-Lee, Hammerton and Philips (1985), used an interview questionnaire on a stratified random sample (of 1,150) of the UK population to ask about the valuations they placed on various road user risks. For example, they were asked how much extra they would be prepared to pay to travel by safer means of transport, or how much money-saving they would require to induce them to travel by a more dangerous means of transport. The answers given to the various questions indicated the average implied value of saving a statistical life to be around £1.5 million (in 1982 prices). Since such studies use hypothetical scenarios the respondents may, of course, have weak incentives to reveal their true preferences.

Indirect inference has been used to derive a similar result from calculation of the extra payments that workers receive for occupations that carry excess mortality risk. With some jobs, such as steeplejack or deep sea diver, the risks are expected to be high and risk premiums on wages may be paid explicitly. However, there are many other occupations that also carry high risks. Marin and Psacharopoulos (1982) calculated the implicit premiums on wages paid for excess risks, after standardising for numerous other factors that would be expected to influence wage levels (schooling, work experience, unionisation, and an occupational desirability ranking), using data from the UK General Household Survey 1975 (OPCS, 1978a) and occupational mortality data (OPCS, 1978b). They concluded that workers facing an annual 1 in 10,000 risk of a fatal accident at work were paid a premium for this risk of £60 to £70 (in 1975 prices) per annum. Thus the implied value of a statistical life was £600,000 to £700,000, or about £1.25 million in 1981 prices (Marin, 1983). This last figure is remarkably similar to that derived by Jones-Lee, Hammerton and Philips (1985) but this may be coincidence. (See Tables 5.2 and 5.3 for other results.)[2]

The empirical evidence thus suggests that these workers would on average be indifferent between having £150 (1982 prices) or a reduction in risk of 1 in 10,000. However, this assumes that workers make choices with reference to the objective risks of the occupation, whereas cognitive dissonance ('It'll never happen to me') may be common (Akerlof and Dickens, 1982). Marin and Psacharopoulos (1982) failed to detect any correlation between implicit risk premiums and occupational cancer risk. Hence although cancer risks may, objectively, be present, if workers underestimate such risks there may be little or no compensating risk premium.

This methodology also assumes that workers make trade-offs to maximise expected utility. In fact, however, studies (see for example Sugden, 1986) have shown that when faced with a choice between an uncertain loss (e.g. an occupational accident or disease risk) and a certain loss of equivalent expected value (e.g. a job with no health risks and low pay) most people prefer the uncertain loss.

Also as noted in chapter 2, it may not be possible to extrapolate from such studies to other contexts, for at least three reasons. First, the workers in risky jobs are self-selected and may have different risk preferences from other groups of individuals. Second, in these jobs the average risk of fatal accident was 1 in 10,000 and, given an increasing marginal disutility of risk, the value placed on higher risks cannot be inferred by linear extrapolation. Third, at high levels of risk the disutility of risk function may be bounded, and individuals may be completely unwilling to trade-off risks for compensation (Jones-Lee, 1976).

These caveats apply equally to the measurement of morbid risks as to mortal risks, at least in theory. Hence the same reservations must hold about extrapolating from the measurement of the value of QALYs at any given risk level amongst any given group, to other risk levels or other groups.

These points merely add emphasis to the argument that special research studies may be needed to answer particular questions.

5.4.6 Discounting future costs and benefits

It was suggested earlier that there are three basic reasons why individuals hold positive time preference rates. The first – myopia or impatience – would seem as likely to apply to health improvements as to anything else. The second – risk of never enjoying the benefits – would imply that individuals' time preference rates should increase with their age, although in practice the difference that this makes may be negligible. However, the third – diminishing marginal utility – may suggest a negative rate, at least for certain periods of deferment. For example, since old people are generally less healthy than young people, a given health improvement, *ceteris paribus*, may have a higher marginal value to an old person than a young person, and hence people may prefer (again *ceteris paribus*) to defer such improvements. Thus it is conceptually possible that individuals' time preference for health improvements could be lower than for other economic commodities. In practice it is not clear whether individuals do in fact have different preferences concerning the timing of health improvements from those they hold for the timing of other goods.[3]

It is sometimes argued that while it makes sense to discount the costs of a project, the benefits should be left undiscounted. This is, however, untenable. For example, it would mean that any project could be improved simply by postponing it, because this would decrease its costs but not its benefits, and in turn this would make the logical strategy never to undertake a project in the present period.

5.4.7 Assessing risk and uncertainty

Measurement of costs and benefits should allow for individuals' aversion to risk in gaining benefits, or preference for risk in accepting costs – that is, that the CV will diverge from the expected value of a risky benefit or cost. It is not known whether risk aversion is greater or less in the case of health improvements than for other economic commodities, or risk preference greater or less in the case of health deteriorations. It is also unknown how doctors' aversions to or preferences for risk compare with those of patients. This last point will be of special importance if it is doctors who are making valuations on patients' behalf.

Even less is known about how patients, and doctors, cope with uncertainty, as opposed to risk. For example what strategies do they adopt, and how do these strategies affect the values of the possible outcomes?

Uncertainty in economic appraisal can be dealt with by sensitivity analysis, where all known possible outcomes are tried successively in the calculations, to show to what extent the analysis is sensitive to the uncertainty. However, this cannot overcome the problem, which may be common in medical care, of ignorance – that is, even the possible outcomes may be unknown. Again it is not clear how ignorance affects patients' or doctor' values.

5.4.8 Assessing equity

This stage involves examining the distribution of costs and benefits of each project to determine the gainers and losers and whether the gains and losses seem fair – whether the project benefits (or imposes costs on) particular groups such as the old or the young, the ill or the handicapped, higher or lower social classes, city-dwellers or country-dwellers.

Summarising the equity of a project in terms of a single measure may be as difficult as summarising efficiency in terms of the social aggregate CV. Some measure such as the variance of health care access costs may be appropriate, or a Gini coefficient of health status levels might be constructed and used to compare the equity of health care interventions (see previous chapter, especially section 4.2.3).

5.4.9 Choosing

In CBA a project will be declared socially efficient if the gains exceed the losses or, if a choice must be made between several such mutually exclusive projects, the one with the largest excess of gain over loss would be chosen. In CEA or CUA, one project will be declared technically efficient if it maximises the benefit obtainable from the given budget or minimises the cost of attaining the given objective.

In CEA or CUA if there is the possibility of undertaking more than one project then the projects may be ranked in terms of their output:cost ratios – for example, 'QALYs gained per £1000 spent'. Selecting projects by working down such a ranking is, however, only valid if the measure of benefit is fully comprehensive and if the projects selected exactly exhaust the available budget. Where the projects selected do not exactly exhaust the budget then it is possible that some other selection may produce greater benefits.

It is also possible that marginal costs may increase and marginal benefits decrease as projects are implemented. For example, patients who have the greatest capacity to benefit may be treated first, and subsequent patients may derive less benefit, or the cost of factor inputs may rise as demand increases and they are in inelastic supply. Hence 'QALYs gained per £1000' may change after any finite level of implementation.

The decision-makers responsible for the final choice of project(s) may not, of course, choose the project(s) declared to be efficient. The data on which the analysis was based may be inaccurate and the decision-makers may feel that, with their more extensive knowledge, some other project is more efficient. Or they may disagree with the value judgements that the analyst will necessarily have introduced into the appraisal – as in the way in which different costs and benefits have been valued or allowance has been made for uncertainty. Or they may decide that a more equitable, but less efficient, project should be chosen.

Thus the claim of CBA, CUA, and CEA is not that they *make* decisions, rather it is that they assist in the decision-making process. Perhaps their chief merits (which should not be undervalued!) are that they make health care planning comprehensive rather than partial, systematic rather than piecemeal, and value judgements explicit rather than implicit.

5.5 Conclusions

Some of the problems surrounding the cost-benefit approach apply to any field of application. Others, however, may be special to health care. In chapter 3 the idea of 'irrational' preferences by the consumer/potential patient was discussed. Preferences may be incomplete – individuals may be incapable of ordering preferences over states of health or consumption of health care. Preferences may be non-convex – individuals may have increasing rather than diminishing marginal utility of health. Preferences may be lexicographic – individuals may not trade-off health improvements or health deteriorations with other goods, particularly if the changes are relatively large. Finally they may not try to maximise expected utility in situations of risk or uncertainty and it may not be clear how they do value and respond to risky and uncertain gains and losses.

At the social level the social welfare function, which indicates how to decide what is best for society given the preferences of the individuals who make up the society, may not be well-defined. For example, it may not be clear how changes in efficiency may be traded-off against changes in equity, or even whether such trade-offs are permissible – perhaps equity may dominate. It may be that social decision-makers are irrational in deciding about health care provision, or they may be constrained by the vested interests that dominate health services, or by powerful political forces or allegiances. However, rather than making the cost-benefit approach redundant, such problems make the approach yet more useful owing to its merits of being comprehensive, systematic and explicit. The process of working through all the stages of economic appraisal, using consistent criteria, and reporting the results of every stage, may, by generating further information, lead to less 'irrationality', less uncertainty, more carefully considered choices, and thus better resource allocation. Whether this happens in practice is examined in chapter 6.

6

The cost-benefit approach in practice

6.1 Introduction

This chapter is about how the cost-benefit approach has been applied to problems of health care resource allocation. Against the background of the aims, process and complexities of CBA outlined in chapter 5, section 6.2 presents examples of how particular appraisal studies have attempted to specify alternatives and objectives, to identify, measure and value costs and benefits, to incorporate allowance for differential timing, uncertainty and considerations of equity, and to promote decision-making which is more firmly based on recognition of efficient and equitable projects. The subsequent section (6.3) describes more fully a case study in which we have been involved and assesses its contribution to decision-making.

6.2 The process in practice

In chapter 5, section 5.4, the cost-benefit approach was divided into a nine-stage process. Here those nine stages are illustrated by case-studies drawn from the expanding number of applications of economic appraisal to health care (Drummond, 1981; Warner and Luce, 1982; Drummond *et al.*, 1986; Blades *et al.*, 1986). The studies have been chosen to exemplify some of the problems and complexities discussed in 5.4 and their amelioration or resolution.

6.2.1 Specifying alternatives for appraisal

Screening for breast cancer may increase women's life-expectancy through early detection and treatment of the disease. Evidence from randomised controlled trials is accumulating to support this. One set of alternatives to be considered in a breast cancer screening programme is how to screen, for example through using specially developed X-ray machines – mammography – or by clinical examination. Within these alternatives there are others – e.g. who should perform the clinical examinations or who should read and interpret the X-ray films. Different alternatives may be used singly or in combination. Logically, where there are n alternatives, there are:

$$\sum_{x=1}^{n} \binom{n}{x}$$

possible ways of using them alone or in combination.

This approach to specifying alternatives for appraisal is illustrated by Gravelle, Simpson and Chamberlain's (1982) analysis of the cost-effectiveness of different screening regimes for breast cancer. These included clinical examination by a doctor (D) or by a nurse (N), and of mammography with the result read by a junior radiologist (R1) or by a senior radiologist (R2). These authors considered all the possible combinations of these alternatives:

$$\sum_{x=1}^{4} \binom{4}{x} = 15 \text{ options}$$

(Some of their results are given in Table 6.1.)

This is a good example of assessing all the possibilities within a tightly constrained set of alternatives. There are other options, however, that could have been considered within broader constraints, and that would be relevant to the optimal allocation of resources – permutations of self-examination, other diagnostic technologies, locations, timing, frequency and risk group selection. Determining the applicability of such dimensions of choice is not for economists alone, which re-emphasises the multidisciplinary nature of appraisal.

There may be many reasons for limiting appraisal to a narrow

Table 6.1 Breast cancer screening: NHS cost per year of life saved (£s, 1980 prices)

Test	Observer(s)	Cost per woman-year of life saved
1	N	979
2	D	832
3	R1	1,010
4	R2	819
5	D, N	990
6	N, R1	1,223
7	N, R2	1,065
8	D, R1	1,138
9	D, R2	1,066
10	R1, R2	893
11	N, D, R1	1,359
12	N, D, R2	1,249
13	N, R1, R2	1,200
14	D, R1, R2	1,147
15	D, N, R1, R2	1,299

Source: Gravelle, Simpson and Chamberlain (1982).

set of alternatives – from practical constraints, such as the availability of equipment, to policy constraints, such as a policy of making a service universally standard for all clients, whatever their risk status, to resource constraints on the appraisal itself. However, the broader the set of alternatives appraised, the more confident it is possible to be that the most socially efficient, or equitable, solution will be found.

Williams (1985) assessed the cost-effectiveness of coronary artery bypass grafting operations for different groups with more and less severe heart disease. He also considered the possibility of other treatments that might be contenders for more resources – pacemakers, heart transplant, kidney transplant, kidney dialysis and artificial hip replacement. Thus the analysis addressed the broad issue of determining the most socially efficient uses for extra funds available for specialised treatments.

Another set of alternatives to treatment may be interventions at other stages of the disease – primary prevention to prevent its onset, or secondary prevention (screening) to catch it in its pre-symptomatic phase. Feldstein, Piot and Sundaresan (1973) examined possibilities for the control of tuberculosis (TB) in Korea, covering not only domiciliary or hospital treatment, but also screening to find the disease in its early stages and BCG vaccination of children to prevent it. They looked at how these options might be applied to different age groups and to urban and rural residents. They thus showed that there are many ways of tackling even a single objective such as control of TB.

6.2.2 Specifying the appraisal objective

In economic appraisal of alternatives for health care resource allocation, there should be an explicit statement of the objectives of the study in general and, in particular, of whether the study is to address questions of technical efficiency (CEA) or of social efficiency (CBA). This will be partly determined by the constraints upon the alternatives – narrow constraints can determine that the appraisal must be a CEA, or non-constant cost levels and non-constant benefit levels that it should be a CBA.

In one study with decision-makers in an NHS district in England, Ludbrook (1986) assisted in the formulation of the objective of the study. The health authority had decided to allocate an extra £1 million to community services and were puzzling over which set of 'norms' to adopt as a means of spending this extra money. However, Ludbrook persuaded the authority to identify the sorts of community services that were just on the margin of being provided and to ask what the extra benefits of expanding these services would be. Thus the objective was changed from being specified in terms of throughputs to outputs and became a CEA study seeking to maximise the benefits obtainable from the additional budget.

Feldstein *et al.* (1973) in their study of TB control went even further in their efforts to ensure that the maximum benefit was sought. They specified all the constraints that existed within the Korean health service, in terms of both money and resources: labour (doctor/nurse) availability and supplies of hospital facilities, drugs and so forth. The objective of the study was then one of optimisation, subject to the constraints of local money and resource availability.

6.2.3 Identifying all effects

While most studies identify the effects of health care projects on the use of health service resources, not all of them take into account how patients and their families are affected. This again illustrates the way in which epidemiological and clinical information, ideally from randomised controlled trials, is needed – particularly to identify how health status will be affected. But it also illustrates that the underlying aims of CBA should be more closely integrated with the design of trials themselves – to promote broad definitions of health status as perceived by, for example, patients, and to include other ways in which patients and their families are affected. Thus patients may derive utility from extra knowledge about their own health (or perhaps disutility if their prognosis is poor) and from alleviation of the burden of decision-making (Berwick and Weinstein, 1985; Strull, Lo and Charles, 1984).

Anxiety and inconvenience, time and travel and impacts upon consumption and leisure possibilities are all of concern to patients and their families. Hence adopting the consumer sovereignty perspective in CBA requires all such effects to be included.

Russell *et al.* (1977) considered the social effects of day case, as opposed to in-patient case, surgery for hernias and haemorrhoids. They looked at length of time before resumption of work, family time off work or school, housework, costs of visiting hospital and costs of post-operative care at home, as well as the health service resource implications.

Mooney (1982) in a study of the cost-effectiveness of different ways of screening for breast cancer identified the intangible costs to women of not only correct screening results for women who did have abnormalities (true positive results), but also of being incorrectly identified as having an abnormality (false positive results). Thus he described the possibilities of anxiety or distress associated with the true positive and false positive test results and in addition the reassurance of a true negative test result.

6.2.4 Measuring the identified effects

The identified effects can only be valued directly if they command a price in undistorted markets. However, for many of the most important effects this will not apply and, therefore, special measurement and shadow pricing will be required.

The study of day case surgery by Russell *et al.* (1977) referred to above was linked to a randomised controlled trial, which measured the effects upon the patient and family by means of a home interview before and after the operation, for the two (day case and in-patient) groups of patients. Thus economists have often found it necessary to undertake special studies to ascertain the extent of the social effects of different options, because routine data sources for such effects usually do not exist.

Mooney (1982), however, was able to rank, by method, the intangible costs of the different methods of screening for breast cancer. This enabled him to draw conclusions on the technical efficiency of the different methods without the need for a special survey or measurement – rather the ranking of intangible costs was ascertained from the information supplied by medical staff involved.

The techniques of measuring the impact of health care upon health status in quantitative terms have been discussed in chapter 2. As noted in section 5.4.4, choosing which measure of benefit or health improvement to use, when several alternatives are available, involves value rather than technical judgements, which may be most appropriately made by public decision-makers acting as society's representatives.

Rather than use a single measure of the benefit of TB control, Feldstein *et al.* (1973) used four: avoided life years of temporary disability (bed confinement); avoided life years of permanent impairment through reduced lung function; avoided premature deaths; and avoided losses of paid-labour output. They then calculated the TB control strategy that would maximise each different measure, arguing that, ultimately, responsible government officials or public health administrators were the people best placed to judge which objective would maximise social welfare. (Although they found that the differences in strategy implied by switching from maximising one measure of benefit to maximising another were relatively small. Thus in this case the alternative ways of measuring benefits did not affect the ability to suggest the most technically efficient strategy.)

Although measuring QALYs requires further research and

development, cost-utility analysis is becoming more widely used and will continue to gain credence as clinicians and planners become more familiar with it. Williams (1985) measured the benefits of coronary artery bypass grafting in terms of QALYs gained, by first asking three cardiologists to give him 'their judgement on the comparative profiles of health of various patients with angina who had or had not undergone coronary artery bypass grafting' (op. cit., p. 237). He combined these with the ratings of different levels of disability and distress derived by Kind, Rosser and Williams (1982) (see chapter 2, Table 2.7). The gains in QALYs are depicted in Figures 6.1 and 6.2. Williams also measured the QALYs produced by heart transplant, pacemaker implantation, valve replacement for aortic stenosis, kidney transplantation, hospital haemodialysis, home haemodialysis and hip replacement operations. Measuring health service outputs, such as quality of life, is certainly possible, and while still by no means perfect, will undoubtedly be improved as it is tackled more often.

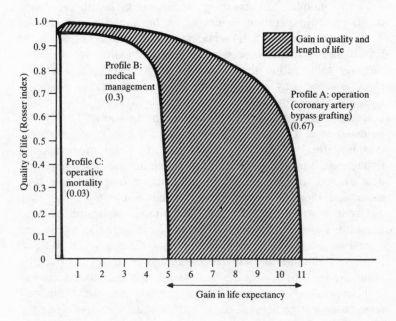

Figure 6.1 Expected value of quality and length of life gained for patients with severe angina and left main vessel disease

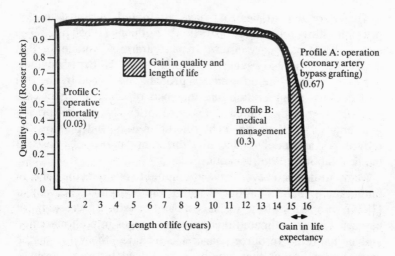

Figure 6.2 Expected value of quality and length of life gained for patients
with severe angina and one vessel disease
Source: Williams (1985)

6.2.5 Valuing the measured effects

The process of valuing the effects of projects can involve shadow pricing or direct elicitation of individuals' willingness to pay to gain benefits or avoid costs. As discussed in the previous chapter, shadow pricing of resources consumed, or released, is both a theoretical and a practical problem. In the study of day case surgery by Russell *et al.* (1977) the patients operated on as day cases fared no worse and had lower costs than those operated on as in-patients. Therefore the day case option was the more cost-effective. One of the effects of treating patients as day cases rather than in-patient cases was to release space within the hospital. Rather than try to value the released space by trying to apportion the joint costs – e.g. by average costs per square metre – for which there would be no theoretical justification, they considered how it might realistically allow the hospital to save resources, through either closing a small ward or avoiding having to build a small ward extension. This is a better way of estimating the value of the space released than by trying to apportion joint costs.

There are few studies that have attempted to adjust market prices to allow for market distortions. Williams (1985, p. 327) in his study of coronary artery bypass grafting comments that American studies have suggested higher costs than British studies, but that 'much of the difference is probably explained by the fact that doctors' remuneration and the costs of acute inpatient care are fairly high in the United States of America'. No shadow pricing is attempted to reconcile such cost differences, but perhaps the differences accurately reflect the different opportunity costs of medical labour in the two countries.

Many studies, however, have attempted to estimate the value of unmarketed services produced within the household. Schweitzer (1974), in a study of the social costs and benefits of screening for cervical cancer, estimated the value of changes in both marketed and unmarketed resource usage. He included the value of the extra future output that would be produced by women whose cervical cancer would be prevented, in paid employment and housework. In addition the costs to the women of being screened were estimated: travelling, waiting and the procedure itself would take around 1 hour 30 minutes, while a diagnostic biopsy following a positive screening test would involve 2 hours of a woman's time. Whether or not the woman worked this was costed at the hourly average female wage rate, as a measure of the opportunity cost of time.

Sometimes proxy measures have been used in shadow pricing. For example, Geiser and Menz (1976) wished to value the benefits of routine annual examination of school children's teeth for early signs of dental caries. They argued (op. cit., p. 192) that the objective of dental care is 'to enhance the appearance of the mouth and to maintain a dental structure conducive to comfort and effectiveness in chewing'. Since a permanent false tooth would satisfy this objective, with the exception of appearance, they argued that a minimum estimate of the benefit of the dental programme could be represented by the cost of replacing those natural teeth that would be lost, in the absence of the programme, with false teeth. Using this minimum estimate of the benefit they were able to conclude that the benefits exceeded the costs.

Buxton and West (1975) estimated the implied value of the benefits of home and hospital blood dialysis for kidney failure. They measured the costs of these services in terms of health service resource use, the costs to patients and their families of adapting their home for a dialysis machine and the gains to society of extra output owing to patients being enabled to work. Thus they derived the net social cost (at 1972 prices) of home dialysis (£2,600 per annum) and hospital dialysis (£4,720 per annum). They argued that since society is prepared to provide these services to people with kidney failure, these sums 'may be considered to represent one estimate of the price society is prepared to pay to maintain life' (op. cit., p. 376).

Direct valuation of willingness to pay to gain the benefits of projects that have a major impact upon risk of death or quality of life may be difficult if not impossible to elicit and may encounter the problem of boundedness discussed earlier in section 5.4.5. For example, Bush, Chen and Patrick (1973) measured the improvement in physical and mental functioning brought about by early detection and treatment of phenylketonuria, as part of the benefits of screening newborn infants for this disease. As shown in Figure 2.3 of chapter 2, quality of life is improved enormously. In such cases there may be no amount of compensation that would make a person indifferent between the two prognoses: the value of ΔQ may be infinite. In such circumstances decision-making may have to appeal to criteria other than willingness to pay.

6.2.6 Discounting future costs and benefits

The rate of discount can play a major role when comparing treatment and prevention, since resources for prevention usually need to be committed much earlier (*vis-à-vis* receipt of benefits) than those for treatment. Cretin (1977) compared the costs and effectiveness of different ways of preventing death from heart attack. He considered the alternatives for a cohort of 10-year-old males. One option was to screen the boys and treat those with high blood cholesterol levels. Other options were to wait 20 years and then provide hospital coronary care units (CCUs) to prolong life after a heart attack, or mobile coronary care ambulances. While the CCUs and ambulances had high nominal costs, costs 20 years in the future have a present value, at a 5 per cent discount rate, of only 0.377 of their nominal value. Using such a rate Cretin estimated that the cost per life year gained by the ambulance would be about half the cost per life year gained through screening and, by the hospital CCU, only one third the screening cost. However, at lower discount rates screening had the lowest cost per life year gained.

6.2.7 Allowing for risk and uncertainty

Given that most individuals are averse to risk, preferring certain benefits to uncertain benefits, economic appraisal that adopts a consumer sovereignty approach should not treat uncertain benefits as if they were certain. However, studies commonly do treat uncertain prospects as if they were certain. The practical significance of this will be negligible where the risks involved are small. However, in the case of the possibility of large increases in quality of life or reductions in mortality, or large risks in these prospects, the divergence between the utility of the expected outcome and expected utility of the possible outcomes may be significant.

Using the standard gamble approach (see chapter 2) to elicit individuals' preferences or willingness to pay can take this divergence into account. Pauker and Pauker (1977) have shown how the standard gamble may be used to help prospective parents to decide whether or not to have prenatal diagnosis by amniocentesis. Without prenatal diagnosis there would be greater uncertainty as to whether the fetus would be handicapped, e.g. by Down's syndrome (mongolism), but with prenatal diagnosis there are other risks – amniocentesis carries a risk (of about 0.005 to 0.01) of causing a miscarriage. By getting the prospective parents to make a series of hypothetical trade-offs between different possibilities, Pauker and Pauker show how they may be helped to choose the alternative that best reflects their risk aversion and preferences.

Thompson (1986) reported the results of a study also using a standard gamble. Individuals suffering from chronic rheumatoid arthritis were invited to choose between two hypothetical scenarios – a drug which could cure their condition but which carried a risk of death, and the certainty of their current condition. The median risk of death at which the respondents were indifferent between the two scenarios was 0.27.

A technique that is adopted to deal with uncertainty in assumptions, estimates and possibilities, owing to lack of ideal data for the appraisal, is sensitivity analysis. This involves substituting alternative assumptions, estimates and possibilities into the appraisal to determine whether the conclusions are robust, or are changed by the substitution.

A good example of sensitivity analysis can be found in the study by Buxton and West (1975) of blood dialysis for kidney failure. They noted that (ibid., p. 378):

> While the values of the parameters we have used represent in each case the 'best estimate' from available data, there is no doubt that some of these values (for instance, survival or rehabilitation rates) may prove inaccurate when evidence from a greater number of cases becomes available, and other values (discount rate or average earnings) may prove inappropriate in future economic environments. We have therefore tested the sensitivity of our findings . . . to gross changes in the values of the major variables.

These sensitivity analyses gave net costs ranging from £10,320 p.a. to £1,920 p.a. for hospital dialysis and £16,410 p.a. to £700 p.a. for home dialysis.

Henderson *et al.* (1984) compared the costs and benefits of screening to prevent congenital toxoplasmosis (which can cause mental and visual handicap) in a context where the incidence of the disease was not known with any accuracy. Also there was uncertainty about the typical degree of harm caused by the disease, and about the effectiveness and costs of screening. Therefore, they used a series of maximum and minimum figures from the range of possibilities. They were able to conclude that screening would be unlikely to save resources except under the most optimistic assumptions. Thus even where variables are subject to considerable uncertainty, much can be learned by using sensitivity analysis.

6.2.8 Assessing equity

Rich, Glass and Selkon (1976) examined the cost-effectiveness of screening all schoolgirls in a city for asymptomatic bacteriuria. Collection of urine specimens, at the school, with extensive efforts to reduce non-attendance, yielded 96 per cent coverage at a cost of 77p (1973 prices) per girl screened, or, with less effort to reduce non-attendance, 85 per cent coverage at 55p per girl screened.

This compared with home dipslide screening which yielded 70 per cent coverage at a cost of 26p per girl screened. Thus for the first 70 per cent of the girls the home dipslide method was the most cost-effective. Glass (1979) also calculated the marginal cost per girl screened of increasing coverage beyond the 70 per cent achieved by the home method. This was £1.93 per girl for an additional 15 per cent coverage and £2.45 per girl for the next additional 11 per cent coverage. However, as well as the extent of the coverage obtained, decision-makers may also be interested in the distribution of the benefits, in terms of, for example, the social class composition of the groups of girls covered by the more and less comprehensive screening options. In the home dipslide option 42 per cent of girls whose fathers were unskilled manual workers or unemployed were not screened, whereas the most comprehensive option managed to screen a much higher proportion of these girls. Thus if decision-makers have an objective of achieving social class equity as well as efficiency, they may decide that the higher marginal costs of more comprehensive options are worth paying to achieve this additional goal.

6.2.9 Choosing

Williams (1985) presents his results in the form of a ranking of options in terms of their cost:utility ratios – £s per QALY gained – which suggest that to maximise the QALYs gained from limited resources, extra resources should first be put into, not coronary artery bypass grafting, but pacemaker implantations and hip replacements. Such rankings ought to be useful to decision-makers in helping them to determine priorities. But to what extent do decision-makers base their decisions on results such as these?

There have in the past been economic evaluations of aspects of health policy whose results have been unequivocal. Over a decade ago it was shown that the benefits of adding fluoride to water supplies to prevent dental caries outweighed the costs (Nelson and Swint, 1976). For over a decade it has been known that vasectomy is one of the most cost-effective forms of contraception that health services can supply (Trussell, 1974). Yet in the UK there is little fluoridation of water and there are long waiting lists for vasectomy from the NHS. Generally it appears at present that economic appraisal has not had a great influence on the decisions that have been taken. Yet as we stated in the previous chapter economic appraisal can only be an aid to decision-making. There may be sound, non-economic reasons for ignoring the results of economic studies. Of course, on the other hand, there may not!

6.3 A case-study

In this section we describe and discuss an exercise in economic appraisal with which we were closely involved (Henderson, McGuire and Parkin, 1984a, 1984b; Parkin and Henderson, 1985). The study concerned the provision of a District General Hospital for the area of Fife in eastern Scotland, north of Edinburgh. Our intention in presenting this case-study is not only to show how economic appraisal has been used in practice, but also to raise some important issues – a particular example being the potential for conflict between objectives of efficiency and equity.

6.3.1 Introduction

NHS acute hospital services are defined as including all specialties other than obstetrics, mental illness and mental handicap. 'Demand' for acute hospital services is regulated by referrals from general practitioners and by hospital doctors, on the basis of their perceptions of patients' needs. 'Demand' in many areas is growing due to increasing numbers of elderly people. Supply of hospital services is planned by health authorities in response to current and anticipated 'demands' and in the light of the resources made available by central government.

Fife's main problem was a 'shortage' of acute hospital beds – i.e. in-patient services were 'under-bedded' by Scottish NHS 'norms', and some of their existing accommodation in Dunfermline in West Fife caused dissatisfaction because of its age, condition and layout. Options for improving and increasing the acute in-patient accommodation would consume substantial amounts of NHS capital and revenue resources and would have important implications for patients, local communities and other health services.

The main purpose of this section is to draw attention to the differences that the application of the cost-benefit approach can make to consideration of this sort of project. This approach involves the better analytical formulation of issues, better data, and greater concern for evidence (Henderson, 1968). This study shows what improvements can be brought to health service planning through the application of the cost-benefit approach.

6.3.2 The problem

'The problem' might have been defined locally as 'being without a modern District General Hospital (DGH) of adequate size'. To have done so would, however, have suggested only one solution: build a modern DGH of 'adequate' size.

More fundamentally, the roots of the main problem were that the Fife hospital admission rate was 8 per cent below the Scottish average, the number of acute beds per 1,000 population was below the average, and the two hospitals in Dunfermline were old and inconveniently laid out (with the implicit presumption being that the health or welfare of the people of Fife was thereby poorer). Various other concerns were identified but these 'sub-problems' were capable of being set aside until a later stage, allowing these main issues to be tackled first.

Identifying both the main problem to be addressed by the study in hand, and those 'sub-problems' that can be set aside, are crucial at the first stage of appraisal. This, together with the expression of the problem in terms of its harmful effects on those actually suffering because of it, will usually direct the subsequent stages.

6.3.3 Setting the objective of the appraisal

With the problem defined in terms of the low admission rate and the deficiencies of the old Dunfermline hospitals, the objective was set as being to find the best way of increasing access to in-patient accommodation and services and of improving conditions for staff and patients in hospital. The purpose of the appraisal was therefore to compare the costs and benefits of options for solving or ameliorating the above problems to help health service decision-makers to decide what change in quantity and quality of in-patient services for Fife would be most socially efficient and equitable.

6.3.4 The options

The three shortlisted options were:

A   closing the existing two acute hospitals in Dunfermline and increasing the number of Fife patients treated in Edinburgh;
B   upgrading the existing two acute hospitals in Dunfermline, with a smaller increase in the number of Fife patients treated in Edinburgh;
C   building a new DGH in Dunfermline to replace the existing two acute hospitals.

6.3.5 Identifying costs and benefits

This process can make a difference to health care planning because of the economic definition of costs as opportunities forgone rather than cash outflow. Opportunity costs include, for example, time, travel and inconvenience to patients and their relatives, as well as the capital costs to central government and running costs to the local health service.

For the options on the shortlist, the capital costs of the new developments involved not only the construction costs but also professional fees for designing the building, undertaking surveys, etc. The revenue costs involved changes in the costs not only to Fife Health Board but also to Lothian Health Board, which includes the Edinburgh district, and the Scottish Ambulance Service. The benefits involved not only new facilities and ease of liaison for staff but also improvements in care and changes in travel costs for patients and their visitors and in the lost output at work. Such aspects would not have been included if the appraisal had been a simple financial appraisal of the effects upon Fife Health Board.

6.3.6 Measuring and valuing costs and benefits

The first problem to be resolved here was how to measure those costs and benefits that were identified as being relevant to the study. Trying to value the costs and benefits of the options made us critically aware of the need for better data, particularly for the costing of changes in hospital throughput.

Capital costs

Typically in health service appraisals of major developments at least one option will concern investment in fixed capital stock. In this study the size of new capital facilities was measured in terms of the number of beds they would contain. Indeed bed numbers are generally taken as a measure of capital stock although clearly they can only be considered as a first approximation. The rationale behind using bed numbers lies in the assumption that there is a fixed proportionate relationship between the number of beds and the cost of the capital. To try to be more realistic, calculations also include the number and type of back-up facilities for broad categories of beds, for example distinguishing between acute and non-acute beds. Capital costs will also vary between sites and between different hospitals on the same site, if the specialty mix is different.

In this study the Building Division of the Scottish NHS provided rough estimates of the capital costs of each option. This proved more difficult than we had anticipated because they were unfamiliar with the kind of precision (or, more accurately, relative lack thereof) required in this sort of study. For many appraisals the capital costs are less crucial to the final outcome than the revenue costs and sensitivity analysis can show whether estimates of building costs need be more than approximate.

Revenue costs

The revenue (running) cost calculations were of fundamental importance to this exercise, yet the accuracy of their measurement left much to be desired. This problem was not unique to this study, and highlights the lack of a suitable data base for appraisal exercises (Ashford, Butts and Bailey, 1981). (Having said this we believe that by approaching and gaining very full cooperation from the health boards concerned we were able to attain a high level of accuracy, within the time available, in the specially-undertaken cost projections.)

The publications on health service costs give total hospital running costs, average costs per case by hospital and a few costs by specialty. However, these statistics are inadequate for most appraisals. Where an option involved the closure of in-patient services but the retention of those for out-patients such data did not allow a calculation of the proportion of support service costs that would be saved through the closure. Where fewer patients were to be treated in Edinburgh hospitals, it was not possible to calculate the saving that these hospitals would make through the reduction in throughput. Where Edinburgh hospitals were to treat more patients, the statistics were of little assistance in calculating the extra costs that these hospitals would thereby incur. It is of course marginal costs that are relevant.

The sort of information required was which costs would be affected, and to what extent if, for example, two or three extra patients per week were to be treated in some particular ward. Thus for the following it was necessary to know whether expenditure would increase and, if so, by how much:

- meals
- drugs
- cleaning
- laundry
- nursing
- physicians
- diagnostic tests
- heating
- administration

Published costs give only the total costs of the above categories of expenditure averaged over all cases treated. But treating an extra few patients on a ward is unlikely to mean, for example, that extra nurses are employed or that extra cleaning staff are hired. Linear extrapolation from average costs will produce a biased estimate.

The length of the period concerned may also be relevant. In the short-run it is less likely that extra staff can be employed, for example, than in the long-run. In this study the relevant period was 25 years, by the end of which marginal costs might be the same as the average costs, since, when decisions are taken about the level of, say, nurse staffing to provide for the hospital in ten or more years' time, then extra patients would be included in the staffing norms and so extra expenditure (the same as for the other patients on average) would be incurred because of them. This would be unlikely in the short-run, however.

With discounting, costs in the near future will be given more weight. Therefore knowing how long it takes for hospital costs to change in response to a change in the number of patients is relevant. Again this was not known.

Patients, their visitors and society in general

Some of the options to be costed would have involved extra return journeys of thirty miles or more for many patients. Hence transport costs, inconvenience, lost work time and lost leisure time were potentially major aspects of the study. However, there were no existing data on how patients travelled to hospital, how much it cost, how long it took, how many visitors they received, or their visitors' travel costs.

The initial assumptions made were that most people would travel by private car, that the cost of car travel could be measured by the mileage allowance paid to NHS staff and that patients would receive on average 1 to 2 visits per week during their stay in hospital.

The survey, which was later conducted, revealed errors in these assumptions in a number of ways. Most patients travelled by private car, but a large proportion – around 20 per cent – by bus. Many hospital visitors shared cars. Overall, however, the NHS mileage allowance seemed to be a reasonable proxy for the average transport cost per person per mile. The initial assumption which was most out was the number of visits that patients received – ranging from 8 to 16 visits per week according to the survey. Finally there were several people who had taken substantial amounts of time off work to travel to visit relatives in hospital in Edinburgh.

We found this survey – quick and unsophisticated as it was – to be very useful in filling some important gaps in our knowledge.

Utilisation

A further inadequacy of the data related to the issue of utilisation rates. The utilisation of acute hospital beds by the people of Fife was significantly below the Scottish average. Why was not clear. Ideally we wanted to determine the impact upon utilisation of both the availability of acute hospital beds and, separately, the distance, and travel costs, of journeys to health service facilities. We would then have attempted to determine the expected variation in utilisation rates for the different options. To this end we sought information on the impact of the opening of other new hospitals in Scotland, looked at research on the effect of distance from the point of service upon utilisation of acute in-patient services, and undertook statistical analyses of the returns from our own survey and hospital utilisation data, supplied by the Information Services Division of the Scottish NHS. Unfortunately the end result was that we still did not know the effects of the different determinants of utilisation rates. We surmised that distance would depress utilisation a little but had no empirical evidence to support this view.

6.3.7 Sensitivity analysis

Costs were calculated for the three options, using the methods outlined above. We then undertook sensitivity analysis of all figures calculated, varying each estimate by at least ±10 per cent and varying visitors' journey and time costs by ±30 per cent, on the basis of the survey we had undertaken. (The main results are shown in Table 6.2.) We also tested higher and lower discount rates (3 per cent and 7 per cent) as well as the 5 per cent rate recommended by the UK Treasury.

The results were unequivocal. The option (C) of building a new DGH would cost around £45 million (±£12 million) more than (B) upgrading the existing Dunfermline hospitals, which in turn would cost around £45 million (±£10 million) more than (A) treating the patients in Edinburgh and closing the existing Dunfermline hospitals (figures using 5 per cent discount rate).

Table 6.2 Case study results: net present value over period 1985–2010 of the costs: £ millions at 1982/83 prices using 5 per cent discount rate

OPTION	Sensitivity analysis	Capital	Fife Health Board Revenue	Lothian Health Board Revenue	Scottish Ambulance Service	Patients	Visitors	Time	TOTAL
A	+10%/high est.	3.6	−69.8	22.2	0.8	1.8	22.8	7.1	−11.5
	Central est.	3.2	−63.5	20.2	0.7	1.7	16.4	5.5	−15.8
	−10%/low est.	2.9	−57.1	18.2	0.7	1.5	10.0	3.8	−20.5
B	+10%/high est.	7.6	4.9	8.9	0.4	0.7	9.2	2.9	34.4
	Central est.	6.9	4.4	8.1	0.3	0.7	6.6	2.2	29.2
	−10%/low est.	6.2	4.0	7.3	0.3	0.6	4.0	1.6	24.0
C	+10%/high est.	21.6	62.0	−1.15	0.05	−0.07	−0.96	−0.30	81.2
	Central est.	19.7	56.3	−1.05	0.05	−0.07	−0.69	−0.23	74.0
	−10%/low est.	17.7	50.7	−0.94	0.04	−0.06	−0.42	−0.16	66.9

6.3.8 Assessing equity

Having reported valuations of as many as possible of the options' costs and cost savings, and identified, described and discussed the other benefits and disadvantages, the findings clearly indicated that the least cost way of increasing access to in-patient accommodation and services and of improving conditions for patients in hospital was to close down the acute hospitals in Dunfermline and to increase substantially the flow of patients to Edinburgh. This result raised two important and separate issues of equity.

Distribution and compensation

The first issue concerns the fairness of saving Scottish NHS expenditure at the expense of the people of Dunfermline. If the least cost option were chosen, the Scottish NHS would probably save over £500 for every patient treated in Edinburgh instead of in a new DGH in Dunfermline. If these patients were to be offered compensation of £500 then they would, no doubt, prefer to make the extra journey to Edinburgh and spend the £500 on something else, rather than have it spent on building and running a new DGH in Dunfermline. There seems, however, to be no chance that they would be offered the £500. If Fife Health Board were to keep the savings and spend them on improving and extending other acute, long-stay and community health services in Dunfermline then the people there would benefit from these services. While these services might not be used by precisely the same group of people who would make the journey to Edinburgh, there would be considerable overlap. This, therefore, could be one way of compensating them.

As arrangements stand at the present, however, Fife Health Board would not be able to keep any savings realised in the long run through the least cost option being chosen; rather these would accrue to Lothian Health Board, owing to the way in which the resource allocation formula redistributes revenue for acute services between the Health Boards (on the basis of average costs not marginal costs). Hence, in the long run, if the least cost option were chosen the people of Dunfermline would have a worse health service and would receive no compensation.

Equity

The second issue concerns the extent to which the promotion of equity should be an objective of economic appraisal in health care, and the most appropritae definition of equity to use in assessing the attainment of this objective. As has been demonstrated (see chapter 4) there are several definitions of equity that could convincingly be argued to be appropriate in health care, but which have different, and at times contradictory, implications for resource allocation. Three particular definitions that would seem appropriate are:

- equality of resource input for equal need
- equality of opportunity of access to services for equal need
- equality of utilisation of services for equal need

The first definition is (largely) the one by which the resource allocation formulae operate for NHS hospital facilities (DHSS, 1976; SHHD, 1977). They provide equal resources for acute health service inputs for NHS Areas, or Regions, with equal needs for acute health services (where need is defined by the size of the population weighted by its age and sex distribution and standardised mortality ratio).

The second definition is one which many health service decision-makers profess to believe in (and indeed is the stated goal of the resource allocation formulae). Its implication is that either health services should be equally accessible, for equal need, for every member of the population – which would mean, for example, providing the same level of service for people living in rural areas as for people living in urban areas – or compensating those who face higher access costs, such as travel costs, for example by reimbursing their fares.

The third definition implies, for example, that hospital admission rates should be equalised for Areas, or Regions, with equal needs. Hence not only must access costs be equalised but also the 'demand' for services must be the same, or else access costs must be manipulated to ensure that the use of services is equalised – that is access costs must be raised if 'demand' is 'too high' or lowered if 'demand' is 'too low'.

In the present case all three equity objectives conflict with the choice of the least cost option, because this option would redistribute resources to another Area, further decrease access to services for Fife residents and probably further reduce utilisation. Hence by the above three definitions the least cost option would be inequitable.

The appropriate decision-makers must decide, however, how much it is worth paying to achieve equity, for what sort of equity the health service should strive, how much weight should be attached to costs falling on patients, how much weight should be attached to under-utilisation, and in what services Health Boards/Authorities should be self-sufficient.

6.3.9 Choosing

This appraisal opened up an unresolved debate within the NHS about the importance of issues of equity and distribution *vis-à-vis* cost-minimisation and efficiency. Not unnaturally, Fife Health Board attached greater importance to equity and the distributional consequences of the options, while the ministry of health attached greater importance to cost-minimisation and efficiency. At the time of writing no final decision had been reached on the option to be implemented. However, it was clear that the analysis that was undertaken for this study helped to focus decision-making on the broad strategic choices, on the divergence of interests between patients and their relatives on the one hand and NHS budget holders on the other, and on the potential conflict between equity and efficiency.

6.4 Conclusions

In this chapter the various stages of applied economic appraisal have been illustrated with examples of case-studies drawn from the literature on health care resource allocation. In conclusion we present a checklist of questions that are intended to promote critical assessment of any case-study (Stoddart and Drummond, 1984, p. 1543).

6.4.1 Ten questions to ask of any published study

1. Was a well defined question posed in answerable form?
   (a) Did the study examine both costs and effects of the service(s) or programme(s)?
   (b) Did the study involve a comparison of alternatives?
   (c) Was a viewpoint for the analysis stated or was the study placed in a particular decision making context?

2. Was a comprehensive description of the competing alternatives given (i.e. can you tell who did what to whom, where and how often?)?
   (a) Were any important alternatives omitted?
   (b) Was (should) a 'do-nothing' alternative (have been) considered?

3. Was there evidence that the programmes' effectiveness had been established? Was this done through a randomised controlled clinical trial? If not, how strong was the evidence of effectiveness?

4. Were all important and relevant costs and consequences for each alternative identified?
   (a) Was the range wide enough for the research question at hand?
   (b) Did it cover all relevant viewpoints (e.g. those of the community or society, patients and third-party payers)?
   (c) Were capital costs as well as operating costs included?

5. Were costs and consequences measured accurately in appropriate physical units (e.g. hours of nursing time, number of physician visits, days lost from work or years of life gained) prior to valuation?
   (a) Were any identified items omitted from measurement? If so, does this mean that they carried no weight in the subsequent analysis?
   (b) Were there any special circumstances (e.g. joint use of resources) that made measurement difficult? Were these circumstances handled appropriately?

6. Were costs and consequences valued credibly?
   (a) Were the sources of all values (e.g. market values,

patient or client preferences and views, policy-makers' views and health care professionals' judgements) clearly identified?

(b)   Were market values used for changes involving resources gained or used?

(c)   When market values were absent (e.g. when volunteers were used) or did not reflect actual values (e.g. clinical space was donated at a reduced rate) were adjustments made to approximate market values?

(d)   Was the valuation of consequences appropriate for the question posed (i.e. was the appropriate type, or types, of analysis – cost-effectiveness, cost-benefit or cost-utility – selected)?

7.   Were cost and consequences adjusted for differential timing?

(a)   Were costs and consequences that occurred in the future 'discounted' to their present value?

(b)   Was any justification given for the discount rate used?

8.   Was an incremental analysis of costs and consequences of alternatives performed?

Were the additional (incremental) costs generated by the use of one alternative over another compared with the additional effects, benefits or utilities generated?

9.   Was a sensitivity analysis performed?

(a)   Was justification provided for the ranges of values (for key parameters) used in the sensitivity analysis?

(b)   Were the study results sensitive to changes in the values (within the assumed range)?

10.   Did the presentation and discussion of the results of the study include all issues of concern to users?

(a)   Were the conclusions of the analysis based on some overall index of ratio or costs to consequences (e.g. cost-effectiveness ratio)? If so, was the index interpreted intelligently or in a mechanistic fashion?

(b)   Were the results compared with those of other studies that had investigated the same questions?

(c)   Did the study discuss generalizability of the results to other settings and patient/client groups?

(d)   Did the study allude to, or take account of, other important factors in the choice or decision under consideration (e.g. distribution of costs and consequences or relevant ethical issues)?

(e)   Did the study discuss issues of implementation, such as the feasibility of adopting the 'preferred' programme, given existing financial or other constraints, and whether any freed resources could be used for other worthwhile programmes?

7

The demand for health – a household production theory approach

7.1 Introduction

A major conceptual advance in the analysis of the demand for health care has been the recognition that the fundamental demand by the consumer is for health and not health care *per se*. The demand for health care is a derived demand. A similar proposition holds for the demand for health insurance. However, it may also be argued that for certain purposes the demand for health is also a derived demand. Health is demanded not just for its own sake but also to enable individuals, for example, to participate in the labour market. This small, but influential insight was utilised in an important study by Grossman (1972a, 1972b) which represents a direct application to the demand for health and health care of the new theories of consumer demand. Such theories were themselves important extensions of the neoclassical approach to consumption theory. The earlier, revealed preference approach, resting upon the individual's taste not changing and a number of simple accompanying assumptions, demonstrated that demand could be analysed simply through observing how a consumer's purchases varied with prices and incomes. These assumptions, as they relate to choice under uncertainty, were outlined in chapter 3, where it was noted that they imposed severe limitations upon the economic analysis of the commodity health care. In particular the informational requirements demanded of the consumer and the associated problems relating to the uncertainty of consumption were seen to be central to the consideration of this commodity.

129

Unfortunately, as we shall see, the application of the new theories of consumer demand to the demand for health have failed to resolve these basic problems, although they have generated a substantial literature.

These new theories were developed through the removal of the artificial separation of consumption and production, particularly in analysing service commodities, necessary (conceptually) to allow price and income to enter as the major independent explanatory variables in the household consumption function. Becker (1965), for example, suggested that consumers are simultaneously involved in production, as well as consumption activities.[1] This new approach to consumer behaviour also suggested that demand is associated not only with inherent qualities within commodities, which led to the study of characteristics and hedonic pricing,[2] but also in particular with basic or fundamental commodities. Thus the household becomes the basic decision-making unit with regard to production as well as consumption (Grossman, 1972b, p. 224).

Consumers produce (fundamental) commodities with inputs of market goods and their own time. For example, they use sporting equipment and their own time to produce recreation, travelling time and transportation to produce visits, and part of their Sundays and church services to produce 'peace of mind'. Since (purchased) goods and services are inputs into the production of fundamental commodities the demand for these goods and services is a derived demand.

In applying this approach to health and health care Grossman perceives health as a fundamental commodity. The analysis of the demand for health care, it is argued, must be undertaken after an initial analysis of the demand for the fundamental commodity – health. The model suggests, in line with our earlier exposition, that the demand for health care is a derived demand and focuses upon the primary demand – the demand for health. Consumers are held to demand health for two reasons. As a consumption commodity, health enters their utility functions directly. As an investment commodity, it determines the amount of time available for work, which allows consumers to produce money earnings, and the amount of time available for leisure, with leisure time being combined with other commodities which in turn produce commodities which directly enter their consumption functions. Grossman has tended to concentrate upon the investment demand for health, possibly as the consumption model analysis leads to inconclusive findings. This chapter will also concentrate upon the investment model.

This then is the methodological background to the household production model first developed by Grossman (1972a). We may now consider the analytics associated with the model in some more detail. That it is merely an extension of the neoclassical approach can be seen diagramatically or algebraically. Section 7.2 considers the diagrammatic outline. Section 7.3 then considers the algebra. Section 7.4 considers criticisms of the model. Section 7.5 considers the approach within a wider context.

7.2 The household production model: a simple exposition

The consumer is presumed to be a utility maximiser. This can be represented through indifference curve analysis, such behaviour being constrained by income level, the price of health inputs, consumption activities, and the opportunities for transforming health inputs into health. In other words, the individual's objective is to attain the highest consumption possibility contour, subject to the conditions that he operates on both his budget constraint and his health production function. The individual's utility maximising behaviour can be analysed, following Wagstaff (1986b), with regard to the four-quadrant diagram given as Figure 7.1.

Quadrant II outlines the health production function which, as is shown, encompasses the law of diminishing marginal product. This function shows how much health can be obtained for a given quantity of health input, given technical knowledge. Quadrant III outlines the budget constraints upon the individual's utility maximising behaviour. As neither health inputs nor consumption activities are costless, the consumer, in line with traditional neoclassical economics, must allocate his income between these activities. The slope of the curve reflects the relative costs. Note that the consumer is assumed to have perfect knowledge over these costs.

Inclusion of the budget constraint and health production in the same diagram allows determination of the combination of consumption and health input activities that the consumer will actually

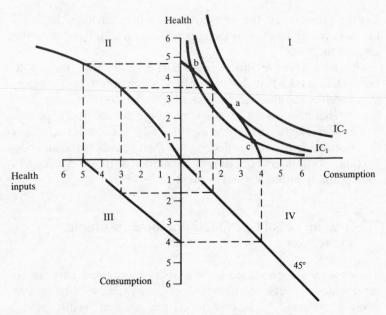

Figure 7.1 The household production of health.
Source: Wagstaff (1986b)

choose. This is shown in Quadrant I, which transforms the information given in Quadrant III through the 45° line of Quadrant IV. The IC_1 and IC_2 curves outline part of the consumer's indifference map. The concave curve is the consumption possibility frontier. Equilibrium is given at point a.

This presentation is useful in examining *ceteris paribus* assumptions. Figure 7.2, for example, outlines the effect of changing income under this assumption. It is assumed that the individual's income falls, as in Figure 7.2, resulting in a parallel movement towards the origin of the budget constraint. Moving round the quadrants, we can follow through the effects of this fall in income. Not surprisingly, given the underlying assumptions, a lower income means that the number of feasible combinations of health input and consumption activities open to the individual are diminished. Equilibrium at a is no longer possible, the individual's new equilibrium is at b, at which point he has a lower level of health and consumes less. His health stock is reduced because he has less to spend upon health inputs. Thus, for the particular

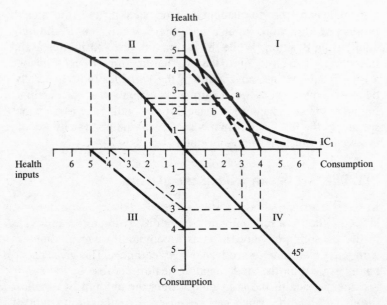

Figure 7.2 The effect of falling income on the household production of health.
Source: Wagstaff (1986b)

example given in Figure 7.2, a fall in income is predicted to result in a reduction of the quantity of health inputs employed and a deterioration in the individual's health status. A similar exposition could be outlined for changes in the price variable.

It will of course be recognised that a number of basic assumptions underlie this simple exposition of the household production model. It is assumed, for example, that the consumer is able to make comparisons between consumption activities and health levels in such a manner that he can decide on his preferred consumption patterns and health production to allow consistent preference orderings to be made. This of course necessitates the consumer having adequate information to allow rational decisions to be made. The ability to acquire such information may be questioned. It should also be noted that the equilibrium points attained in our examples are a function of the shape of the curves drawn. Thus, for example, if the marginal efficiency of the presumed capital stock, health, were different, then the health production function would suggest different elasticities of substitution between the fundamental good health and the health production function inputs, and there would be a different equilibrium position. While the diagrammatic exposition is useful in outlining the basic approach, the implied directions of change arising from specific movements in the variables may, generally, be more explicitly arrived at through examination of the algebraic formulation. The algebra also enables us to outline the assumptions specific to the full Grossman model, i.e. to examine the household production function in greater detail.

7.3 The Grossman model: the algebra

In the Grossman model, as was stated above, health may be viewed either as a fundamental commodity giving direct utility, as in the consumption model, or as a commodity which combines with, *inter alia*, time to produce money earnings. This gives rise to an investment motive in demanding health, because by increasing his stock of health the individual lowers the amount of time lost through ill-health, which can be devoted to the production of market and non-market activities. Health, the durable capital stock, produces an output of healthy time per period, as measured by healthy days. Grossman argues that this output differentiates the capital good health from other forms of human capital. For example, the individual's stock of knowledge influences his market and non-market productivity, whereas the stock of health actually determines the total amount of time he can spend producing money earnings and commodities.

The full formal Grossman model is considered below before we turn to analyse the investment model. As in the simple diagrammatic exposition, the individual's objective is to maximise utility. However, in this case it is life-time utility. This is a function of Z_t, a composite consumption good, and h_t, the services which flow from the health stock. In other words H_t represents the healthy days derived from the stock of health. The maximand is therefore of the typical neoclassical form:

$$U = f(h_0, \ldots, h_t; Z_0, \ldots Z_t) \qquad (7.1)$$

The service flow, healthy days (h_t), is produced from the health stock (K_t^h), such that:

$$h_t = \Phi_t(K_t^h): \Phi'_t > 0, \Phi'' < 0 \qquad (7.2)$$

where Φ'_t may be considered as the marginal product of the stock of health as measured in healthy days. The stock changes over time may be shown by:

$$K^h_{t-1} - K^h_t = I^h_t - \delta_t K^h_t \qquad (7.3)$$

where I^h_t is new investment in health and δ_t is the rate of depreciation of the capital stock, health. The rates of depreciation are assumed to be exogenous.

A constraint upon capital stock exists such that:

$$K^h_t > \bar{K}^h \qquad (7.4)$$

where $\bar{K}^h$ is a given minimum; the 'death stock'. At the last period, T, $K^h_t < \bar{K}^h$ of course.

It is further assumed that consumers produce the gross investments in health and the other commodities in the utility function from the following household production functions:

$$I^h_t = I^h_t (X^h_t, T^h_t, E_t) \qquad (7.5)$$

$$Z_t = Z_t (X^z_t, T^z_t, E_t) \qquad (7.6)$$

where X^h_t is health care and X^z_t is the market goods input in the production of Z; T^h_t is time spent investing in health and T^z_t the time input in producing Z; E_t is the stock of human capital, essentially education, which operates upon the efficiency of household production, in a manner analogous to the operation of technology upon the efficiency of industrial production processes. Note that Grossman, whilst acknowledging in a footnote (1972b, p. 226) that health care is not the only market good relevant to gross investments in the capital stock health, has abstracted away the effects of all other market goods, for example, cigarette smoking, diet and housing, upon health.

A time constraint is introduced such that the total amount of time in the period, Ω, is exhausted by all possible uses:

$$\Omega_t = T^w_t + T^z_t + T^h_t + T^u_t \qquad (7.7)$$

where T^w_t and T^u_t are working time and sick time respectively, in time-period t. Using equation (7.2) we can show that:

$$\Omega_t - T^u_t = h_t = \Phi_t(K^h_t) \qquad (7.8)$$

The life-time budget constraint equates the present value of

135

purchases to the present value of life cycle earnings plus initial asset endowments:

$$\sum_{t=0}^{T} \frac{P_t^z X_t^z + P_t^h X_t^h}{(1 + r)^t} = \sum_{t=0}^{T} \frac{W_t T_t^w}{(1 + r)^t} + A_0 \qquad (7.9)$$

where r is the opportunity cost of capital, i.e. the constant rate of interest, P_t^z and P_t^h are the prices of X_t^z and X_t^h respectively, W_t the wage rate and A_0 the discounted value of capital income.

Maximising the utility function (7.1) subject to the constraints (7.3), (7.4), (7.7) and (7.9), taking into account (7.2), (7.5) and (7.6) gives, after rearranging, the marginal condition for new health investment as:

$$\frac{U_{\Phi t}(1 + r)^t}{\lambda} \cdot \frac{\Phi'_t}{MC_{t-1}^h} + \frac{W_t \, \Phi'_t}{MC_{t-1}^h} = r + \delta_t - \overline{MC}_{t-1}^h \quad (7.10)$$

where $U_{\Phi t} = \delta U / \delta \Phi_t$ which is the marginal utility of health time; λ is the marginal utility of wealth; Φ'_t is the marginal productivity of health as measured by healthy days: MC_{t-1}^h is the marginal cost of health investment in period $t - 1$; and $\overline{MC}_{t-1}^h$ the percentage rate of change in marginal costs between periods $t - 1$ and t.

Equation (7.10) is the essential equation of the Grossman model. As the inherited health stock and rates of depreciation are given, the optimal quantity of gross investment determines the optimal quantity of health capital. In short this equation merely sets, at the margin, the user cost of health capital equal to the discounted marginal benefits of health. In other words, at the margin, benefits must equal costs in equilibrium: that is the total rate of return, both the monetary rate of return and the 'psychic' rate of return, to an investment in health must equal the user cost of that capital as expressed by the price of gross investment. Thus reading equation (7.10) from the left, the first term expresses the monetary rate of return (or the investment benefit), the second term expresses the 'psychic' rate of return (the consumption benefit), while the RHS term expresses the user cost as determined by the real own-rate of return ($r - \overline{MC}_{t-1}^h$) and the depreciation rate.

Grossman assumes that the capital stock, health, cannot be traded, in a capital market, implying that gross investment must be non-negative. However, he does envisage that the individual is able to rent the capital stock from himself over different time periods, giving rise to a user cost of health capital. Thus trade is possible through the individual varying his own pattern of gross investment in health over time.

Grossman continues his analysis by abstracting out, separately, the consumption benefits to be gained from the capital stock of health and the investment benefits to be gained from the stock. Thus to analyse the consumption aspects the second term on the left-hand side of (7.10) is set to zero. The equilibrium condition is then:

$$\frac{U_{\Phi't}(1+r)^t}{\lambda} \cdot \frac{\Phi'_t}{MC^h_{t-1}} = r + \delta_t - \overline{MC}^h_{t-1} \qquad (7.11)$$

To analyse the investment benefits, the consumption benefits are set to zero, i.e. the marginal utility of healthy time equals zero, such that the equilibrium condition becomes:

$$\frac{W_t \Phi'_t}{MC^h_{t-1}} = r + \delta_t - \overline{MC}^h_{t-1} \qquad (7.12)$$

The right-hand side of this equation may be thought of as the marginal monetary rate of return on an investment in health, or the marginal efficiency of health capital. It should also be noted that Grossman assumes a constant marginal cost of investment in health in the investment model, which allows the equilibrium stock of health at any age to be determined by setting the marginal monetary rate of return on health capital equal to the opportunity cost of this capital.

The investment model is then completed by the specification of a demand for health care derived as follows. As we noted above the output of health capital has a finite limit of 365 days per year, and therefore the marginal product must diminish. Thus the production function of healthy days (equation 7.2 above) may be specified as

$$h_t = 365 - B(K^h_t)^{-C} \qquad (7.13)$$

where B and C are constants. From this, the marginal product of health (Φ'_t) is given as;

$$\Phi'_t = BC(K^h_t)^{-C-1} \qquad (7.14)$$

Now

$$\ln\Phi'_t = \ln BC - (C + 1)K_t^h \qquad (7.15)$$

and, from (7.12) we may define the marginal efficiency of capital, γ_t, in terms of the hourly wage rate and the marginal cost of gross investment in health:

$$\gamma_t = \frac{W_t \Phi'_t}{MC_{t-1}^h} \qquad (7.16)$$

and of course for equilibrium

$$\gamma_t = r + \delta_t - \overline{MC}_{t-1}^h \qquad (7.17)$$

If we substitute $\ln\gamma_t - \ln W_t + \ln\overline{MC}_{t-1}^h$ for $\ln\Phi'_t$ in (7.15) and solve for $\ln K_t^h$ we get:

$$\ln K_t^h = \ln BC + \epsilon\ln W_t - \epsilon\ln\overline{MC}_{t-1}^h - \epsilon\ln\gamma_t \qquad (7.18)$$

Replacing γ by the equilibrium condition $r + \delta_t - \overline{MC}_{t-1}^h$ and assuming as Grossman does that $r - \overline{MC}_{t-1}^h$ is zero, gives:

$$\ln K_{t-1}^h = \ln BC + \epsilon\ln W_t - \epsilon\ln MC_{t-1}^h - \epsilon\ln\delta_t \qquad (7.19)$$

as the demand for health capital or marginal efficiency of health capital schedule. This equation forms the basis for an estimatable reduced-form demand for health equation.

Usher (1975) points out that it is essential to assume a constant marginal cost of investment if the demand for health is not to depend upon future values of the exogenous variables, in particular the rates of depreciation in future years. Indeed he suggests that it is more plausible to assume that the marginal cost of investment in health *is* an increasing function of the investment in health. If this is true then the demand curve would depend upon future values of the exognous variables, in which case the demand for health today becomes a function of 'all the parameters in the model, all wages, all depreciation rates, and all prices of health capital from now until the end of one's life' (Usher, op. cit., p. 219). Of course the restriction upon the marginal cost is necessary to ensure that the algebra does not become unduly complicated.

Grossman continues by considering how changes in particular variables will affect the analysis, which remains based upon the pure investment model. He considers the impact of age upon the demand for health, with a *ceteris paribus* assumption holding. As marginal costs are constant and therefore not age-dependent (7.12) reduces to:

$$\frac{W_T \Phi'_t}{MC^h_{t-1}} = r + \delta_t \tag{7.20}$$

i.e. we ignore $\overline{MC}^h_{t-1}$. It is then assumed that depreciation increases with age for each individual. As the depreciation rate (δ_t) increases, the marginal cost of producing healthy days increases. In other words there is a rise in the shadow price of health. Of course as the depreciation rate increases the individual moves out of equilibrium, as the costs of investing in health exceed the benefits. From (7.2) above we know that $h_t = \Phi_t(K^h_t)$, and assuming that the marginal productivity of health (Φ'_t) is lower the higher the health stock (K^h_t), the individual will choose a lower stock of health thereby increasing his marginal productivity which will, eventually, bring the individual back into equilibrium as the marginal rate of return is equated with the increased marginal cost. Note that nothing is said about the dynamics of the adjustment process as this is, after all, an exercise in comparative statics. Presumably, however, as the individuals are acting with complete certainty the process is instantaneous. Thus as Grossman puts it 'Biological factors associated with ageing raise the price of human capital and cause individuals to substitute away from future health until death is "chosen"' (op. cit., p. 240).

Of course an increase in the shadow price of capital, caused by the depreciation rate, reduces not only the demand for health capital, but also the amount of health capital supplied to them by a given amount of gross investment. The cost of investment, having increased, reduces the supply of health capital. However, given a relatively inelastic demand curve for health, individuals will offset part of the reduction in health capital, caused by an increase in the rate of depreciation, by increasing their gross investments. Therefore, the demand for health care, for example, being one of the inputs in the health investment function, will increase as long as the price elasticity of the demand for health capital is less than one. In other words there will be a negative relationship between health and health care if the demand for health capital is inelastic. This predicts that people who are less healthy will increase their consumption of health care!

Grossman then turns to consider wage effects. The value of the marginal product of health, $(W_t\Phi'_t)$, obviously depends upon the wage rate. Thus as wages increase, this will increase the monetary equivalent of the marginal product of the health stock. In other words the higher an individual's wages then the higher will be the value to that individual, *ceteris paribus*, of an increase in healthy time. But the gross investment function also requires an input of time and if more time is spent in the labour market there is less time to devote to investing in health, for example, through consuming health care. As a consequence the costs of investment must increase. However, as time is not the sole input in the gross investment schedule the percentage increase in wages will always be greater at the margin than the percentage increase in investment costs. The exact return to health capital of an increase in wages will, therefore, depend upon the elasticity of demand for health and the share of time in the gross investment schedule.

Finally, Grossman examines the investment model with respect to the role of education. The model, as we have seen, assumes that education acts, in a manner similar to technology, by shifting the production function. Thus it is postulated that education shifts the marginal efficiency of capital schedule (i.e. the demand curve for health) by increasing productivity. In other words the demand curve for health shifts to the right not as a result of changes in consumers' tastes, not a relevant mechanism in household production analysis, but rather because more efficient production has reduced costs. Thus the marginal efficiency of the health capital schedule is seen to depend upon the elasticity of that schedule and the elasticity of investment with respect to education.

Making further assumptions concerning factor neutrality in the production process, Grossman shows that if the elasticity of the marginal efficiency of capital is less than one, the more educated will demand more health but less medical care (1972a, p. 28). This occurs because the better educated will increase their demand for health at the margin as their education leads to a fall in the cost of production of health. However, this increase in health, gained through more efficient production, will also give individuals an incentive to decrease health care purchases.

While the Grossman analysis is pursued predominantly in the context of the pure investment model, some analysis of the pure consumption model is undertaken. Thus it is found that, as in the investment model, the process of ageing causes individuals to 'substitute away from future health until death is chosen' (Gross-man, 1972a, p. 34). However, a major difference is that, in the consumption model, the existence of time preference for the future might outweigh the rise in the depreciation rate which accompanies age and lead to a temporary increase in health capital. The elasticity of substitution between present and future health, rather than the elasticity of the marginal efficiency of capital schedule, becomes the parameter determining life-cycle behaviour. In analysing wage effects with regard to the consumption model, these are found to be difficult to determine. Wages affect both the marginal cost of gross investments and the marginal cost of consumption goods. There is, therefore, an ambiguity over the wage effect. Similarly the introduction of wealth effects in the consideration of education in the consumption model leads to an ambiguity in the effect of this variable. As a consequence the comparative static predictions associated with the consumption model are inconclusive.

7.4 Summing-up the Grossman case

The Grossman model has been detailed here because it has been extremely influential in the study of health economics. This remains the case although a number of criticisms have been made of the model. A major criticism is that the model assumes the existence of certainty. This is particularly relevant in the investment model to the definition of user cost and the concept of renting stock attributable to a later period. However, its relevance may be pursued at a more general level. It has been argued previously that one of the most distinguishing features associated with health is the inherent uncertainty associated with it. In the Grossman model the depreciation rate is presumed known, and indeed this leads logically to the conclusion that every individual can choose his own time of death. This is clearly a convenience dictated by the assumptions of the model. Grossman in fact acknowledges that the model must be developed to incorporate uncertainty. He suggests that the simplest manner would be to subject the depreciation rate to probability distributions in each period, thus creating dispersion in time of death expectations. Indeed this suggestion is pursued by Phelps (1973) and by Cropper

(1977). However, Dowie (1975) has argued that this is unnecessarily crude as, if one has to choose where uncertainty should be incorporated, then it would be better placed upon the gross investment variables. He suggests this on the grounds that the process of ageing is seen to be a continuous and largely determinate one, whilst the effect of a given input upon a specified health stock is largely uncertain. He, therefore, suggests that the gross investment function with regard to health should be specified to include not simply health care, but also other health related commodities, for example, diet and smoking. This would enable a portfolio approach to be undertaken with regard to health care. In doing so, however, the model, to be properly specified, would have to take account of the further complication of joint production, given that market commodities would enter both of the household production functions defined by Grossman as (7.5) and (7.6) above.[3] However, this portfolio approach does not overcome the fundamental difficulty of dealing with the inherent uncertainty in relation to health.

With respect to this latter point it is worth distinguishing, as we did in chapter 5, between risk – where individuals are able to attach probabilities to events – and uncertainty – where individuals are unable to do this. In suggesting that consumers would attach probability distributions to depreciation rates, Grossman is overcoming difficulties associated with risk rather than uncertainty. It may well be suggested that it is uncertainty *per se* that is fundamental to analysis of the consumption and investment decisions associated with health. Notice, however, that if such a stance is adopted it becomes impossible to 'trade' health across time-periods in the manner suggested by Grossman.

It is also worth considering the role of health care in Grossman's model in a little more detail. As Usher (1975) points out, health care is purchased, according to the model, solely to yield a flow of illness-free days each year for the rest of the consumer's life. The purchase is, therefore, not made to alleviate sickness but rather to invest in health. Two points arise from this. First, the model abstracts from the complications of the mechanics of the health care insurance market. Just as the demand for health and the demand for health care can be separated, it may be analytically useful to separate the demand for health care insurance and health care consumption. Certainly such a separation would explicitly acknowledge the randomness – the uncertainty rather than the risk – associated with health and illness, as well as complicate the role of health care in the gross investment function. Second, it is not clear that the benefits from health care consumption, let alone health care expenditure, may be assumed to be realised steadily and constantly over time by the consumer. As Usher (op. cit., p. 215) remarks, to obtain a positive rate of return from radiation treatment the consumer must first be sure of having cancer. Moreover while some illnesses may be recontractable and self-limiting, e.g. the common cold, others may be so acute that health care is necessary to sustain life, e.g. acute appendicitis. In other words the consumption of health care does not necessarily lead to a constant long-term investment in illness-free days. To some degree it is constantly necessary to remind oneself of the simultaneity of consumption and production in health care and the heterogeneous nature of this commodity.

Muurinen (1982) has criticised the basic Grossman model on two specific grounds. First, she argues that it is not credible to assume a dichotomy of health stock benefits. The splitting into consumption and investment benefits are, as she states, 'clearly treated as rival hypotheses of the "true" nature of health services' in Grossman's discussion (op. cit., p. 7). To an extent this dichotomy is obviously an analytical convenience arising from the specification of the commodity health as a fundamental or basic good and as an input in the household's gross investment function. On a conceptual level, Muurinen argues, this convenience appears intuitively wrong if the health benefits are viewed as alternative specifications, that is as substitutes. In her own extension of the Grossman model, she retains the analytical convenience of the separation of health benefits, but views these benefits as complements rather than substitutes. Her argument is that it is both for its consumption benefits (enjoying good health) *and* for its investment benefits (freedom from illness to participate in selling labour value) that health is demanded.

Muurinen's second criticism is that the health stock is not the only durable capital good which produces flows of services. She argues that both the stock of education and the stock of wealth also produce flows of services and, importantly, that all three capital stocks may be interchangeable to a degree. This would obviously affect the depreciation variable in the original specification. Indeed she correctly states that the relationship between education and health is not made fully explicit in the Grossman model, and this remains an under-researched area. Grossman assumes that education may be treated in a manner analogous to the treatment of technology and entrepreneurial capacity in the industrial production function, namely as a production function efficiency factor. Assuming linear homogeneity, the model shows that education raises the marginal product of the direct production inputs. In other words the quantity of direct inputs required for a given level of gross investment is reduced which, *ceteris paribus*, lowers the marginal cost of gross investment in health. As Muurinen notes, there is little justification for this assumption which emphasises the better use of inputs arising, for example, from better knowledge concerning their relationships and ignores the role of education in the specification of the gross investment process itself through, for example, the determination of life-style.

Indeed the aim of the household production function literature generally is to explain non-market and market activities utilising conventional economic analysis but without resorting to explanations which rest upon intangible mechanics, such as changing tastes. Yet the change in household technology, attributable to increased education in the Grossman model, may be viewed simply as analogous to a change in tastes. Certainly it is the formal equivalent.

Such criticisms are specific to the Grossman model yet on a more general level the basic approach of the household production model may be questioned. The model assumes that the consumer is sufficiently informed and rational to make utility maximising choices with regard to his investment in health care and his stock of health; and with regard to the timing of and disutility associated with the depreciation of that stock; and with regard to the income elasticity of substitution between health care and other inputs in the health production process; and with regard to the marginal efficiency of current and future investment in health which requires knowledge *inter alia* of future technical change. Given more realistic appreciation of the characteristics of the commodity health care, in particular the essential role of uncertainty, it is difficult to see that such assumptions can represent an accurate description of the demand for health. A particularly important aspect, to be developed in later chapters, is the effect that the uncertainty associated with both the unpredictability of illness and the future cost of health care has upon the decision-making process. By assuming that households can rationally choose utility maximising paths, the model avoids important questions regarding risk-bearing in decision making with regard to both health and health care. All such problems are abstracted away by assuming perfect informational flows.

Of course the unreality of the assumptions need not necessarily subvert the model, provided they can be relaxed without destroying the basis of the argument erected upon them, and the model holds some predictive content. Certainly the Grossman model is an elegant example of an application of household production theory and its starting point, the defining of the basic commodity and its relationship to the demand for health care, is to be commended. That the model does not rely upon changing tastes and 'explains' the ageing process in terms of conventional economic analysis is remarkable only to the extent that the predictions are not. At least within the confines of the investment model, the predictions do accord with intuitive knowledge. However, it must be stated that overall the model remains restrictive and underdeveloped.

In empirically attempting to substantiate the model, certain difficulties also arise. Certain variables remain unobservable in empirical specifications necessitating the use of reduced-form rather than structural estimates of the demand for health. Indeed because the model relates to life-cycle utility, critical assumptions have to be made concerning variables such as lifetime earnings, time preference rates and interest rates. The data requirements, therefore, strictly demand the use of panel data. In short the empirical specifications and model testing directly associated with the model are also complicated.

The empirical testing of the original model was based upon reduced-form demand for health equations with health specified in terms of healthy days. Not surprisingly given our discussion of the consumption model predictions, estimation of the consumption model gave rise to ambiguous results. In contrast the estimation of the investment model led to results which were consistent with the predictions of that model. In particular the results, based upon reduced-form equations, upheld the user-depreciation and education-efficiency hypotheses.[4] Specifically with regard to the latter result the schooling parameter was positive when other variables were held constant and was interpreted as supporting the hypothesis that education raises the efficiency with which health is produced. However, as Grossman (1975) points out, if schooling is correlated with the initial period depreciation rate or if it is an imperfect measure of the stock of human capital, both of which are plausible, then this result is not as powerful as it first appears. In his later work Grossman attempts to overcome such criticisms by developing a more general model, in which the amount of schooling and an individual's health status during school years are entered as endogenous variables (op. cit., 1975). This model allows Grossman to examine the 'pure' effect of schooling upon health. The empirical estimation of this model upholds the positive and significant effect of schooling upon health.

Further empirical studies have applied the household production function approach to the analysis of the determinants of the utilisation of paediatric care and neonatal mortality rates (Colle and Grossman, 1978; Corman and Grossman, 1985). In the former study the mother's schooling and the number of children in the family were found to be the major determinants in the utilisation of paediatric services, with income also found to be significant. In the latter study the availability of abortion services, neonatal intensive care facilities and female schooling were indicated to be the most important determinants of neonatal mortality rates, with a poverty measure also found to be significant. Shakotoko, Edwards and Grossman (1981) have gone a step further in examining the educational efficiency parameter in their study of the relationship between health and cognitive development. They conclude that the single most important contributor to cognitive development is the mother's schooling and that cognitive development does have a positive effect upon health in adolescence.

The emphasis upon education as a major determinant of either individuals' own health or their children's health should not be dismissed lightly. Generally the empirical significance of such a relationship is supportive of the claim that health care is only one determinant of health status, and, indeed, that it is not the major determinant. More specifically, hypothesising that education is the major efficiency factor in the health production function releases economic analysis from a reliance upon tastes to explain differences in the level of demand for health. Yet it is essential to recognise that the mechanisms through which education is held to affect health have not been explicitly identified. In other words the explanations relying upon taste differences and those relying upon educational differences may not be so different after all. Certainly we are still relying upon a process that is not fully specified to explain differences in demand levels. Moreover while the parameter estimates gained from the estimation of the various models are generally consistent, in terms of sign and significance, with the predictions, the predictions themselves are less than revealing.

In general, the most powerful pedagogic message is that it is wrong to emphasise the effect of health care as a determinant of the demand for health and neglect all other factors. However, this does not mean that the relationship between the commodity health care and health status is any less distinctive. Indeed the recognition that this relationship is peculiar has implications for the Grossman approach. Thus, for example, chapter 3 noted that health care is normally only demanded when health status falls. Yet in the Grossman model health care yields a continuous flow of services. The acceptance of this small, but important point would alter the Grossman model in a fundamental manner. Similarly the acceptance of, for example, the importance of the agency relationship or of health insurance would have a significant impact upon it.[5]

7.5 Postscript

It may be considered by some that the space devoted to the Grossman model is unwarranted. In answer it must be stated that the model represents a lucid example of the application of rigorous economic analysis to the study of health economics and that it has formed the basis for a considerable amount of literature in the discipline. We have tried to relate the model, through diagrammatic exposition, to the well known axioms of consumer theory associated with choice under certainty. In particular the consumer is held to be sovereign with regard to such choices. The algebraic outline of the model was presented in an attempt to characterise its conventional elegance.

There have, however, been some studies which have examined the production of health at the aggregate level which, perhaps not surprisingly given the epidemiological evidence, confirm Grossman's specific predictions, if not his underlying approach.

The starting point for these models is that the production of health should be seen in the context of broad resource substitutions in the provision of health, thereby taking account of non-medical inputs, such as environmental factors, as well as health *per se*. One particular example is the study by Auster, Leveson and Sarachek (1969). This study specified a Cobb-Douglas form for the health production function, which was regressed on cross-sectional (state) data in the USA. Age–sex adjusted death rates were used as a proxy measure of health status. The results showed, amongst other things, that income is positively related to death rate, education is negatively related to death rate, and environmental factors, such as the percentage of the population living in a manufacturing area or smoking, are also positively related to mortality. Specifically, the model indicated that a 1 per cent increase in the quantity of medical services was associated with a reduction in mortality of 0.1 per cent. Moreover the finding of a negative income elasticity is in agreement with Grossman's own empirical work. Environmental variables were seen to be much more important however in the explanation of inter-state mortality variations. Over 50 per cent of the variation among states in age–sex-adjusted death rates was associated with the combination of medical and environmental variables. Education, for example, was seen to be almost twice as effective as medical care in reducing mortality. Income as noted above was positively related to the death rate. This was held to reflect the fact that an increased standard of living can be detrimental to health. From the results it was estimated that, given the 35 per cent increase in health care expenditure over the period 1955 to 1965, we should have expected a decline in the mortality rate of around 4 per cent. That this did not occur was explained by the offsetting factors; cigarette consumption would have increased mortality by 2 per cent and the increase in real income would have increased mortality by up to 6 per cent.

The methodology employed by Auster, Levenson and Sarachek is itself open to some criticism. First, we must question how accurate a proxy to health status are age–sex-adjusted death rates. To some extent, as the authors acknowledge, it is a one dimensional proxy which emphasises mortality rather than morbidity. The model adopted also assumes that the amount of health services produced in any area equals the amount consumed (i.e.

there is no excess capacity), and more importantly that the state of the population's health is a function of the current year's health care only. In other words health is not affected by the life cycle consumption of health care commodities or environmental factors. The initial regression results, based upon ordinary least squares regression, are subject to simultaneity bias, and the more refined two stage least squares regression are suspected of containing multicollinearity, although it is unclear how severe this is. Note that a possible consequence of multicollinearity is that the signs on the estimated coefficients can be affected. The results also pertain only to the white population, even although data on some variables were only available on the whole population. Once again the empirical work needs to be extended. However, it is supportive of the general conclusions of the analysis by Grossman – health care services only have a marginal impact on health, which in turn is supportive of the earlier evidence from epidemiological and medical studies (see section 2.2).

8

Is there a demand for health care?

8.1 Introduction

There has been an increasing awareness in the health economics literature that the application of the conventional theory of demand to health and health care is misleading. The characteristics of uncertainty and informational impactedness of the commodity health care, as introduced in chapter 3, have a fundamental effect upon demand analysis in the sector. The usual economic approach is to specify the consumer as sovereign and relate demand to willingness to pay, constrained by the tangible role of budget considerations. Uncertainty is managed by expression of von Neumann-Morgenstern expected utility maximisation and market analysis continues through the study of supply in the light of the specified demand constraints. The existence and nature of the information impactedness in health care is such that, although the consumer remains strictly sovereign over the basic utility choices, in that it is only the consumer who can convert health status changes into utility gains or losses, he lacks the necessary information over the technical relationship between health care and health status to make consistent preference comparisons as well as the information which would allow him to define the expected *ex post* state of the world. This information is relevant to both the direct consumption of health care and the investment effects of that consumption. Health care is, of course, a hetero-geneous commodity. Nevertheless it may still be suggested that health care is broadly bad in consumption, in that its consumption *per se* involves disutility. There are few people who, in the normal course of events, would willingly consume health care purely for its consumption effects on their utility function. Information on the form of health care necessary for its investment effects is required, however, to allow the consumer to evaluate net utility and make rational choices.

Evans and Wolfson (1980) express the problem in terms of a nested utility function:

$$U = U(X, \ldots ,HS(HC, X, E))$$

where U is utility, X is a composite consumption commodity other than health care (HC), E represents environmental goods and HS health status. Consumers alone may determine the relationship $\delta U/\delta HS$, but they must seek information on the relation $\delta HS/\delta HC$ prior to this utility evaluation. Not only is this information highly technical, in a number of cases it may also be excessively costly to acquire in terms of associated search costs. Further the anxiety costs involved in holding the information may also be high. The fundamental demand for health and its specification remain the property of the consumer, with decisions in this respect remaining sovereign to the consumer. For example, even if the consumer is aware of the health risks involved in smoking, the decision to smoke remains his. However, the derived demand for health care relies upon the decision-making capacity of the provider. Informational impactedness means that the provider becomes instrumental in specifying the consumption pattern of the consumer.

The crucial role of the supplier in the ordering of the consumer's preferences has long been recognised in the literature.[1] However, the first and earliest response to the peculiarities associated with the consumption of health care revolved around the discussion of need as a demand concept. Later, the explicit introduction of the supplier in the consumption process arose from the recognition that, given information impactedness, the supplier could manipulate the consumer's demand levels. We shall examine each of these issues in this chapter. Section 8.2 discusses the concept of need. Section 8.3 is devoted to discussion of the agency relationship and section 8.4 considers the importance of supplier-induced demand. Section 8.5 then considers the empirical evidence on supplier-induced demand.

8.2 Need

The ambiguity of the concept of 'need' has attracted a lot of past attention (e.g. see Culyer, 1976). It is not our intention to cover the full intricacies of the discussion over the concept of need; rather we consider the usefulness of this concept with regard to a better understanding of the operation of the health care sector. Need can be related to the concept of demand by arguing that demands are nothing more than expressions of felt needs or desires reflecting a given taste. In other words every demand is a need by someone of something for some purpose. Of course if the consumer is not the best judge of his own needs this will affect his revealed preferences, i.e. his demands, for goods and services.

However, it may also be argued that need is a much more heavily value laden concept. As Boulding (1966) remarks, need is associated with a mechanistic view of consumption which is to be contrasted with the libertarian concept of demand – 'Only the slave has needs; the free man has demands' (op. cit., p. 31). The concept also has overtones of equality if only in its association with the dictat 'from each according to his ability, to each according to his need'. In the extreme the concept of need may be utilised to reject that of consumer sovereignty altogether. It may be argued that certain commodities, including health care, are so fundamental that individuals have a 'right' to their consumption.[2] The ethical bases of such judgements, as well as being open to dispute, are certainly different from the utilitarian arguments advanced to defend government intervention in the provision of health care on efficiency grounds. Largely because of, rather than in spite of, such inherent biases need has remained an influential concept in determining health care levels. This is unfortunate from an economic viewpoint because the concept remains underdeveloped.

For instance from a medical stance needs tends to be viewed simplistically as an absolute quantity, as opposed to a relative measure. Of course the reverse is true. The range of health care provision is not infinite and each new procedure or advance in medical technology creates a higher level of need. Moreover the levels of unmet need are difficult to ascertain. An individual's need for health care normally relies upon identification of that need, by clinical examination. However, various studies have shown that the number of individuals presenting themselves for treatment may be far less than the number estimated to have treatable illnesses.[3] One study found that, of 1,000 individuals examined, over 90 per cent had treatable conditions, yet only 20 per cent were in fact receiving any health service treatment (Wadsworth *et al.*, 1971). Finally, and perhaps most importantly, the concept of absolute need defies analysis of resource consequences in the provision of health care: if a need exists then surely it must be treated! There is little room for the examination of opportunity cost if such an argument is advanced.

Perhaps the most succinct outline of need as an economic concept is given in Williams (1978) where need is considered from the point of view of both supply and demand. In respect of the former, he suggests that a need exists so long as the marginal productivity of treatment is positive, the implication being that there is no benefit to be gained by considering policy instruments which have zero or negative productivity. A word of warning, however, is necessary here on the definition of productive. While a treatment may have little physiological impact on a particular condition and may, therefore, be thought to be ineffective, the actual process associated with the treatment may still be beneficial to the patient, for example, if he receives utility from the caring, as opposed to curing, aspect. This points to the importance of defining why any good or service is needed and in this respect Williams highlights the question of who is to assess need. In doing so at least three potential decision-makers are identified: the individual, the technical expert and society.

As noted above, defining the level of need is difficult because the individual does not normally hold information on the technical relationship between health care and health status. As such the individual may be quickly ruled out as a competitor for the status of assessor. The technical expert, the doctor, is obviously better qualified and indeed this may explain the attraction of the concept of need to the medical profession – it helps maintain their monopoly position. However, when conflicting needs arise, as they are bound to once we recognise that needs are relative and resources limited, then the individual and society both have a role to play in determining priorities. Deciding who plays which role in making decisions about health care resource allocation clearly matters, and ensuring a legitimate distribution of property rights over such decision-making must be the central focus of any economic analysis of health care markets (McGuire, 1986).

Need as an economic concept does appear to be helpful in providing insights into the nature of the decision-making process. Primarily the advantages of using the concept lie at the level of definition and like most definitional problems the gain in resolution is one of clarification. Need, as a concept, recognises that supply and demand do not interact in the health care sector in the conventional manner. Indeed, as we shall see, the operation of demand constraints upon supply is severely constrained in the health care sector. Before demand can be specified, need, used in the sense to define the technical relationship between health care and health status, must be determined, although even here the process utility elements in the act of consumption may be of importance to the definition of need. The concept of need thus recognises that the demand for health care is not autonomous – at the minimum the supplier plays an integral role in specifying consumption levels. With the exception of the receipt of the utility associated with any health status gain, in all other respects there appears some restriction on the autonomy of the consumer – in judging benefit, judging cost, decision-making and, because of the involvement of others in the decision-making role, the bearing of risks associated with outcome.

The recognition that need is a relative concept does, however, involve the individual, as well as society, in making judgements over the relative valuation of costs and benefits. It is in this sense that the ambiguity associated with need remains. Clarification of the roles to be played by the various actors remains to be resolved and the importance of the opportunity costs of treatment require to be more fully acknowledged. Opportunity cost and the weights attached to them have to play a more explicit role in defining the decision making process. Thus while the concept of need is useful in highlighting the restrictiveness of the concept of demand, analytically it remains somewhat redundant. Its major value lies in illuminating the limitations of the conventional approach to the analysis of consumption.

8.3 The agency relationship

The question of who is to determine need, specifically concerning the relationship between health care and health status, leads on to an analysis of the agency relationship. In discussing the characteristics of the good health care in chapter 3, it was noted that because of information impactedness the consumer and supplier initiate an agency relationship, in which the doctor's specialised knowledge of the relationship between health care and health status is made available to the consumer to aid utility maximising behaviour. As with a number of service commodities, the act of consumption is individualistic in nature, and production and consumption activities tend to occur simultaneously. However, unlike the act of consumption as applied to the majority of goods and services, in the consumption of health care the consumer lacks adequate knowledge of the effects that such consumption will have upon his utility. Furthermore a significant number of outcomes associated with consumption are uncertain as medicine is not an exact science – in many circumstances even the agent is not able to predict the outcome with certainty.

Thus the consumer is not well placed to judge the utility gains (or losses) to be attached to the consumption of health care. Certainly after the act of consumption the consumer can normally judge the utility derived from any change in his health status. However, as Weisbrod (1978) explains, what he can not judge, *ex ante* or *ex post*, is to what degree, if any, the consumption of health care is associated with the change in health status and therefore utility. Weisbrod points out that the human body is endowed with its own ability for recovery. Consequently a consumer of health care who experiences a gain in health status after treatment 'does not know whether the improvement was because of, or in spite of, the care that was received. Or if no health care services are purchased and the individual's problem becomes worse, he is generally not in a position to determine whether the results would have been different, and better, if he had purchased certain health care' (op. cit., p. 52). Moreover, as Weisbrod continues, the patient/consumer, not being a medical expert, may gain little in the way of information from his experiences of illness and may not be able to convert information gained from others into knowledge. In short it is difficult for the consumer to judge quality both before *and* after consumption. On the other hand the supplier of the good, the doctor, specialises in knowledge concerning the technical relationship between health care and health status. The doctor is better placed, through his knowledge, training and experience, to perceive *ex ante* how consumption of health care will affect utility, in terms of both the direct disutility aspects (for example, the impact of any side-effects associated with a treatment), and the expected, derived, effects upon health status. Unlike other goods and services, therefore, the supplier is better placed to inform the consumer not only of the technical information necessary to aid consumption, but also of the likely outcome in terms of net utility gains associated with that consumption.

In addition the search costs to the consumer associated with the acquisition of information may be very high, particularly if there is an uncertain relationship between health care and health status. There may be little point in acquiring a second opinion if this only increases uncertainty. If these costs are coupled with what may be termed anxiety costs arising from the cause of the demand – the fact that the consumer is ill – then it is not surprising that the consumer becomes reliant upon the supplier. In fact if the anxiety costs become too high the consumer may be unwilling to participate in the choice process and default on making decisions, in which case the doctor/supplier takes over this decision-making role. Similarly in other circumstances the consumer may be so ill that he is unable to participate in the decision-making process.

Reflecting upon this it should be noted that the agency relationship in health care is not the same as the normal economic relationship posited to hold between economic principal and agent. In the usual relationship the utility functions of these actors are separate and the principal hires an agent to perform an act which affects his utility. Contractual arrangements are arrived at through bargaining to ensure, hopefully, that the interdependent but separate objectives and utility functions of both the principal and agent are maximised. In contrast in health care, the objectives and the utility functions are no longer, or at least ought not to be, distinct or separate and it becomes difficult to distinguish the utility functions of the principal and agent.

The perfect agency relationship is, however, clearly difficult to attain. The doctor's task is to aid the utility maximising behaviour of the consumer. This requires that the doctor has full knowledge of the patient/consumer's relevant tastes, preferences, income, production and consumption possibilities. In other words it relies upon the doctor, in effect, assuming the personage of the consumer. This is unlikely to occur. Essentially the problem is that both doctors and patients/consumers may be making certain types of judgement, the reconciliation of which becomes extremely difficult, especially under the circumstances of duress which often accompany illness. This difficulty would almost certainly manifest itself even if the arguments in the doctor's utility function involved no possible conflict with those in the patient/consumer's utility function.

It is unlikely then that the perfect agency relationship will exist. The doctor can help the consumer in the understanding of the technical relationship between health care and health status, as well as aid in the evaluation of different consumption patterns as they may affect utility. But the position is complicated by the fact that individual consumers may vary in the extent to which they wish to have information and to make their own decisions. In other words the perfect agent has to consider not just the utility associated with the health status outcome but also the process utility associated with information receipt by the patient and with responsibility for decision-making by the doctor on behalf of the patient.

The concept of process utility, as we noted in chapter 3, is not one that is readily accepted by many economists.[4] However, it may be argued that, in considering such topics as the valuation of human life and health care generally, the concept is fundamental. In fact in the debate over the valuation of life, discussed in section 5.3, Buchanan and Faith (1979, p. 246) certainly appear to accept the importance of process utility. In adopting the *ex ante* willingness to pay approach they argue that this approach relies upon allowing people to take risky decisions (i.e. over the risk of death involved with any consumption or production activity) for themselves and that this should be valued for its own sake. In other words the process utility attached to the freedom to choose whether or not to take a risk with their life is important in and of itself.

Similarly in health care, the fact that the agent affects consumption plans in a fundamental manner also gives importance to the concept of process utility. Even where the individual wishes to make, and retain liability for, the choice he will be aware that he must rely upon the agent for information on both the technical relationship between health care and health and on the definition of the expected *ex post* state of the world. In other words it is difficult to arrive at subjective probabilities to attach to the outcomes without a significant input into the decision-making process by the agent. Furthermore for many choices that affect health the consumer may wish to default upon decision-making. The means by which the outcomes are achieved are then obviously important.

These aspects of process utility are often not given sufficient weight in discussions about the agency relationship. Yet, as raised in chapter 3, they are important features of it. One of the major difficulties in any analysis of such a relationship is that it is likely to be highly 'customised' in the sense that it will vary according to the individual patient, the individual doctor and the individual health condition being considered. In other words different patients will place more or less utility on the process of receiving information and more or less utility on the process of delegating decision-making to the doctor, and for the individual patient this will vary depending on the individual doctor and the nature of the ill-health condition involved. (While we are concerned here with the patient's utility function it is also relevant to note that the utility function of the doctor is also likely to influence how much information he is prepared to give and how much decision-making to undertake.)

While a perfect agency relationship is, therefore, unlikely, the agency relationship which has evolved between consumer and supplier in health care leads to the supplier gaining powerful property rights holdings in the consumer's utility function. Of course the blurring of property rights in the determination of the consumer's utility function leads to the potential for exploitation. Doctors hold a position such that they can determine the costs and benefits of alternative patterns of health care consumption, and express them, if they wish, so that consumers' willingness to pay for treatment may be exploited.

This gives added importance to the role of ethical codes of conduct in health care. The ethical standards of the medical profession are used, at least in part, as a means of specifying that the agent will undertake all that is necessary and possible to fulfil individual patient needs. As Arrow (1974b, p. 37) states:

the usual reasons why the market acts as a check to ensure quality operate here with very weak force. It is for this reason that the ethical indoctrination of physicians is of such crucial importance. The control that is exercised ordinarily by informed buyers is replaced by internalized values.

The consumer, entering into an agency agreement with the supplier of health care, cannot evaluate the performance of this relationship *ex ante*. The codes of medically ethical conduct help in this respect by reassuring the consumer in as much as they state that the doctor will work in his (the consumer's) best interest. There is of course the problem, alluded to above, that the best interest of the consumer may be misspecified by the doctor, whose specialisation is in the technical relationship between health care and health status, and who may have little knowledge of the true preferences of the consumer or the nature of the constraints facing the consumer. The doctor may indeed determine the relationship between health care and health status and help the consumer evaluate the expected utility gains from different forms of treatment, i.e. help define the expected utility associated with the probable outcomes. However, only the patient occupies the position from which, after all relevant information has been appropriated, *net* utility gains can be properly evaluated. In this respect the patient may have the final say, in that he may refuse to comply with the specified treatment.

Of course the further problem remains that consumers may be unable both to understand fully or evaluate the relevant information, either because the costs of doing so are prohibitive or because it is not technically possible – the consumer may be unconscious, mentally disturbed, in a state of anxiety or even unborn as of yet. Even when the patient is able to make rational choices, if the anxiety costs associated with the decision-making process are prohibitive he may be unwilling to evaluate the information. Thus even if the consumer is in a position to make decisions he may well consider the costs associated with this to be so high that he is willing to default and pass responsibility to the doctor/agent. It is, however, important to remember that health care is a very heterogeneous commodity and that the costs associated with the decision-making process will typically be strongly correlated with the degree of complexity and uncertainty associated with the particular form of health care under consideration. For minor ailments these costs will be negligible. However, the slope of this particular cost curve is likely to be steep and the potential to pass the costs of decision-making over to the agent is in itself a source of process utility.

The importance of ethical codes of behaviour may be linked to the assurance that, given the role of the supplier, at the very least if the consumer's best interests are not being maintained, the supplier's conduct is determined by medical rather than economic objectives. In this sense ethical conduct is, at the minimum, an attempt to abstract away the economic arguments in the supplier's utility function. To the extent that this does not occur there is obvious concern regarding exploitation.

8.4 Supplier-induced demand

One means of analysing this potential for exploitation is through the concept of supplier-induced demand where the supplier, in acting as agent for the consumer, brings about a level of consumption different from that which would have occurred if a fully informed consumer had been able to choose freely.

The concept of supplier-induced demand should be distinguished from overtreatment. Overtreatment relates to a technical judgement concerning the difference between the treatment deemed technically necessary and that actually provided. It should be noted that overtreatment may exist when supplier-induced demand does not, if patients prefer what is technically considered to be too much treatment. Obversely supplier-induced demand may occur with no overtreatment if patients prefer less than the technically necessary treatment but are persuaded by the supplier/agent to consume more (see Parkin and Yule, 1984). The importance of this distinction arises, once again, from the question of who is to evaluate the consumer's utility function.

The existence of supplier-induced demand may be interpreted as a demonstration of an imperfect agency relationship. Specifically it is a display of the monopoly potential of the medical profession and has been linked to the hypothesis that individual doctors aim to maximise a target income and the observation that *per caput* consumption of doctors' services tends to rise roughly in line with increases in the doctor:population ratio. To the extent that the concept is linked to the personal remuneration derived from health care services it is predominantly a phenomenon arising from the organisational structure of health services delivery. A commonly asserted manifestation of supplier-induced demand is that a 'built bed is a filled bed', which is sometimes referred to as Roemer's Law after the name of the investigator who first examined this hypothesis (Roemer and Shain, 1959). Thus supplier-induced demand is a phenomenon worth investigating to ascertain whether or not, as the supply curve shifts, there are accompanying shifts in the demand curve. Supplier-induced demand may be thought of as a shift in demand, induced by the supplier in response to underlying changes in the supply (or demand) conditions.

However as Reinhardt (1978) has pointd out, it is difficult to determine whether or not demand inducement is occurring under conditions where both the demand and supply curve are shifting. He examined the situation where the supply of doctors increased. This can be illustrated graphically as in Figure 8.1. The initial demand and supply curves are given by D and S. If the supply of doctors' services increases – to S' – the equilibrium point would move, assuming competitive conditions and no inducement, from A to B. Price would fall as quantity increased. With inducement,

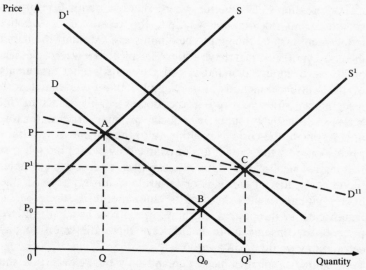

Figure 8.1 Effect of supplier-induced demand?

however, as supply increases demand would also increase, let us assume from D to D'. Again prices have fallen as quantity increased, yet the equilibrium point is now at C.

The primary point to be made is that the two models cannot be distinguished using data which are held to reflect equilibrium positions. If the data are consistent with the equilibrium moving from A to C, one of two explanations may be suggested. Either demand inducement is occurring with a consequent shift in demand from D to D'. Or, assuming a competitive structure, the market demand may be represented by D", rather than D as originally envisaged. We are then merely witnessing a shift in equilibrium under competitive conditions.

The relevance of the concept of supplier-induced demand to systems where the consumer faces zero prices at the point of consumption or which are based upon the concept of need, may of course be questioned. Where doctors are paid under a fee-per-item of service system the rationale for supplier inducement is clear. Considerations of health insurance merely complicate the picture to the extent that the doctor/supplier may feel less obligation to restrict demand inducement if costs are covered by third-party insurers, which in turn raises questions about the ability of the insurers to pass price increases on to consumers in the form of higher premiums. In systems where there is national insurance coverage and doctors are salaried, the relevance of supplier inducement may be thought to be diminished. Certainly the target income hypothesis may have little relevance[5]. However, doctors may wish to induce demand in order to satisfy other arguments in their utility functions, for example, those associated with teaching activities or even if the doctor simply wants to 'fill beds'. Alternatively supplier inducement may arise if doctors underestimate the costs of health care to the patient. Any money prices borne by the patient are of course only part of the full cost to them of health care. Other relevant costs are, for example, travel costs, loss of earnings or leisure and anxiety costs. If the doctor underestimates these costs, and, therefore, the price of health care to the patient, he may, in his role as agent, induce patients to consume more health care than willingness to pay calculations would deem appropriate.

Of course supplier-induced demand only has relevance in the context of consumer sovereignty. Yet, as we have seen, it is possible for the basis of health care consumption to be related to the concept of need. In this respect supplier inducement is irrelevant as long as the 'needed' level of care is provided. As such it is overtreatment, rather than supplier inducement, that becomes a matter of concern.

More generally the concept of supplier-induced demand raises questions concerning why a particular level of demand is necessarily associated with any given level of supply. If this were not the case then there would appear to be no constraint upon the medical profession's continually raising consumption levels. In addressing this issue Richardson (1981) suggests a number of explanations. He dismisses the hypothesis that doctors always seek to increase demand as much as possible. He also dismisses the explanation that political constraints inhibit medical behaviour with respect to supplier-induced demand as this fails to explain, *inter alia*, geographical variations in demand-shifts. Another explanation is that the medical profession act collectively to set demand as a means of maximising individual incomes. However, as Richardson points out, this does not explain the constraints, it merely states that they operate at a collective rather than individual level. He then suggests that doctors are satisficers, and that the only constraints upon demand generation are self-imposed behavioural constraints. Again he finds this implausible in that it fails to explain systematic differences in doctors' incomes and work patterns.

The explanation Richardson finds most plausible with regard to medical behaviour and induced demand is that additional arguments in the doctor's utility function limit the degree of inducement. In particular he argues that the ethical codes of conduct respected by the medical profession impose constraints upon the use of the profession's potential monopoly power. In this sense there may be an 'ethically acceptable' level of induced demand. Richardson believes, however, that this constraint may operate with only weak force. The entry of the patient's welfare into the doctor's utility function and the belief that health care is income elastic are also posited as restrictions on the medical profession from pushing inducement to the limit. Indeed Richardson maintains that this is even more likely if doctors' utility functions are held to include status as an argument and status is associated with reasonable pricing policies and ethical conduct.

8.5 Empirical evidence on supplier-induced demand

It appears plausible then that supplier-induced demand can exist without any inherent tendency to be pushed to the limit. Of course the acceptance of the concept is only part of the picture; there also remains the problem of empirical validation. This has been attempted at both the aggregate health sector level and the disaggregated individual practice level. Both are subject to similar problems. A starting point for the testing of the hypothesis of supplier-induced demand must be separation of uninduced and induced demand. Given the involvement of the agent in the specification of any level of demand this is extremely difficult. One method proposed by Wilensky and Rossiter (1981, 1983) is to differentiate between patient-initiated and doctor-initiated visits and then to examine the importance of market characteristics upon demand. However, to the extent that effective demand is only realised after visiting the doctor, this is a somewhat false distinction between uninduced and induced demand. Further, not all post-consultation demand should be thought of as induced. The Wilensky and Rossiter studies find that doctors initiate treatments predominantly on the basis of their patients' health status and considerations relating to their patients' income rather than in a manner reflecting their own self-interest, i.e. there is little evidence of inducement.

A further problem in the empirical testing of supplier-induced demand is that the predictions associated with this presumed behaviour are very unclear. Under the normally posited circumstances where an increase in supply is associated with an accompanying increase in demand, price may increase, decrease or remain constant. Price changes will depend upon the exact movements in the supply and demand curves and their elasticities, as well as any effects that insurance coverage has upon distorting the market price of health care. Even assuming that the health care market may be analysed with reference to the normal monopolistic model, it is unclear, as we saw graphically above, as to where the predicted equilibrium should lie. A further problem encountered at the aggregate level of empirical testing relates to the lack of identification of induced shifts in demand from other causes. A number of studies, including Sloan and Feldman (1978),

Pauly (1980) and Auster and Oaxaca (1981), have noted that the target income hypothesis and the importance of changes in doctor-to-population ratios can only be properly tested if one abstracts from the effect of tastes, income, insurance coverage and population health status. In other words it is difficult to isolate the effects of supplier-induced demand from those of other factors. The paucity of data represents a further problem. It is difficult to measure output, for example, and to identify the appropriate fee scale for treatments.

At the disaggregated data level, while similar problems exist, there appears to be considerable support for the hypothesis that supplier-induced demand exists. Evans, Parish and Sully (1973) and Evans (1974) find that high individual medical fees and gross billings are correlated with high doctor-to-population ratios and, after discussing data and definitional problems, accept this as evidence of supplier-induced demand. In one of the few non-North American studies, Richardson (1981) found evidence of a strong and significant association between the supply of doctors and the demand for their services in Australia. Steinwald and Sloan (1974) present evidence that supplier-induced demand may exist among obstetricians but not general practitioners in the USA, while Fuchs (1978), controlling for demographic factors, shows a significant positive relationship between surgeon-population ratios and consumption levels. In contrast Pauly (1980) finds no evidence of supplier-induced demand, while Bunker and Brown (1974) and Hay and Leahy (1982) both indicate that medical practitioners and their families have as many treatments as other consumers, calling into question the hypothesis that supplier-induced demand arises from information impactedness.

The conclusion is that, although there is some supporting empirical evidence, given the problems discussed above, it is not surprising that, as Parkin and Yule remark, 'it remains possible to dispute the existence of supplier induced demand' (1984, p. 19). What is not in doubt is that, given the existence of the agency relationship and the consequent property rights holdings in the consumer's utility function, the supplier of health care does have the potential to exploit the consumer. It is, after all, only after consultation with the supplier that the consumer's demand for (most) treatments is specified.

8.6 Conclusions

This chapter has considered how conventional demand analysis has to be altered to cope with the peculiarities of the mechanics of the health care sector. It has been shown that the blurring of the decision-making process across the demand and supply sides of the sector, and the acknowledgement of the role played by the supplier in the specification of consumption decisions, through the agency relationship, lead to supply side responses dominating the resource allocation process in this sector. The literature on need, the agency relationship and supplier-induced demand can all be seen as amendments to traditional demand analysis, borne out of an acknowledgement of the special characteristics of the commodity health care. Uncertainty relating to the timing of consumption and the benefits to be gained and the costs borne in the process of consumption, result in a diffusion of property rights holdings associated with decision-making over patterns of consumption. All the analytical extensions recognise that the supplier of health care gains property rights in the consumer's utility function arising directly from the impacted information on the relationship between health care and health status held by the provider.

It is also possible to reintroduce the interdependent utility concerns at this point as part of the evaluation of the decision-making process and the associated allocation of resources at a social level. Thus the measurement of need, for example, becomes a wider issue than one constrained to decisions made by individual consumers over their own health status or by doctors acting as agents on their behalf. Decisions taken at a social level reflecting the concern of individuals for others' health must also be made. This chapter although confined to demand issues has emphasised the importance of the discussion of the supply of health care by highlighting the role of the supplier on the demand side of the market. However, we are not yet finished with demand issues as we have so far taken little explicit account of the effect health insurance has upon the demand for health care. However, in considering the actual utilisation of health care there is little doubt that this is affected by insurance coverage. It is to this that the next chapter turns.

9

The utilisation of health care

9.1 Introduction

It should be clear by now that one effect of the supplier's involvement in the consumption decisions of the patient is that it becomes difficult to specify a pure demand variable in empirical studies. As a result a particularly poignant criticism of the demand for health care literature is that the dependent variable in empirical specifications of the demand function normally reflects utilisation rather than demand *per se*. Therefore, a number of purportedly 'demand' studies are in fact utilisation studies. This is a more serious problem than simply one of identification, in that in this case demand does not exist independently of supply. Thus as Stoddart and Barer (1981, p. 149) remark, given the existing evidence that health services utilisation is not compatible with the normal economic definition of demand, it is surprising to find the distinction between demand and utilisation so seldom made explicit in the literature. The conventional notion of demand, as applied to the health care market, is not acceptable even if the perfect agency relationship exists. However, if there any exercising of discretionary power by the clinician, which as we have seen is likely in the real world, then it is certainly inappropriate to define demand in terms of consumption. The acceptance of utilisation as the relevant concept acknowledges that with consumption choices in the health care sector the consumer relies upon information provided by the supplier. This phenomenon is not of course unique to health care – although the degree of reliance is more significant in this sector, particularly given the supplier's role in defining the expected utility to be attached to the possible outcomes.

While recognition of the significance of supplier decisions in defining consumption levels and the importance of such recognition to the empirical specification of demand equations and to consequent policy implications led to the definition of consumption in terms of utilisation, there have also been attempts to reconcile utilisation with the conventional notion of demand. This has, in turn, led to the consideration of an 'episode' of medical service as the appropriate unit in which to define health care utilisation. Essentially an episode relates to a particular combination of health care services which form the complete flow of services for a particular treatment. Stoddart and Barer (1981), raising concern over policy initiatives aimed at changing consumer behaviour which are based upon empirical studies relying on traditional demand analysis, proposed such an episodic measure.[1] Acknowledging that utilisation comprises a consumer-initiated as well as a medical practitioner-generated phase and that consumption relates to combinations of services rather than specific services, they argue that utilisation normally comprises a number of episodes of treatment. It is these individual episodes which are held to correspond most closely to conventional measures of demand. Empirical specification of the utilisation process, as based upon this episodic approach, requires the collection of a different information set. The data requirements, however, are no less demanding than those associated with more conventional analysis.

The redefinition of health care consumption in terms of utilisation rather than demand is useful not merely in acknowledging the influence of the supplier in that process. It also allows proper acknowledgement of the role of health insurance. The unpredictability associated with the timing and the form of health care requirements leads to a demand for health insurance. Thus, as the health insurance is the prior purchase, the consumption of health care becomes dependent upon the level and form of insurance coverage. This again removes analysis from the conventional microeconomic approach where demand – in this case the demand for health care – is held to respond to a specified, easily defined, market price. The fact that the consumer may have purchased insurance prior to his utilisation of health care services means that it is difficult to define willingness to pay and the market price of the health care actually utilised. The net price paid by the consumer is dependent upon the gross price charged by the provider plus the extent of insurance coverage (Feldstein, 1974). Of course the gross price charged by the provider may itself be influenced by the fact that a third party (the insurer) is meeting costs at the point of consumption. Furthermore the extent of insurance coverage will be dependent upon, amongst other things, the individual's degree of risk aversion, the form of insurance available and the price of that insurance which, as we noted in chapter 3, is unlikely to be actuarially fair. Thus the purchase of insurance may distort calculations of willingness to pay for the commodity health care and the price of that commodity. Certainly in evaluating the price elasticity of 'demand' for health care both the gross price to be met and the insurance coverage are relevant. As such the analysis of the 'demand' for health care becomes further complicated in that the demand for health care insurance, as well as the influence of provider behaviour, is seen to be relevant. The replacement of the term demand with utilisation recognises the relevance of both.

Section 9.2 analyses the welfare implications associated with the introduction of third-party payment, focusing upon how utilisation is influenced by this. Section 9.3 covers the empirical evidence on utilisation.

9.2 Utilisation and welfare

The background to any discussion of utilisation accepts the importance of uncertainty as an essential concept in understanding the operation of the health care sector. Uncertainty leads to reliance upon the agency relationship as discussed in chapter 8. However, there is another form of uncertainty which arises in health care associated with the actual act of consumption rather than the accompanying decision-making process. The patient is uncertain over the timing of this act because illness itself is unpredictable. He is also uncertain about the consequent cost implications. Insurance coverage is normally adopted to cover the risks associated with the potential treatment costs, as we discussed briefly in chapter 3. A basic consequence of this is that we may not presume that, *ceteris paribus*, consumption responds to cost changes in the commodity health care. Payment for health care purchases is normally made, in part or in full, by a third party (the insurer) rather than directly by the consumer. The effect of this third party intervention upon consumption is unclear *a priori*.

One argument that is commonly advanced is that, if the insurance coverage is complete (i.e. comprehensive for all risks with all expenses covered) then there will be no incentive for an individual's consumption to be restricted by willingness, let alone ability, to pay. In other words fully comprehensive insurance will mean that, at the point of consumption, the price to the individual patient/consumer of purchasing health care is zero. The consumer then has an inherent inducement to consume more of the commodity than if he had made a direct purchase of it. In other words, he may be induced to move down his 'demand' curve. Arrow (1963) describes this situation as one of moral hazard whereby the welfare gains achieved by insuring against health care costs may be partially offset by the lack of incentive, arising from the third-party coverage of costs, to contain the purchases of health care.

Pauly (1968) has stated that the potential existence of moral hazard is a reason for not providing fully comprehensive insurance coverage arguing, in effect, that social welfare is increased if the consumer is left to bear some of the risk of health care costs. His argument adopts a conventional demand function where consumption is held to depend upon income and tastes, the degree of illness and the price of health care. He argues that even if the incidence of illness is a random, unpredictable event, Arrow's welfare proposition (i.e. that moral hazard will reduce the welfare gains from insurance coverage) only holds strictly if health care costs are random also. It is suggested that the effect of insurance upon the randomness of health care expenses depends upon the elasticity of demand for health care. As Pauly states, only if this demand is perfectly inelastic with respect to price in the range from the market price to zero is an expense insurable in the strict sense envisioned by Arrow's welfare proposition (op. cit., p. 532).

Pauly continues by arguing that if the demand curve is elastic to any degree over this range, the consumer must take account of the positive cost of care which is subsumed in the price of his insurance. Each individual will come to recognise that the existence of moral hazard increases the price of his own insurance premium. This gives rise to inefficiency as individuals are forced to cover moral hazard, i.e. the non-random effects in insurance coverage. He proposes, therefore, that some price-rationing at the point of service will be necessary to ensure efficient allocation. This implicitly assumes that, given the consequences of moral hazard and the existence of some degree of elasticity of demand, the consumer could improve his welfare position by bearing some risk himself.

This is a perfect example of squeezing the analysis of health care into the neoclassical paradigm. The analysis of moral hazard, as carried out by Pauly (1968), assumes the complete separation of supply and demand. This is of course in line with concept of the rational, sovereign economic patient. Demand, as an economic concept, relates to willingness and ability to pay, as determined by a fully informed consumer. In the health care market, however, the actual consumption of the commodity relates to the utilisation of a service based upon information acquired from the supplier, information for which search costs may be prohibitive. As such the act of consumption is dependent, to a significant degree, upon the supplier. Therefore, a more realistic analysis of the health care sector allows moral hazard to arise from decisions undertaken by the suppliers. In other words if the providers of health care are instrumental in specifying consumption levels they may also be instrumental in inducing moral hazard. Thus analysis should focus upon the combinations of services determined by the supplier. There is then, as Enthoven (1981) notes, little call for the analysis of the purchase of individual units of treatment by the insured sovereign consumer; the normative significance of the demand curve is diminished.

While there would appear to be little controversy in this last statement there is nevertheless a considerable empirical literature on pricing incentives to contain the consumption of health care; a policy incentive which follows directly from the accceptance of arguments of the kind proposed by Pauly. Perhaps not surprisingly such literature is predominantly US-based, the majority of which takes a conventional demand analysis, amended to account for the effect of insurance coverage upon incentives, as its starting point.[2]

Price rationing, in an attempt to increase welfare, or the introduction of prices to aid incentives, forms the focus of some of this literature. However, most of the studies are concerned with merely the estimation of elasticities rather than their normative significance. Both forms of analysis materialise in much the same form: a discussion of cost-sharing in the insurance coverage. Several forms of cost-sharing are in fact possible. It can take the form of, for example, a deductible where the consumer pays a set amount before any benefit occurs. The exact nature of the deductible may vary, in that it may be either a pre-specified fixed amount or it may be tied to the value of a specific service. Alternatively the cost-sharing could be in the form of a co-payment, i.e. a fixed amount to be paid with each service consumed. Finally another common form of coinsurance is payment as a set proportion of the cost of each service.[3]

9.3 Utilisation: the empirical results

Given that the form of insurance coverage is an important component in determining the elasticity of 'demand' for health care it is not surprising to find that a number of empirical studies have focused upon the effects of the introduction of particular forms of cost-sharing. The studies which have had access to the largest databases have examined the effect of changes in insurance patterns on actual insurance schemes. Such studies differ in their structure but all indicate that changes in insurance coverage do appear to affect the consumption of health care services. In most cases, however, it is difficult to distinguish between changes in consumption patterns based upon ability to pay as opposed to willingness to pay, i.e. to distinguish between income and price effects. In one of the earliest studies, Beck (1974) analysed the effect of the introduction of a co-payment plan after a period of comprehensive insurance coverage in the Canadian province of Saskatchewan. The plan took the form of fixed charges – a payment of $1.50 for visits to the offices of medical practitioners and $2.00 for home, hospital out-patient or emergency visits. The results indicated that these charges did produce a fall in consumption and in particular consumption fell further for lower income families. One problem with the study, which is common to all studies which cover the total population of an area, is that it was difficult to differentiate pure price effects from other effects. Thus the consumption rates may also have been affected by supply influences after the introduction of the co-payment rate.

A widely reported insurance change was the introduction in 1967 of a 25 per cent coinsurance rate for clinical visits in the Palo Alto Group Health Plan which had previously offered comprehensive insurance coverage to Stanford University employees. The motive for the introduction of this coinsurance rate was explicitly to try to contain consumption. A number of studies found that consumption dropped significantly after the introduction of this scheme (see Phelps and Newhouse, 1972; Scitovsky and McCall, 1977).

One of the most important studies of this kind is the recently concluded RAND Health Insurance Experiment. This experiment ran from 1974 to 1982 with the participation of 2,005 families in six centres of population across the USA. Families were assigned to 14 experimental insurance plans. These plans can be grouped into four categories; one providing free care and three requiring different forms of cost-sharing. The experiment was controlled, as far as possible, for selection bias. Self-selection bias was avoided through the random allocation of individuals to particular schemes. Although population characteristics did differ across the study centres, for example, in terms of racial composition, the design of the experiment did allow some analysis of the effect that variations in population characteristics had upon service uptake. However, families on supplemental security income, disabled on Medicare and family members over the age of 61 were excluded from the experiment. Supply influence was held to be negligible as the participants formed only a small percentage of the covered population, thus changes in their insurance coverage were assumed to have an imperceptible impact upon supplier behaviour and incentives. The estimated effects were, therefore, regarded to be as close as possible to an examination of price-effects.

The results tend to confirm the view that consumption is dependent upon the form of insurance coverage and specifically that consumption increases as out-of-pocket expenses decrease. Consequently expenditure *per caput* was found to be higher as coinsurance fell. For adults, cost-sharing resulted in one-third fewer ambulatory visits and hospitalisation rates were approximately a third lower. It was also found that the largest difference between the highest cost-sharing plan and the comprehensive plan was in the incentive to delay treatment (Newhouse *et al.*, 1981).

The RAND study also considered the relationship between insurance and health status, which is obviously a fundamental variable in its effect upon consumption. Not surprisingly health status is generally held to have an inverse effect upon health care consumption. The cautiously presented conclusions in the RAND study were that comprehensive coverage had no effect upon major health-related habits or on the general health of the subjects as measured by crude health status measures. Of most importance, perhaps, it was found that it was only for those subjects with easily diagnosed symptoms and well-established treatments, for example, those with hypertension, that there were substantial benefits, realised in the form of gains in health status, from comprehensive insurance coverage (Brook *et al.*, 1984; Keeler *et al.*, 1985; Ware *et al.*, 1986). From this evidence the authors conclude that for the population in general, whilst there may well be legitimate arguments for the provision of health care being free at the point of consumption, such arguments are not justified by recourse to the health benefits involved.

This particular study, based as it was upon a controlled social experiment and through extending its analysis to health effects, is the most important of its kind. It overcomes a number of difficulties experienced by studies analysing insurance effects, particularly those founded upon individually based data rather than, as in the studies discussed above, aggregate data (see Newhouse, Phelps and Marquis, 1980; Newhouse, 1974 and 1981).

There have in fact been numerous studies relating to individually based data. Normally these have focused upon household insurance and the use of services, or have been restricted to the analysis of the consumption of particular services. Such studies have used widely different databases and methodologies, thereby rendering comparison difficult. Yet most agree with the results of aggregate studies that consumption increases as coinsurance falls.

Particular problems with such studies relate to the definition of the price of health care. Commonly the insurance premium paid by the consumer is taken as a proxy. This can only ever be considered a crude measure of the price. Strictly the premium relates to the commodity health insurance and not health care. It is, therefore, difficult to distinguish the price effects associated with health care itself as opposed to the distortions introduced by insurance coverage and third-party payment. In any case welfare effects are difficult to specify given the reliance upon average rather than marginal insurance rates. Alternatively price may be calculated as expenditure divided by quantity, but of course insurance distortions may again affect the measurement of expenditure. Moreover quantity consumed may be inherently difficult to measure across a sample (e.g. are all bed-days to be taken as the same commodity?). The presence of moral hazard in consumer behaviour will of course lead to additional measurement complications. As such measurement error is liable to be serious and, subsequently, to bias the calculated price elasticities.[4]

Table 9.1 gives an indication of the range of estimated price elasticities. Due to methodological and measurement differences, as well as the fact that these studies relate to different types of health care, it would be inappropriate to compare them directly. The fact that the studies are, for the most part, rather dated largely reflects the change in emphasis more recently away from the analysis of pure price effects and consumer reactions towards recognition of insurance distortions, the importance of supplier decisions in acts of consumption and the use of utilisation, rather than demand *per se*, as the dependent variable in empirical specifications. Reflecting this movement some recent studies have concentrated upon the effect that tax subsidies have upon the amount of health care insurance purchased.[5]

Not surprisingly, given the conceptual and empirical problems discussed, the estimation of price elasticities for health care is difficult. The own-price elasticities of health care should be negative, and although some studies have found positive elasticities these are probably due to misspecification or measurement error. Negative price elasticities are expected because, even though the actual consumption of the commodity health care may involve disutility, the consumer/patient is relating this derived demand to the presumed overall net utility gain. Despite the methodological difference the consensus of the evidence is that the introduction of price rationing will reduce consumption.

The empirical literature has extended the analysis to consider time prices. It is argued that the *real* price of health care services,

Table 9.1 Selected own-price elasticities of demand: hospital and ambulatory services

Study	Elasticities	Service	Price measurement	Data	Notes
Rosenthal (1970)	−0.24 to −0.70	Patient-days (length of stay) in medical categories	Cash payment as proportion of total hospital charge	Cross-section	Price criticised by Fuchs (1970) as not measuring price of service to consumer. Variation in estimates due to estimation being based on various specialties.
	−0.11 to −0.65	Patient-days (length of stay) in surgical categories	As above	As above	As above
Feldstein (1971)	−0.626	Hospital admissions	Net price calculated as insurance multiplied by gross price of service (proxied by average-cost deflated by RPI)	Pooled cross-section and time-series	Estimates relate to basic equation
	−0.49	Mean length of stay			
	−1.12	Bed-days			
Davis and Russell (1972)	−0.19 to −0.46	Admissions	Variation in estimates reflects various price definitions	Cross-sectional	
Newhouse and Phelps (1974)	−0.29 to −0.13	Patient-days	Net price as proxied by gross price of bed multiplied by coinsurance rate	Cross-sectional	Variation in estimates reflects estimation procedure OLS or 2SLS
	−0.04 to −0.03	Hospital room and board	Coinsurance rate	Cross-sectional	As above
Newhouse and Phelps (1976)	−0.062	Patient-days	Net price as proxied by gross price of bed multiplied by coinsurance rate	Cross-sectional	Variation reflects different estimation procedures. 2SLS produced positive signed elasticities for patient-days equation

Study	Elasticity	Dependent variable	Price variable	Data type	Comments
Newhouse and Phelps (1976)	−0.22 to −0.005 −0.24	Room and board Admissions	Coinsurance rate Coinsurance rate	Cross-sectional	Estimates relate to basic equations
Feldstein (1977)	−0.13 (long-run) −0.01 (short-run)	Bed-days Bed-days	Net price proxied by average cost of service multiplied by insurance rate deflated by RPI	Pooled time-series and cross-sectional	
Newhouse and Marquis (1978)	−0.05 −1.00	Hospital day Physician office visits	Coinsurance	Cross-sectional	Estimates relate to 1970 data
Carrin and van Dael (1984)	−0.22	Medical treatments	Reimbursed insurance cost as proxy for price	Time-series	Medical treatment is limited to certain technical treatments
Colle and Grossman (1978)	−0.106	Physician visits	Adjusted coinsurance rate	Cross-sectional	
Davis and Russell (1972)	−0.98 to −1.03	Out-patient services	Revenue from out-patient visits	Cross-sectional	
Fuchs and Kramer (1972)	−0.15 to −0.20	Physician visits	Average price of insurance	Cross-sectional	
Rossett and Huang (1973)	−0.35 to −1.15	Physician visits and hospitalisation		Cross-sectional	
Newhouse and Phelps (1974)	−0.15 to −0.20	Physician visits	Coinsurance rate	Cross-sectional	
Manning et al. (1981)	−0.20	Total medical treatment	Coinsurance rate	Cross-sectional	Medical treatment includes all in-patient and out-patient care plus services provided by non-physicians e.g. pharmacists

particularly important when some resource costs are being met by a third party insurer, should include the cost of time, for example, travel and waiting time to the consumer. As such this represents a further application of household production theory to health care economics. The general conclusions from studies analysing time prices are that they may be as significant as money prices in determining consumption and that the relationship between the two variables is such that the effect of the time price on consumption is normally larger the lower is the money price effect (Acton, 1975; Newhouse and Phelps, 1974). Interestingly Coffey (1983) reports that the relative time price effect is more important in the choice of provider than it is upon the number of visits.

Of course another variable that is considered to be important in its influence upon demand is income. Again the empirical evidence relates largely to the structural setting of the United States and therefore the distortions introduced by the insurance market will affect the results. Bearing this in mind an early study by Andersen and Benham (1970) analysed income effects while attempting to control for a number of variables, including price variable, the most important component of which represented insurance coverage. The study also relied upon a measure of permanent income in some of the estimated equations. Newhouse (1981) argues that this is the only theoretically acceptable measure of income given that current income may be presumed to be endogenous because of the effect of illness upon both income and the demand for health care. The inclusion of permanent income does involve the usual measurement problems, however.

Among the more important conclusions to be drawn from the Andersen and Benham study was the recognition that, given the heterogeneous nature of health care and the considerable differences in the determinants of demand for different aspects of this commodity, future studies should concentrate upon the individual services provided rather than the compound commodity 'health care'. A study by Hershey, Luft and Gianaris (1975) did indeed find that income was differentially important for different measures of utilisation. Specifically it was found that income was a useful predictor of the demand for initial visits and check-ups. Manning *et al.* (1981) appear to go some way to add further confirmation in their suggestion that income has a strong explanatory effect upon the decision to seek health care. Andersen and Benham also note that one effect of insurance coverage is to diminish the role of income as a determinant of the consumption of health care.

As with the evidence relating to price elasticities, comparison of estimated income elasticities is difficult. Studies differ in terms of the independent variables analysed, the specified dependent variable, estimation technique, level of analysis and the decision making unit selected for analysis. Yet the evidence is remarkably robust in so far as the estimated income elasticities are normally found to be positive and less than one. The general conclusion is then that health care consumption is income inelastic (for example, see Andersen and Benham, 1970; Grossman, 1972b; Rossett and Huang, 1973; Newhouse and Phelps, 1974; Newhouse and Phelps, 1976; Manning *et al.*, 1981).

As the empirical literature has converged to a broad agreement over the relationship between cost-sharing, consumption and expenditure levels there has been a noticeable shift in policy emphasis. Early studies were very much geared towards an emphasis on the importance of the results to changing consumer behaviour. The implicit assumption was that, with consumer sovereignty over choice, introducing or increasing out-of-pocket prices – essentially attempting to correct for the distortions of the insurance market – would act as an incentive to the consumer to inhibit moral hazard. With the recognition of the supplier's role in aiding in the specification of consumption levels and the consequent possibility of moral hazard arising from the supplier's behaviour, there has been increasing doubt that changes in incentives which are constrained to attempting to change the consumer's behaviour alone, will affect the mechanics of the relationship between insurance coverage and consumption levels.

The RAND Health Insurance Experiment is particularly important in this respect in its emphasis upon the empirical evidence on the direction of change in this relationship under controlled conditions and in its attempt to analyse the effect of different patterns of coverage upon health. Furthermore economists were able to have a large input into the experimental design of the study making it of methodological interest as well (see Newhouse, 1974). However, the RAND experiment, along with the other earlier studies, was restricted to examination of consumer behaviour. In other words the experiment was of a partial nature in that it was not explicitly concerned with the responses of suppliers to any changes in insurance conditions. If the influence of suppliers upon consumer behaviour is strong this is a large caveat, although the study was designed in such a way that the potential for the change in the insurance conditions to affect supplier behaviour was minimised.

The identification of potential inefficiency is only part of any story. In addition one must be convinced that the incentives to change behaviour offer real gains. Acknowledgement of the role of the supplier in the utilisation process has led to arguments that the introduction of cost-sharing as an instrument for reducing moral hazard and consequently consumption and expenditure levels is, at best, a partial answer. Incentives must also be geared towards the supplier. This has led Enthoven (1978, 1981) to argue that incentives should be introduced to ensure that medical practitioners contain health care costs. He suggests that organisations providing comprehensive health care should be encouraged to minimise costs, with the providers of medical care given a financial incentive by allowing them to retain residual profits. In other words if a competitive structure were maintained, based upon profit maximisation as a constraint, this would ensure the maintenance of quality and the minimisation of costs. Such proposals recognise that the analysis of demand issues in the health care sector leads to the conclusion that supply and demand cannot be as easily separated as is normally assumed by economists. Although this of course means that ensuring competitive conditions are maintained in the supply of health care is difficult. In such circumstances it is difficult not to reach the conclusion that supply decisions tend to dominate the analysis of the health care market.

9.4 Conclusions

This chapter has continued the arguments of the previous chapter that the analysis of the 'demand' for health care is far removed from conventional microeconomic analysis. In particular the use of the term 'utilisation' was seen to be useful in acknowledging both the role of the provider in the consumption process and the role of insurance coverage in specifying the level of consumption. The failure to recognise the importance of these arguments will lead to misconstrued analysis and misinterpretation of empirical results.

Both of these may end in the pursuit of mistaken policy proposals. The topics discussed in both chapters lead to areas of fruitful discussion not least because there has been an underinvestment in the theory of consumption as compared to the research investment in empirical studies. Of course, not surprisingly, given the structure of the US health care sector, the majority of the empirical work which has been undertaken is confined to that country. The chronology of the analyses of the consumption of health care reflects a willingness to become more realistic by acknowledging both the role of the provider in the process and the role of health insurance in determining consumption levels. As such policy initiatives are increasingly recognising that regulation of incentives on the supply side of the sector is fundamental.

10

The supply of health care

10.1 Introduction

In previous chapters it has been noted that supply is the dominant side, if sides can be distinguished, of the health care sector. To bring this process of clarification one stage further this chapter now turns to reflect upon the market process and its failure to provide health care efficiently. This draws upon earlier discussion of the nature of the commodity health care. The chapter thus includes some topics which we have considered earlier. It is largely contextual in that it emphasises, for example, the important role that the characteristics of the commodity play in determining supply conditions. With this intent, the chapter begins with section 10.2 discussing the difficulties imposed by the characteristics of health care upon efficient market provision. The non-market responses to this failure and the structural consequences are then discussed in section 10.3. Finally the modification placed upon conduct which arises from these responses is considered in section 10.4

10.2 Markets and failures

In the traditional market allocation process the activities of producers are co-ordinated with each other and with the demands (as distinct from the needs) of consumers by means of information conveyed by market signals. Producers, in competitive market conditions, will expand production of every good and service up to the point where the costs of producing any extra good become equal to the market price for that good. Given an assumption that producers wish to maximise profits, there will be an incentive to keep production costs at a minimum; production will be most cost-effective. As price is a reflection at the margin of consumer valuations of the good or service demanded, *ceteris paribus*, the higher are consumer valuations of a good the higher its price will be. Allowing producers to be guided by means of price signals will also ensure therefore that the pattern of production matches consumer wants. In this way a mix of goods and services will be provided, at lowest possible resource costs, which is compatible with consumer demands.

The market, again by means of price signals, will also ensure the orderly distribution of the goods and services, based upon a reflection of the underlying distribution of wealth. At given market prices, consumers will purchase extra units of a good where, assuming an ability to pay, their valuation of these extra units is reflected in their willingness to pay for the good. The distribution of the good will therefore be related to the ability of the consumer to pay for it, i.e. by his wealth. Distribution will then be determined, not just by demand *per se*, but by the existing structure of wealth holdings.

Prices, by conveying relevant signals on both demand and supply, act as a simple mechanism for the resolution of an immensely complex allocation problem. Prices are useful in 'invisibly', but not costlessly, allocating resources. Of course under other accompanying assumptions, in particular the lack of any externalities, the simple two agent transaction between producer and consumer results in not merely prices clearing the market but also the attainment of social (economic) harmony.

Implicit in this analysis is the assumption that, as well as there being no imperfections in the pricing system and no externalities, property rights are clearly defined and privately held. The supplier produces a commodity which is taken to the market place and exchanged, at a clearing price, such that the consumer gains the property rights holdings in the commodity. This simple exposition of exchange focuses upon the market relations existing between two transactors – the producer and the consumer – who act independently, notwithstanding the aggregate demand constraints upon supply.

Previous chapters' explanations of the economics of health care, although confined to the consumption process, raised particular difficulties in the application of this conventional analysis to this sector. As we have noted earlier, given a choice, the overwhelming majority of people would not want to participate in the consumption of health care. Not only do consumers have to be ill to consume health care – and illness is itself a source of disutility – but on occasion the cure can seem worse than the disease. The utilisation of health care services is only undertaken because consumers hope it will contribute to their health status. It is defined to be a bad in consumption and the 'demand' for health care is a derived demand from the basic desire for health.

There is, however, as noted in chapter 3, no market in health. A market for health care exists – resources are allocated and exchanged directly for health care provision on the assumption that they will contribute to health status. Yet this market is characterised by overlaps in property rights and the existence of important externalities as well as imperfections in the pricing system arising from significant transactions costs. This serves to undermine the efficiency of market allocations and provides considerable interest for the study of the economics of health care.

Market analysis is not, of course, omnipotent. Indeed Williamson (1973, 1975) has argued that the focus should be upon 'transactions', as the basic unit of microeconomic analysis, rather than market exchange *per se*. Transactions may or may not be conducted within a market setting. If transactions costs are substantial then, according to Williamson, the market becomes redundant and analysis of hierarchies, essentially internal organisational forms of resource allocation (e.g. the 'firm'), becomes essential. Williamson suggests that transactions costs will become significant if a number of conditions dominate the resource allocation process. He identifies these conditions as:

(a)   bounded rationality
(b)   uncertainty and/or complexity in decision-making
(c)   small numbers of actors being involved in any transaction environment

(d)   opportunism in behaviour arising from the pursuit of self-interest through the lack of candour or honesty in transactions
(e)   informational impactedness and
(f)   atmosphere, which relates to the fact that decision-making and the transaction process itself may directly affect utility.

A little reflection on these conditions and on the commodity health care, in particular the characteristics outlined in chapters 3 and 8, brings out the subsequent significance of transactions costs in the health care sector, as well as highlighting the likelihood of substantial market failings in this sector.

As has been argued throughout, individuals lack information concerning the timing of most of their health care consumption and also about the effectiveness of treatment. Utility assessment by the consumer relies on the information supplied by the provider, on the relationship between health care and health status and on the expected outcome (i.e. on the expected *ex post* state of the world). As a result of this, information impactedness and the agency relationship are formed. In this sense the agency relationship is an institutional response to market failure in the provision of information. However, this response can itself lead to further market failure if the potential for opportunistic behaviour by the agent, for example, in the form of supplier-induced demand, is not mitigated. Such considerations give rise to the importance of ethical medical behaviour which was discussed briefly with regard to supplier-induced demand in chapter 8 and is discussed further below.

Of course the degree of consumers' reliance upon an agent will depend upon both the uncertainty and the complexity surrounding the decisions to be taken. In this respect it is worth emphasising again that health care is a heterogeneous commodity. In the consumption of some health care, although the unpredictability associated with the timing of consumption may remain, the uncertainty and/or complexity in the decision-making process with regard to the relationship between health care and health status may not be a problem. Most of us have suffered from one or more of the most common ailments (e.g. the common cold). Such ailments involve little uncertainty/complexity in their treatment; they also lead to repeat purchases of health care and are normally such that self-diagnosis and self-prescribed treatment are capable of restoring health status to its original level. In some cases specific health care may be purchased (e.g. paracetamol). Nonetheless there may be a role for the agent even at low levels of uncertainty and/or complexity, if only in reassuring the consumer that he is making the right decision. However, as uncertainty and complexity increase, the cost of gaining information also increases to the extent that information impactedness is attained relatively quickly in the health care sector. Moreover, the potentially high costs associated with the actual process of decision-making in the consumption of health care and those associated with making wrong decisions (i.e. anxiety costs) leads to a heavy reliance upon an agent. Indeed these costs may become so high that the consumer is willing to default upon the decision-making process completely. In any case, as we have argued throughout, property rights in the consumer's utility function will not be as well-defined (with respect to the consumer and producer) as market efficiency requirements would dictate.

The uncertainty associated with the timing and form of health care utilisation will affect supply in as much as production in this sector must be, for the most part, directed towards short-run allocation. Health care is difficult to store in that, being a service commodity, it is difficult to build up inventories. It is also poorly substitutable across broad categories of consumer as it is an inter-mediate commodity relating to the production of health status. Production will, therefore, vary across diagnostic categories and possibly even across individuals within the same diagnostic category. Certainly as the complexity of treatment grows the commodity becomes increasingly 'customised'. Moreover the intermediate nature of health care and the heterogeneity of treatment mean that consumers must have ready access to all levels of health care production.

Thus consumers rely upon information gained from the supplier concerning both the nature and outcome of the consumption process, which is specific to the case (i.e. the contract). It may also be necessary to reconsider earlier decisions about both diagnosis and treatment (i.e. to recontract) in a sequential manner particularly as the consumption/production process can have any number of idiosyncrasies (i.e. every case is potentially different from every other). All of this emphasises the nature of the exchange problem. In other words the supply of health care represents 'a complicated sequence of adaptive responses in the face of uncertainty' (Harris, 1977, p. 469). Of course the degree of complexity and uncertainty will differ but the intermediate nature of health care means that production must be organised in such a manner that what is produced (i.e. diagnosis, information given to the consumer and treatment) is quickly responsive to changed requirements.

The market is unable to cope efficiently with such problems. Pure market solutions would rely wholly upon re-contracting as a means of alleviating uncertainty. However, even assuming the consumer is physically able to re-negotiate, information on the effectiveness of health care and the expected *ex post* state of the world is impacted and re-contracting will not necessarily provide an efficient solution.

A number of alternatives exist. Contracts could be based, for example, upon prepayment either to individual doctors or to a group of medical providers. As Arrow (1963) points out, prepayment is really a form of insurance in that the uncertainty associated with health care, at least with regard to the cost of treatment, is passed on to the medical provider(s). In this sense the doctor also takes the role of insurer. The individual doctor, given the uncertainty associated with health care and its effectiveness, may not wish to assume such risks. Certainly some pooling of risks, through prepayment being linked to a group of providers, for example, would reduce costs. However, as we shall discuss below problems occur even with such pooling and with insurance generally. Moreover the patient/consumer may not wish a doctor, who is after all his agent, to become too closely associated with the costs of health care provision. Certainly such pooling of risks through prepayment does not overcome the potential for the exercise of monopoly power arising from information impactedness. Another solution would be to transfer fully the risks from the patient to the doctor by contracting on the basis of payment by results. Again, given the uncertainty of the effectiveness of medical treatment the doctor might have an aversion to bearing these risks.

A more detailed examination of insurance follows below. Essentially the problem is that ideal insurance is difficult to provide efficiently. Given that this is the case the sector has responded by offering institutional solutions which provide some form of substitute, of which the agency relationship is one of the more important.

Such contractual problems are exacerbated by the transaction problems associated with small numbers exchange. Where exchange is confined to an environment which is limited to a small number of transactors, considerable resources are liable to be expended in attempting to agree upon a (market) clearing price, the problem being that competitive pressures are not operative, and this leads to market inefficiency (Arrow, 1969). Not surprisingly small numbers exchange when coupled with information impactedness increases the potential for opportunistic behaviour.

Although conditions are ripe for the potential for opportunism and other small numbers bargaining problems to be realised, the actual production process, with the consumer not only playing an integral role but also being in a particularly vulnerable position, gives rise to the importance of the atmosphere in which transactions take place. In other words the atmosphere in which consumption occurs may itself affect utility. Indeed process utility may be of such importance that it may influence the nature of production. For example, an attempt may be made to separate out economic aspects from the medical aspects, i.e. to distance the consumer from economic decisions at the time of consumption. No one wants to add to the consumer's disutility associated with illness by engaging him in negotiations over the price of treatment. We shall return to this below.

It would appear then that all the conditions which Williamson (1975) states can lead to market failure are relevant to some degree, and quite often to a considerable degree, in the analysis of the supply of health care. Given this it is not surprising that there is market failure in this sector. The basic problem is that the market cannot deal efficiently with exchanges which are concentrated on the short-run between a small number of transactors where information on both the nature of the commodity and the expected outcome is impacted, where additionally the commodity is poorly substitutable across consumers and where there are potentially severe problems relating to uncertainty and complexity in decision-making. At best, conditions are ripe for the exercise of monopoly power; at worst there will be a complete failure in allocation if this is left to the market. It is then not surprising that various institutional structures have appeared which attempt to correct for these potential and actual market failings.

10.3 Further complications and additional failures

To complicate matters the analysis of the supply of health care must include, as alluded to above, an analysis of insurance. Certainly the occurrence of illness is unpredictable. But individuals are not only uncertain about the timing of their future health care consumption, they are also uncertain about the form and consequently the cost of that consumption. Such uncertainties lead to welfare losses and therefore individuals seek insurance. Welfare is then increased by the spreading of risks. It has also been argued that insurance may increase welfare by releasing the consumer from concerns over health care prices and income constraints at the time of consumption when it is likely that the costs directly associated with decision making, even without such considerations, will in any case be high (Fuchs, 1979).

In considering the welfare losses associated with risk bearing Arrow (1963) shows that risk averse individuals will demand full coverage if insurance is available at actuarially fair prices. In fact Arrow goes further by arguing that even if the insurer is risk averse and loads the premium to cover his risk (i.e. the premium is set at a higher rate than the actuarially fair value) the insurance will still be purchased, provided that the loading is not perceived by the individual to be too unfair. Arrow continues by discussing the conditions under which an individual will prefer a deductible or coinsurance scheme. The former is better suited to cover high loading and the latter to coverage of any uncertainty associated with the risk insured against.

In most circumstances then the demand for health care should lead to a demand for health insurance. If utility is positively linked to income and the cost of health care is seen as a deductible from that income, the risk averse individual is likely to purchase more insurance as the risks increase. Indeed it is also argued that, *ceteris paribus*, events which have a low probability of occurrence but a high associated loss, such as hospital care, are more likely to be insured against than events which have a high risk of occurrence but low loss, such as check-ups (see Hershey *et al.*, 1984; Phelps, 1983).

However, a number of problems prevent the existence of ideal insurance markets. For example moral hazard may occur, with insured individuals having little incentive to restrict their consumption levels to those that would prevail if they faced the full cost of consumption. This subsequently increases the expected loss to be insured against, the essential problem being the effect of insurance upon incentives. It may be argued that the relationship between the doctor and the patient limits the extent of moral hazard in that the professional conduct of the doctor means that he acts, to some degree, as a controlling agent for the insurer. In other words, the doctor will only provide that level of treatment which is strictly necessary.[1] To the extent that moral hazard remains a problem insurers may attempt, as we saw, to exert some control by introducing coinsurance provisions.[2] Thus some of the cost of health care may be shifted back to the consumer. Arrow also points out that the existence of moral hazard can be related to insurance removing any incentive to search out the lowest priced health care. Thus competitive market forces are impeded by moral hazard and 'market forces, therefore, tend to be replaced by direct institutional control' (op. cit., p. 36).

There are a number of additional problems which hinder the efficient operation of the insurance market. The operating costs of an insurance company may exhibit increasing returns of scale. Obviously as insurance involves the spreading of risks there are inherent characteristics which lend themselves to such economies of scale. It is normally assumed that such economies are substantial although little empirical evidence exists (Arrow, 1963; Evans, 1984). Arguments may be forwarded for the public provision of health care insurance, on the assumption that such economies are large and on the grounds of the standard welfare arguments against monopoly. If monopoly power is excessive in the private insurance sector it may mean that the loadings on premiums are high which will result in some individuals not covering the risks associated with the cost of health care. In other words, the existence of economies of scale may result in market failure through the failure of some individuals ensuring that they have adequate insurance coverage.

A further problem with private insurance is adverse selection.

This arises when there is an asymmetry of information between the parties involved in the insurance contract. Specifically, individuals may have more information on their expected health status than the seller of the insurance. The significance of adverse selection stems from the fact that the welfare benefits of insurance are dependent upon the ability to discriminate amongst different classes of risk, the result being that those groups facing a higher risk of illness should pay higher premiums. If this does not occur, (and if adverse selection is a problem it will not), there will be a welfare loss. Thus adverse selection affects the pooling of risks such that high risk parties are paying a subsidised premium, with resultant redistributive consequences. Ultimately adverse selection may lead to gaps in insurance coverage, as competition amongst insurers leads to high risk groups being first distinguished and second omitted from coverage. Of course as the amount of pooling of risk decreases and as a consequence the risk covered increases, premiums will rise and some individuals will indeed be priced out of the market. The chronically ill and aged are the most obvious examples of individuals who may find it difficult to obtain insurance coverage. Once again little empirical evidence is available on the effects of adverse selection upon the supply of health insurance. Although it may be noted that coverage in the private health care sector, for whatever reason, is far from universal.

A further complication is that there is a tendency to equalise risks in the health insurance market. Health care is a very heterogeneous commodity and, therefore, the potential costs covered by insurance cover a wide spectrum. Under competitive conditions premiums would be matched to risks. However, in reality unequal risks tend to be pooled with the result that wealth is redistributed, *ex ante*, from low-risk individuals to high-risk individuals. Not only is this easier to administer for the insurance company, the costs are passed on to the consumer in the form of higher than actuarially fair premiums for low-risk coverage. As a consequence of not fully discriminating between risks, social welfare is, to some extent, diminished. Moreover this may lead to further welfare losses in the form of gaps in coverage if the loading on low-risk individuals becomes, to their mind, unacceptably high.

All of these problems result in the failure of the insurance market to provide efficient solutions – either because of changes in incentive structures or through the exercise of monopoly power leading to the unacceptable loading of premiums and/or gaps in coverage. On top of this the heterogeneity of the commodity health care leads to a tendency for risks to be equalised, which in turn results, as discussed above, in redistributive effects and subsequent welfare loss. The market, therefore, fails to offer individuals comprehensive insurance against the risk of incurring health care costs associated with the possible occurrence of a multitude of illnesses. Not surprisingly alternatives to market provision have emerged. Thus analysis of health insurance leads one to the conclusion, first arrived at by Arrow, 'that the failure of the market to insure against uncertainties has created many social institutions in which the usual assumptions of the market are to some extent contradicted' (op. cit., p. 41).

The uncertainty associated with the costs of health care encourages not only an analysis of health insurance and problems of willingness to pay. Also important are the problems associated with interdependent utility functions and ability to pay. We noted earlier that the market relies upon the ability of the consumer to pay to act as a mechanism to distribute goods and services. This ability is unlikely to be positively correlated with medical need. Clearly if income constraints are severe consumers may not be able to pay, as and when necessary, for some treatments. The market allocation system would operate as if they had put very low valuations on these treatments. Effective demand and, *ceteris paribus*, production would be biased towards those services favoured by those with less constrained incomes. While this is a feature of all market allocation systems, with health care interpersonal utility considerations seem of such fundamental importance that some adjustment to market provision is necessary. Many individuals do appear to be concerned about equity in health care, as discussed in chapter 4. Certainly if interpersonal utility considerations are treated as externalities or if individuals are willing to commit themselves to covering the costs of the health care provision of those in need who are unable to meet such costs, market provision will be inefficient to the extent that it does not account for such behaviour.

It may be argued that interpersonal utility considerations could be abated through the payment of income subsidies – essentially through the enhancement of ability to pay. Such arguments neglect the fundamental failure of the market to provide health care efficiently. The timing of the consumption of health care is uncertain. This may lead to insurance coverage being sought, yet as we have seen such markets may not operate efficiently. Moreover if the subsidised individual should spend the income subsidy on non-health-enhancing goods (or inefficiently with regard to health-enhancing goods) and still required health care at a later date, the continued existence of interpersonal utility concerns might result in a further allocation of resources devoted to the health care of that individual. Such inefficiency would arise because income subsidies are not neutral in their allocative effects.

10.4 Acceptance and response: structural considerations

There would appear then to be the potential for substantial market failures in the health care sector. It is most unlikely that the accident and emergency admission to the hospital will want to collect all the information necessary to evaluate the relationship between health care and health status, work out his demand for the commodity (probably on information given by the supplier), compare his willingness to pay with the market price (if this exists) and then decide whether to accept or reject the service offered. While this may be an extreme example, it is unlikely that this train of events will be efficient for health care generally.

If, as a result of substantial transactions costs and inherent non-marketabilities, health care cannot be efficiently provided by the market it is pertinent to ask what the alternatives are. Most broadly these rely on attempts to internalise transactions and to offer institutional substitutes. We may, therefore, regard the agency relationship as an attempt to internalise transactions. Given the prominence of uncertainty and complexity in a significant number of transactions in this sector, and the possible presence of bounded rationality, the combination of services to be provided will be arrived at through a sequential decision-making process determined by the supplier/agent. If a market solution were pursued, if this were possible, spot market contracting would be the norm. The effect of uncertainty and/or complexity, coupled with bounded rationality, would be that the transaction process would be characterised by substantial re-contracting. However, given the problems imposed upon the market by information impactedness and small numbers bargaining it is likely that market exchange would be costly. Thus the agency relationship may be viewed as an example of vertical integration in an attempt to internalise transactions costs. The supplier of health care integrates forward into the consumption decision-making process to mitigate against transactions costs.

Vertical integration in this sector may also be viewed as a reaction to technological interdependency. Health care is only one of the inputs in the production of health. As an individual's consumption increases the production process is likely to become increasingly complex. However, health care is essentially complementary to other inputs used in the production of health and should be seen as part of a flow process rather than one in which separate component production exists. In other words, the conditions necessary for vertical integration are present in this sector. Indeed vertical integration of health care processes is what appears to have occurred, by way of structural adaptation, in all developed economies. However, the fact that the production of health involves, in an integral way, the presence of the consumer (the doctor cannot perform a tonsillectomy, for example, without the presence of the patient) means that production can never be fully integrated. Moreover in certain circumstances, for example, where production is confined to a GP visit with the result that only part of the production process is required and transactions costs are low, full integration will not always be necessary.

The resultant structure originating from the characteristics of both the commodity and the nature of the transaction in the health care sector has been described by Evans (1981) as one of incomplete vertical integration. He has emphasised that the analysis of exchange is complicated, not only because of market failure and the associated lack of identifiable prices, but also because this particular sector is inadequately characterised by interactions, as exists in many other sectors, at arm's length between pairs of transactors. A clear exposition would recognise the multilateral agreements that are formed in transactions in this sector, which lead to managerial and entrepreneurial functions being allocated across many different actors. These multilateral agreements and the accompanying structure of incomplete vertical integration are both indicative and symptomatic of the preponderance of non-market relationships in the sector, which in turn are themselves a response to the high transaction costs.

The (non-market) agency relationship that exists between the patient and doctor is a key structural feature of the sector. A distinctive relationship also exists between health care suppliers and the government in that the latter, at least in many European countries, provides financial resources while also acting as a regulator of the sector. Even in the USA a significant part of health care expenditure is provided for through government funds and the sector is consequently regulated to a substantial degree. Yet simultaneously governments delegate a substantial degree of regulation to the medical profession who enjoy a large degree of 'self-government'. Doctors' conduct and rights to practise are determined substantially by the medical profession. The existence of these non-market relations, which arise directly from the market failings, are obvious and reinforce the importance of emphasising the need for a non-market-based transactional analysis.

We have already noted important features concerning the structure of this sector, in particular the multilateral relationships and short-run allocation decisions. Therefore it is not surprising that, in analysing the roles of the various actors in health care, we find a conflict of interests arising from property rights holdings with respect to resource utilisation which are spread across different actors in the sector and, as importantly, different time periods.

The major transactors may be identified by referring to Figure 10.1. The left hand side of the diagram identifies the insurance and regulating bodies. Indeed the latter may also be identified as the legislators, if we take the regulators to mean governments. These bodies combine to act as the budget-holders in the health care sector. In playing the roles of legislators, third-party financiers and regulators, these actors determine the quantities of resources available in the sector, for example, through the supply of resources which enable the uptake of specialised labour and capital resources, as well as, in some instances, acting as *de facto* owners of health care resources. Thus the insurance and regulating bodies can influence economic efficiency through their role in providing funds, controlling capacity levels, determining staffing

195

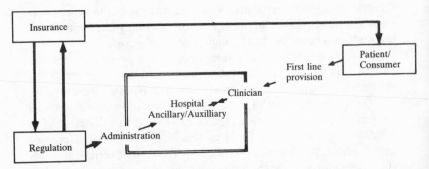

Figure 10.1 Structure of the health care sector (after Evans, 1981)

levels, etc. This control has, at least until recently in most countries, normally been exercised over the long-run period, with such bodies not normally being concerned with short-run allocation problems. In that the regulating bodies are presumably acting for society at large, we may assume that they are attempting to maximise the social welfare accruing from the consumption of health care.[3] Indeed in some countries, for example the UK, this assumption holds for the insurance body as well, since the government has direct control over this function.

The regulation of the sector is further complicated by the fact, noted above, that, although the regulating and legislative bodies do have substantial control over health care, an important delegation of self-government has been awarded to doctors. As Evans (1981) points out, each individual provider's conduct is regulated by the collective medical profession. Thus not only do doctors have strong property rights holdings in the consumption process (as the consumer/patient's agent) *and* in the production process (through the specification of treatment), these property rights holdings are heavily protected through the delegation of self-government. While the doctor is concerned with inputs it is their usage rather than their cost with which he has most regard, and his conduct is regulated by the medical profession accordingly. As we have seen, knowledge of the relationship between health care and health status allows the doctor to make judgements about the effectiveness of health production, and therefore the amount of resources required in treatment. There is not necessarily an interest in the cost of these resources. Indeed the rights to self-regulation held by the medical profession may be seen as reinforcing the agency role of the individual doctor, in as much as they serve to separate medical conduct and performance from resource implications.

In divorcing short-run from long-run resource allocation decisions we may differentiate between tactical and strategic actors. The doctor's behaviour is dictated by the fact that he is operating at the 'coal-face'. His conduct is tactical. In contrast the regulators and insurance bodies, by retaining overall control of long-run resource allocation, operate at the strategic level. Between these levels relationships exist between doctors, hospital administrators, functional budget holders, ancillary departments, and government and insurance agencies which are dictated by reference to their interest in, and control over, tactical and strategic conduct. During periods of financial clemency there may well be little apparent conflict between tactical and strategic approaches. However, during periods of financial stringency, that conflict may become more visible. When government and insurance agencies are tightening resource constraints (e.g. budgets) this will encroach more and more upon short-run allocation decisions. This will occur both directly through the effect that changes in budget allowances have upon the health care production process (e.g. the purchase of technologically advanced equipment) and through putting a strain upon existing relationships and consequently the property rights holdings in health care. Any change in the conditions under which problems of short-run resource allocation are resolved must affect the structure of property rights holdings and consequently the composition of output in the sector.

10.5 The importance of ethical conduct[4]

Having discussed the consequences of market failure in health care with regard to the structure of that sector, we now examine conduct with the emphasis once more placed upon the doctor. His role is complex because he is acting, simultaneously, on both sides of the health care sector. While acting as an agent for the patient in the process of utilisation of treatment, he is also involved in the specification of the supply of treatment. Chapter 8 noted the effect of this integration of consumer and provider interests on demand

197

analysis. It was concluded that demand, as conventionally defined, often had little meaning and that utilisation, based upon decisions taken jointly by the consumer and producer, was often more important. In other words the demand constraints upon supply were frequently ineffective.

If demand does not fully constrain supply, what does? Earlier chapters have alluded to the importance of medical ethics. Budget constraints are weakened, for example, through third-party payment systems; the consumer relies heavily upon the supplier to specify consumption levels; and supplier-induced demand may be limited by ethical behaviour. Thus ethical conduct would appear to be the most obvious form of constraint. Not only do medical ethics act as an internalised check upon supplier behaviour, they are also a key element in the structure of property rights holdings in health care with regard to specification of the production and consumption processes.

The agency relationship is, once again, central to the understanding of the importance of ethical behaviour acting as a constraint. Due partly to the lack of information and the costs associated in gaining such information, but also to the fact that the consumer may actually wish to default on the decision-making process, the agency relationship is entered into as a direct institutional response to market failure. However, *ex ante* because of his lack of information, the consumer cannot evaluate the performance of this relationship. Medical ethics underpin this relationship, providing reassurance that the doctor will attempt to do his best for the individual patient.

In this context Harris (1977, p. 473) in discussing the US hospital sector states that 'one function of the fee-for-service system is to seal the ethical bond between doctor and patient'. This may seem somewhat odd at first glance, but given the US structure, where the doctor is hired by the patient and is not a hospital employee, it does make sense. The separation of the doctor's fees from those of the hospital is a means of keeping the doctor apart from the full consequences of the resource allocation implications of specifying treatment. This process, in effect, helps both to confirm and to clarify the distribution of property rights holdings between the doctor, the patient and the hospital.

In the USA this increase in clarity is indeed enhanced by the fact that the doctor is not a hospital employee but rather an agent employed directly by the patient. In the UK, by way of contrast, the hospital clinician is an employee of the health authority. Thus clinical decisions could, in theory, come under the scrutiny of the employer. If the clinician were using too much of the revenue budget, the health authority could clamp down on him. But enough of the theory!

In reality the position of the doctor both individually and corporately is considerably enhanced by the transfer of property rights holdings from the employers to the collective medical profession in the form of rights to self-regulation. These powers of self-regulation of conduct are, not surprisingly, particularly relevant to medical conduct in that they are geared to the short-run, to the conducting of the agency relationship and to the medical process and outcome. In this manner they reinforce, at an aggregate level, the separation of medical man from economic man which is so important given the individualistic nature of the doctor–patient agency relationship.

This separation of medical and economic considerations which underpins these non-market relations is further supported by the third-party involvement of the health insurance bodies. This payment mechanism also helps to remove the price–exchange–resources aspect from the doctor–patient relationship. The outcome of these institutional transactions is that, unlike other sectors of the economy, there is little, and indeed in some cases no, analysis of the costs of production by the person specifying the level of production (treatments), i.e. the doctor. Such considerations are left, at least formally, to administrators and, in the final event, politicians. In other words, there are strong structural barriers which divorce the medical doctor from considerations of resource allocation.

This may appear strange, but reflection upon earlier arguments should aid understanding. The consumer/patient is concerned with health status and yet, because health is not tradeable, the doctor can only supply health care. The doctor acts both as supplier and as agent for the consumer. In accepting the role of agent, the doctor not only gains property rights holdings in the consumption function but may also have to accept responsibility for the risks associated with outcome. This risk-holding will vary across individual settings both in terms of the medical nature of the case and with regard to the willingness to default in decision-making by

199

the patient. Harris (1977, p. 473), in analysing acute hospital care (essentially circumstances where the patient may not even have the chance or the choice to default), states that the doctor accepts the 'moral burden of ultimate responsibility for the outcome of the case'.

At the same time as underpinning the agency relationship, medical ethical codes of conduct allow individual doctors to know that they have acted broadly as their peers would have done. Strictly this does nothing to reduce the risk-holding by the doctor – but it does affect his perceived cost of doing so. In other words, the non-transferability of the risk holding by doctors to other actors in the production process may mean that medical ethics acts as a substitute for risk sharing.

Medical ethics, when viewed from the perspective of the profession as a whole, may, therefore, be seen as the mechanism for self-regulation. In this sense medical ethical codes aid *ex ante* views concerning performance by reducing the variance of medical outcome. Presumably medical ethical codes and the rights to self-regulation are a form of exorcising quackery!

There are then various dimensions to medical ethics. First and foremost they underpin the non-market relationships, in particular the agency relationship and the medical profession's rights to self-government. They are also a response to the self-regulating ability of the market. The extent of market failure in this sector means that some form of regulation of the institutions which replace the market transactions is required. The fact that such regulation is based upon a separation of medical conduct from economic conduct is a consequence of the dominance of uncertainty, risk and complexity in health care. The inadequacies of the consumer's information and the costs associated with the consumption of health care severely limit *caveat emptor*. The institutional response, in the form of the agency relationship, involves a transfer of this risk to the supplier/agent. The (perceived) ameliorating role that medical ethical codes and conventional medical conduct have upon this risk-bearing by the doctor is a direct institutional response to the handling of uncertainty. Furthermore the integration of the interests of the supplier and consumer through the agency relationship enhances the importance of the process utility associated with transactions in this sector, in other words the 'atmosphere' as Williamson (1975) would put it. Given the potential for economic exploitation that the existence of informational impactedness allows, in this sector, it is perhaps not surprising that professional conduct is regulated with regard to medical rather than economic considerations.

As a consequence, medical conduct, which dictates the nature of the health care production process, has little concern with the resource implications of that process. Moreover, given the dominance of individual need in dictating medical ethics and conduct, we find that the bulk of medical practice is specifically geared to (unique) individual transactions, rather than, for example, preventive community-based medicine. Opportunity cost has little meaning to medical conduct. The constraining effect that medical ethics have upon conduct, and, therefore, resource allocation in the health care sector, is further reinforced by the structure itself. A number of important production/consumption decisions must be made at the 'coal-face' and the resulting decentralised structure of the health care sector serves to augment the role of medical ethics.

10.6 Conclusions: the performance effects

So far we have been concerned with the peculiar structure of the health care sector and the relationship between that structure and conduct. We have highlighted that one of the most important sets of constraints upon supplier conduct, at least at the more sophisticated end of production, relates to the existence of non-market relations. Particularly dominant is the agency relationship between the patient and the doctor and, consequently, it is not surprising to find that the constraints upon conduct are not only concerned with distinguishing economic and medical decisions, but that they are also overwhelmingly individualistic in their nature. They are concerned with the supplier's duty to fulfil his medical obligation to the consumer. In this respect we can see why need, as defined by the medical model, is so important (see chapter 8). A direct result of this is that duty to the individual patient/consumer is emphasised, and performance is related primarily to the manner in which this duty is undertaken and to medical outcome. The resultant resource allocation patterns and social net benefits are, at best, a secondary consideration to the producer/agent. The important role of professional self-governance strengthens this emphasis upon medical performance.

Given the doctor's position in the resource allocation process it may be appropriate that his decisions are limited to medical process and outcome. The doctor, being at the 'coal-face' and concerned with short-run decisions about the individual patient in front of him, is not well placed to make strategic decisions. It would appear appropriate that the social costs and benefits associated with individual treatment are analysed at a more strategic level. Resource implications can then be more efficiently assessed and policy can be formulated aimed at maximising social benefits. It is only at such a level that an overview of the system can be gained which would allow resources to be moved to their most appropriate position. The existence of non-market relations and the associated divorcing of medical and economic decisions have obvious effects, however, on the rationing (or allocation) process in health care.

In the market, the role of prices in conveying information and allocating resources was remarked upon earlier. Unfortunately the price mechanism is unable to undertake either task in the health care sector, as was discussed above. The alternative, basically some form of quantity adjustment, is difficult because it relies upon direct intervention. This does not just introduce the world of the second best, but also the real world with all its political and ideological conflicts. At this level regulation is governed as much by politics as by economics. Health and health care are as much political issues as economic issues. Certainly a starting point for efficient quantity adjustment would be examination of the effectiveness of treatments in an attempt to deal with problems of technical inefficiency. However, even here, conflicts may arise, given that the institutional responses to market failure are not neutral in their allocative role. Medical conduct, founded as it is upon ethical (medical) conduct aimed at the individual transaction to hand and which abstracts from the wider resource consequences, is crucial to maintaining trust in this agency relationship. The process of decision-making, and the reliance upon duty contained therein, is critical to the utility to be gained by the consumer. The collective rights to self-government held by the medical profession underwrite this decision-making process, but also mean that conduct is assessed in medical terms.

Effectiveness *per se* becomes more important than efficiency.

Unfortunately because resources are scarce there will always be constraints; effectiveness may be a necessary condition for the attainment of efficiency but it is certainly not a sufficient one. Certainly the dominance of medical decision-making and its repercussions may be maintained if resources to the health care sector are increased. However, even this 'solution' does not solve the real problem. Throwing resources at the health care system neither contains costs nor means that the resources are necessarily allocated optimally within the sector. At times when budgets are tightened the inadequacy of the reliance upon medical decision-making for allocating resources will be more than recognised. It is during such periods that a fundamental dichotomy in performance can be best observed. Given his individualistic ethical position the doctor tends to stress performance criteria with regard to the relationship between health care and health status, in terms of the effectiveness of treatment at the individual level. The health system planner, on the other hand, ought to have a tendency towards defining performance in terms not only of broad effectiveness, but also of economic efficiency and distributional equity.

Unfortunately again, the picture is further complicated with regard to equity, in that the doctor, working at the 'coal-face', is well placed to operationalise society's policy on equity, through his role as 'gatekeeper' to the health care system. In doing so the doctor is then acting on a distributional and not just a medical level. He may be, inappropriately, making trade-offs between equity and efficiency which are properly the rights of government.

Thus while it may be agreed that prices are not an appropriate device in this sector and that allocation should be based upon some form of quantity adjustment, it is difficult to suggest how such a mechanism should be operationalised at present. Certainly greater concern by the doctor over the effectiveness of treatment and the resource consequences of his decisions would help. However, it may be that this reconciliation of medical and economic behaviour would place unacceptable strain on the agency relationship. Moreover, if the process is important as well as the outcome in the production of health care, it is difficult to see how the efficiency of the production of this element may be measured. The definition of quality, for example, remains an unresolved economic problem.[5] Furthermore we have seen that the response to market failure has been that various institutional bodies have arisen. Not only does this take economics into the domain of public choice, where it has come unstuck so many times, it also means that various health care systems have to be seen in their 'cultural light'. Such complications all take the edge off the ability to abstract with as much elegance when considering allocation mechanisms which relate to quantities rather than price.[6] Consequently this chapter has tried to outline the bare bones of the economics of institutional response to market failure.

11

The hospital as an economic agent

11.1 Introduction

This chapter focuses on the hospital sector. The rationale for a separate chapter on this subject is simple: the hospital is the major consumer of health care expenditures in all developed economies. In 1981 this sector alone accounted for 58 per cent of gross health care expenditure in the UK. Comparable percentages are 49.5 per cent for the USA (1983), 54.0 per cent for Australia (1981), 55.1 per cent for Canada (1982), 58.7 per cent for the Netherlands (1983) (OECD, 1985). The picture is similar from wherever the snapshot is taken. Given the labour intensive nature of health care it is also not surprising that the sector is a large employer. For example in 1951 the UK hospital sector employed just over 400,000 people rising to more than a million by 1983. However, against this must be recorded the fact that the number of hospital beds per 1,000 population in the UK has been falling from 10.8 to 8.0 over the same period, as has the number of average daily occupied beds – from 472,000 to 356,000. Countering the fall in the level of resources used, there has also been a more intensive use of these resources in the UK – for example, deaths and discharges per available bed have risen from 7 to 16 in 1981. Similar trends are evident in other developed countries.

Against this background there has been considerable interest in the economics of the hospital sector. Moreover given that the USA has experienced considerable cost inflation in the hospital sector it is not surprising to find that the literature is predominantly

205

from that country, although another reason may be that the hospital in the USA is a more distinctive economic agent than in other, more integrated health care systems. This chapter analyses the hospital as a firm in an attempt to understand the theoretical basis of the empirical literature which has tended to dominate the analysis of this sector (section 11.2). The structure–conduct–performance paradigm is used as a basis for our analysis. Section 11.3 discusses the literature on hospital costs, while section 11.4 considers the analyses of hospital inflation.

11.2 The hospital as a firm

It is disappointing that we find so few formal models of hospital behaviour. This may arise because there is no typical hospital. Sloan (1979) has raised the point that it is difficult to identify a representative hospital, in that hospitals reflect a wide range of differences with regard to the mix of output. Hospitals, like many firms, can vary not only the scale of their output but also the composition. Moreover the hospital may exhibit varying patterns of ownership, the most extreme variations being in the USA where the sector includes both private for-profit and non-profit institutions. In considering the economic conduct and performance of the hospital it is obvious that ownership patterns will affect the objective functions of this particular agent. Furthermore we also saw in the last two chapters that the health care sector can be identified as a sector where there exists varying degrees of incomplete vertical integration, which may affect the nature of the hospital objective function. We would not, for example, expect to find the NHS hospital, which is part of a general welfare service, to be performing in a manner similar to a private hospital. Such considerations will also affect identification of the relevant decision-makers.

Preliminary analysis of the structure of the hospital sector, therefore, reveals at least two fundamental characteristics. The first is the disparate nature of the agents under study, the hospitals. The diversity of features with which they are associated, for example whether they are proprietary or non-proprietary, the functional type, whether they have teaching facilities, etc., will affect the conduct and the consideration of their performance. A second, and arguably a more important feature, is the difficulty in identifying the decision-maker, given that managerial and entrepreneurial functions will be shared across a number of individuals in this vertically, incompletely integrated sector (Evans, 1981).

11.2.1 The theory of the firm

In discussing the economic models of hospital behaviour, the generic theory of the firm is not very helpful, in a methodological sense, in any search for a useful model. The central problem in the theory of the firm concerns discretion over the behaviour of the decision-maker. The traditional theory of the firm, utilising the assumption of perfect competition and the accompanying constraint of profit-maximisation, allows very little discretion. The market environment is entirely exogenous and independent of the firm, and behaviour is largely deterministic. The defence of this traditional paradigm is that, within its own restricting world, it contains powerful predictive ability, such prediction being confined to relative changes in output, inputs and prices.

On relaxing the assumption of perfect competition the ability to generalise about a firm's conduct becomes more difficult. This occurs largely because in all forms of market structure the firm retains some degree of discretion over its conduct. Indeed such discretion is posited to arise from the firm's internal structure, through the separation of management from ownership, as well as from any degree of monopoly power. The acknowledgement of discretionary power means that profit-maximisation is no longer a binding constraint and that managerial objectives may conflict with the organic firm's objective.

The literature on 'the' theory of the firm has thus evolved such that we have managerial theories which recognise the separation of ownership from management and examine its consequences largely through an extension of the traditional marginalist approach. On the other hand, behaviouralist theories also exist which are not so directly concerned with market behaviour *per se*, but rather emphasise the bargaining processes and organisational structure within the firm. Thus we have two competing paradigms: one focusing on market resource allocation issues and the other on internal allocation issues. The theory of the firm is in fact revealed to be a composite of several theories. That they address a number of distinctive issues leaves some concern over their supposed purpose. This is perhaps the main point to remember in our specific consideration of the theory of the hospital as an economic firm.

11.2.2 The hospital as a firm

One of the more influential theories has been proposed by Pauly and Redisch (1973) who suggest a traditional neoclassical model, built within the structural setting of the USA, where clinicians attempt to maximise residual profit, essentially their own income, thereby performing the traditional role of manager and entrepreneur. Note that hospitals and clinicians are separate 'firms' in the USA. The implication of the model is that hospitals pursue traditional cost-minimisation policies. In this way, the institutional aspects of the hospital sector are used to modify the traditional neoclassical theory of pure profit-maximising. However, the authors take no account of the non-market agency relationship between doctor and patient discussed in detail in chapter 8. Neither is the market structure examined in great detail, it is discussed only to the extent that it is used to justify modification of the traditional model. The amended model assumes that returns to scale exist and that demand is elastic over a wide range of services, even although the empirical evidence relating to these issues is inconclusive. Also, as we have indicated in chapters 7 and 8, demand is itself a misleading concept in this sector. The model is useful, however, as an example to show that even in its 'purest' form the theory of the hospital is forced to accept that certain structural characteristics necessarily constrain the level of abstraction adopted. In particular it could be argued that, in so far as doctors are a specialised labour input in the hospital production process, there is no recognition of the influence of the factor market for this input upon the income- maximising behaviour of this agent.

A number of theories of the hospital focus upon the administrator as the key decision-maker. Given that most of the models relate to the USA this may reflect the fact that the clinician is not a hospital employee. It is also true that a number of such models see the role of the doctor as, somehow, defining quality. Generally hospitals are deemed to maximise output with the quality of output held to be an important consideration. Hospital output might then be seen as a type of Lancastrian good with a number of characteristics, quality being one. This particular characteristic is held to relate to the technical relationship between health care and health status presumably, and therefore the clinician helps to define quality in his role as agent for the consumer/patient (c.f. Reder, 1965). This may be complicated further if we attempt to pursue the Lancastrian approach by separating hospital output into medically necessary treatments and amenities, as does Rice (1966). The latter are seen to be a class of final products and may therefore be treated like any other similar market good. The hospital, therefore, operates in two markets – an intermediate market with health care supplied as a result of the demand for health and in a final market for amenity consumption goods, e.g. food and hotel-type services. This model, like a number of others, is not formally developed, but does raise a number of interesting points about structure and characteristics, not least that the hospital's product markets may be conceptually distinguished.

The separation of the quality from quantity aspects of hospital services is also found in a number of formal models. Newhouse (1970), again focusing upon the administrator as decision-maker, suggests that this actor attempts to maximise both the quantity and quality of output subject to a budget constraint, with the medical staff reinforcing the maximisation of quality levels. The hospital is seen as a single product firm whose physical product is measurable and the decision-making process, that is the maximisation of the quantity/quality trade-off, is conducted by a single actor in the model – the administrator. The author does make it clear that he does not believe that the traditional neoclassical approach can be fully integrated into the theory of the hospital.

Newhouse does consider specific restrictions upon the hospital's market behaviour, such as entry restrictions, but fails to consider the role of interdependency amongst producers. Given that a downward sloping demand curve is assumed and a generally oligopolistic market structure, this failure is a major shortcoming. In effect the model assumes that the hospital can implement market decisions, subject to a budget constraint, without being affected by competitors' reactions. Thus Newhouse does not address the issue of uncertainty in a non-collusive market or whether, through adopting the specified maximand, the structure will lead to collusive action.

The lack of consideration given to the issue of interdependency is a general criticism applicable to all of the 'managerial' theories of the hospital. Given the nature of the products involved and the assumed market structure within which they operate this is a serious deficiency. Consequently there is little discussion as to how the industry's equilibrium level of output is attained and allocated throughout the market. This is especially intriguing given that most of the models of hospital behaviour originated from the US where recent moves suggest that market competition is becoming increasingly important, at least in terms of policy initiatives.

The model proposed by Lee (1971) suggests that inter-dependency is important. Once again the administrator is seen to be the major actor, but utility maximisation is linked to status rather than directly to income. In his model the hospital is seen to be competing not for profits but for status. Such competition is held to lead to inefficient resource allocation as inputs will be utilised without regard to cost-minimising behaviour, in as much as input utilisation reflects status levels. Lee continues by arguing that a kinked demand curve will exist in the factors market, as all hospitals will respond to increased input usage by any particular hospital, but not decreased usage. However, Lee does not fully analyse this interdependency. For example, an analysis of the effect that collusive action will have on the industry, or indeed the pressures in the market to implement collusive action, would seem important. Furthermore attention is focused upon the inputs, although the factors markets are not explicitly modelled, with little discussion of the determination of output levels either at the individual firm level or, possibly more importantly, at the industry level. Nor are the market prices determined, although they are given an integral role in raising status. The price elasticity of demand is assumed to be close to zero and thus revenue can be raised continuously without affecting output levels. However, prices are functionally related to disposable income, health insurance and government expenditure. All these should form some sort of constraint on the level of price increases, but the effectiveness of such a constraint is not considered.

In most formal models of hospital behaviour demand is defined and used in the traditional manner – it may be inelastic over some range, but it is still seen to form a constraint on overwhelming abuse of monopoly power by the supplier. This may, in part, reflect the analytical distinction of hospitals from clinicians in most of these theories. However, such abstractions do not fully acknowledge what Evans (1981) defines as the 'fuzzy boundaries' between actors in this sector. Even in the USA it is stretching abstraction a little too much to consider hospitals as entities distinct from 'clinical firms'. Managerial and entrepreneurial abilities tend to be shared across a number of actors. Nor do such abstractions help in analysing the importance of the non-market relations between actors, particularly the agency relationship, to hospital behaviour. The traditional conceptual use of demand as a constraint restricts discussion of the importance of discretionary behaviour and in doing so avoids discussion of the internal structure of the hospital which is essential to any analysis. Any theory of the hospital must take account of the institutional characteristics of the sector, in particular the medical motives of certain actors. To concentrate upon, for example, administrators as the major decision-makers with regard to resource allocation, is to seriously mislead analysis in that it is precisely the medical motivation and conduct, and subsequent resource consequences, which differentiates this sector from all others.

As a consequence of such criticisms, some models have concentrated upon the internal structure of the hospital. However, most have either not been explicit on the impact that the internal structure has upon conduct, or have introduced such considerations as a means merely to distinguish different objective functions and to compare different input mixes (e.g. see Buchanan and Lindsay, 1970; Clarkson, 1972; Schweitzer and Rafferty, 1976).

In contrast Harris (1977) does detail the effects that the internal organisation has upon resource allocation in the hospital sector. He suggests that the hospital's production process relies upon a separation of internal supply and demand functions. In his role as agent for the consumer, the doctor demands certain forms of health care to be supplied by the other hospital staff, e.g. laboratory technicians, nurses, auxiliaries, etc. Indeed these functions may be separated (at least analytically) to such an extent that the hospital may be regarded as two firms within the same organisational structure.

As important to the economic analysis of the hospital, Harris argues, is the fact that hospital output must be produced and delivered on demand, in that it is a service commodity which is difficult to store and is poorly substitutable between patients. So although drugs and dressings can be stored as inventories, and it may well be the same nurse or specialist who is working with different patients admitted with similar illnesses, the treatment may differ to a marked degree across different individuals. To use Harris' terminology the spot market dominates and the commodity is customised due to the fact that any medical problem can have numerous idiosyncrasies (op. cit., p. 470). As discussed in chapter 10, these characteristics lead to a situation in which decentralised decisions and consequently small numbers dominate resource allocation processes. The role of uncertainty is recognised, as in the analysis of utilisation of health care generally in the previous chapter, by describing the hospital treatment as a sequence of spot demands and deliveries. The agent/doctor is never certain about diagnosis or subsequent treatment and the individual doctor is subject to bounded rationality. As such hospitalisation becomes a sequential process of acquiring more information on the patient, responding to any changes in condition and subsequently ordering different forms of treatment. It is unfortunate that medicine is not an exact science, a case of 'here is the pill, swallow it and it will be all right', but rather involves some detective work and the use of probabilities to assess the diagnosis before treatment is arrived at. The combined effect of such characteristics, which exist to some degree in all forms of health care as we have seen, is that the hospital responds to patient demands through a complicated bargaining process enacted by the doctor and the administration of the hospital.

Such a model is useful in highlighting the temporal and spatial aspects of the production process and in the emphasis that it gives to distribution in this process. The major assertion of the model is that it is the institutional constraints that arise through the medical and associated ethical motives of doctors, as opposed to their economic motives, that are of importance in the analysis of hospital behaviour – 'it should be understood that the organisation is set up to protect the doctor from behaving as economic man' (op. cit., p. 469).

Subsequently Harris suggests that some traditional economic indicators may be misleading in this sector. This arises because of the nature of the commodity and the fact that hospital behaviour is geared towards short-run internal allocation problems. Thus Harris suggests that an internal pricing mechanism will not resolve the problems in allocating hospital resources. The basic problem relates to the fact that the good is customised. Because every case is potentially different and there is an inherent uncertainty with any case, then not only are there severe small numbers problems with the associated lack of competitive forces to ensure a market clearing price is attained (Arrow, 1969), but also it is difficult to assess exactly what resources will be required when treatment begins. What appears to be a straightforward case in the first instance may require a complete re-appraisal if complications develop. There may be a call for further laboratory tests and the initially proposed treatment may subsequently be altered. In such circumstances the intermediate nature of the initial demands made by the agent on behalf of the consumer and of health care itself must be recognised. Under such conditions contractual re-negotiation costs would be bound to occur if prices were utilised as the internal allocation mechanism. There would also be associated adjustment costs further down the production process given the intermediate nature of the health care process. Such knock-on effects occur because resources at other stages of the production process are tied into the negotiation of consumption demands at the 'coal-face' end of production.

Given these conditions it will be difficult to specify exactly the demands to be placed upon the organisation's resources. However, once 'demand' is revealed, given the nature of the commodity involved, it is liable to be highly inelastic. Conversely, it will be difficult for the administrator to determine costs if the 'demand' is not revealed until the last minute. Under such circumstances an internal price mechanism is liable to exhibit such large transactions costs as to be inefficient. Internal behavioural relationships therefore become fundamentally important. Thus Harris states that 'Hospitals with apparent capacity excesses or cost overruns may actually be in a deceptively stable equilibrium' (op. cit., pp. 480–1). In stressing the institutional framework and the behavioural relationship, Harris, therefore, appears to suggest that performance in this sector may not be adequately judged in the economists' traditional manner.

In summarising the literature then we find that the models of

213

hospital behaviour have a strong methodological relationship with the various theories of the firm. It is not surprising that the ambiguities of the latter have been transmitted to the former. The methodological problems of the latter arise from dealing with discretion in behaviour which in turn relates to analysis of structural conditions. These problems are complicated further in the hospital sector by the dominance of non-market linkages between agents and the limited allocative role that prices play. Incomplete vertical integration, as discussed in detail in chapter 10, would appear to extend into the hospital itself if the concept of two firms in one is accepted. If backward linkages are reflected upon it is also unclear whether the hospital can be considered as an individual firm. The analysis by Evans (1981) suggests that the study of the internal structure of the hospital, which is so crucial to an understanding of this agent, must nevertheless take account of the effect of market structure upon behaviour, particularly with regard to how it affects the relationship between the clinician and the hospital.

In common with Harris, the study by Evans also acknowledges that definitional problems arise in the consideration of performance. Such problems are traceable to the nature of the good health care. Thus with regard to efficiency Evans states that 'the allocative efficiency of resource use in the pattern and level of health care production can also be considered as the technical efficiency of health production' (op. cit., p. 343). This may lead to a blurring of efficiency criteria given that the former depends on the agent/clinician who may well be specifying non-minimum-cost production and the latter on the individual consumer.

This, of course, makes it difficult to assess performance in the hospital sector. The structural conditions mean that it is also difficult to identify the decision makers and consequently the objectives of this particular agent, the hospital, particularly given the considerable overlap in responsibilities across agents in the health-care sector generally. Furthermore conduct, at least to a degree, relies upon medical as opposed to economic considerations, with the consumer's agent taking a large responsibility for certain resource utilisation decisions.

11.3 Hospital cost functions

Given the indeterminacy of the theory of the hospital it is not surprising to find that a large part of the empirical literature on hospital costs is concerned with a search for relevant and significant variables. This literature relates not only to questions of performance, however; it is also of interest to the analysis of hospital cost inflation, which is discussed briefly in the last section. This particular section deals mainly with questions relating to both the explanation and the prediction of hospital costs.

The difficulties associated with specifying the objective function of the hospital has resulted in the empirical literature being only very loosely connected with the theoretical literature. The recognition in the theoretical literature of the significance of structural matters in the analysis of hospital behaviour should preclude the use of oversimplified specifications of the hospital's objective function. This in turn would inhibit the predictive quality of the theory in that a very general functional form would be of limited predictive value. However, the traditional economist's definition of predictive power, with its emphasis upon such economic variables as the prices of inputs and outputs, may in any case be of limited analytical value to the understanding of this particular agent. This is not merely because of the problems encountered in the empirical testing of the theoretical models, problems which are discussed below, but also because of the importance of clinical performance to the objective function of the hospital.

The literature on hospital cost functions follows the normal specification of the general cost function with few amendments. Thus total costs (TC) are seen to be an explicit function of fixed costs (F) and the level of output (Q):

$$TC = f(Q) + F \qquad (11.1)$$

Normal cost relations are obtained from the total cost curve. Average total (ATC), average variable (AVC), and average fixed (AFC) costs are defined respectively as total, variable and fixed costs divided by output:

$$ATC = [f(Q) + F]/Q \qquad (11.2)$$

215

$$AVC = f(Q)/Q \qquad (11.3)$$

$$AFC = F/Q \qquad (11.4)$$

Similarly marginal cost (MC) is held to be independent of fixed cost and defined as the first derivative of total cost:

$$MC = f'(Q) \qquad (11.5)$$

However, different analysts, while agreeing with the general outline, have disagreed over the exact specification of the hospital cost function to be estimated. Feldstein (1967), for example, restricts his initial estimation to a long-run variable cost curve defined as $AC = \alpha + \gamma B$ (where B = beds), due to data restrictions inhibiting the collection of data on fixed costs. Evans (1971) and Evans and Walker (1972), in a fashion similar to a number of earlier studies, set average costs as a function of bed levels and activity data:

$$AC = \alpha + \gamma B + \Phi\Sigma(\text{Hospital Activity variables}) \quad (11.6)$$

The activity data relate to patient characteristics and case-mix data. However, as Barer (1982) and Jenkins (1980) point out it is unclear how this relationship, where the independent variables are entered linearly, relates to the total cost curve. Thus Jenkins (1980) views total costs as a linear function of patient-days (P), total admissions (A), capacity (C), and hospital characteristics (H):

$$TC = \alpha P + \gamma A + \psi C + \Phi\Sigma H \qquad (11.7)$$

where the average cost can be found with regard to patient-days, admissions or capacity as in the following relationship:

$$TC/P = AC_p = \alpha + \beta(1/L) + \psi(1/U) + \Phi\Sigma(H/P) \quad (11.8)$$

$$TC/A = AC_a = \alpha L + \beta + \psi(L/U) + \gamma\Sigma(H/A) \qquad (11.9)$$

$$TC/C = AC_c = \alpha u + \beta(U/L) + \psi + \alpha\Sigma(H/C) \qquad (11.10)$$

where:

$L = P/A$ = average length of stay
$U = P/C$ = hospital occupancy rate.

These last two variables are of obvious importance to hospital costs. Note that if we introduce a third variable, throughput (THPT) defined as cases per year divided by the number of available beds, we may specify the following relationship

$$THPT = (365/L)U \qquad (11.11)$$

This in itself is an important measure as it means that inclusion of any two variables in a cost function effectively provides information on the third omitted variable.

Jenkins (op. cit.) argues that the specification given above (equations 11.7 to 11.10) is theoretically more acceptable than those found in earlier studies as these average cost functions are not linear with respect to the variables L or U. As he states, in these specifications the marginal *per diem* cost of increasing length of stay or occupancy rate is dependent upon the value of L and U, as one might expect. Thus:

$$\delta[TC/P]/\delta L = -\beta L^2$$

and

$$\delta[TC/P]/\delta U = -\Phi U^2$$

Barer (1981) suggests an alternative plausible form based upon the following quadratic total cost function:

$$TC = \alpha B + \beta B^2 + \gamma D \qquad (11.12)$$

where $TC = f(B, D)$, with B representing beds and D equal to cases. The squared term is included to pick up any economies of scale. Essentially fixed costs are related to bed levels and variable costs to case levels. Barer then assumes that the variable component is itself a function of a number of factors including hospital activities and patient and staff related characteristics. The average cost (per case) function subsequently becomes:

$$AC = \alpha_o + \beta(B/D) + \psi(B^2/D) + \gamma\Sigma(V) \qquad (11.13)$$

where V represents the variable factors associated with hospital activity, staff characteristics, etc.

Thus the literature on the estimation of hospital cost functions agrees that costs are related to output levels. However, there is less agreement over the appropriate functional form to be fitted. Such specification problems arise because the underlying production process is not well understood and this in turn relates to the lack of well-developed formal models of hospital behaviour. Of course the results of empirical investigation are dependent upon specification and consequently comparison of results across this literature is difficult, added to which a number of practical problems remain unresolved.

The fundamental practical difficulty in modelling the hospital production process is that there is no straightforward definition of hospital output. In other words it is difficult to relate costs to a specified, tangible output. Technically this means that there is liable to be extreme measurement error on the dependent variable which makes quantification of hospital inefficiency, for example, difficult. This complication is primarily related to the fact that hospital output is not homogeneous. Moreover these measurement problems are compounded by the choice of the level of aggregation at which the problem may be addressed. Feldstein (1967, p. 145), for example, states:

> Output may legitimately and usefully be defined in any of the four ways: by an index of the services provided, of cases treated, of the number of successful treatments, or of various measures of the community's health. Each definition is progressively more difficult to implement than the preceding one but comes closer to what we want for welfare-orientated comparisons of output.

The majority of hospital cost studies have concentrated upon intermediate output measures, the first two definitions given by Feldstein, largely because measurement problems are less con-straining. Such difficulties nevertheless remain severe.

The literature on hospital cost functions, associated with the intermediate output approach, is, therefore, dominated by the search for a viable output measure normally based upon either a service-mix or case-mix valuation. The literature is generally not concerned with the effect of hospitalisation upon health status. It is important to note that in confining the specification of the production process to the production of the intermediate com-modity health care we also confine the definition of efficiency. The literature then does not address the relationship between health care and health status. It is a voluminous literature and we shall not attempt an extensive review. However, some studies are cited as examples of the methodology adopted.

Output, as stated above, may be characterised by service-mix and case-mix approaches. The earliest attempts to homogenise hospital output were based on the service-mix approach. Carr and

Feldstein (1967), for example, normalise the effect of service-mix by initially including the total number of services and facilities as an explanatory variable in their regression analysis and also by aggregating hospitals into five 'service-capability' groups and running separate regressions on each group. The authors recognise the limitation of this approach in that it assumes all services and facilities have an equal effect upon costs. Both Berry (1970) and Francisco (1970) used similar grouping techniques in an attempt to define homogeneous output measures. However, such crude measures take no account of differences in hospital size, the technical complexity of the services provided or the rate of utilisation of the facilities.

In his review of the service-mix approach, Tatchell (1983, p. 877) makes the point that this analytical approach essentially relies upon the existence of competitive supply-side forces:

> Each hospital is viewed as a competitive enterprise engaged in selling services to patients and doctors. . . . For the hospital system as a whole, output is only partly determined by an exogenous demand. It also depends on 'marketing' techniques and, for any individual institution, on its success in attracting cases which might benefit from the particular service offers. Case-mix thus depends on service availability rather than the reverse.

The author concludes that such approaches are unlikely to be suitable measures of hospital output for the British NHS or other public service systems. However, even in structural settings where this approach would appear to have merit, empirical evidence suggests that service-mix output measures do not capture much variation in costs (Lave and Lave, 1971).

The alternative intermediate production approach is to standardise hospital output with respect to case-mix data. The essence of the case-mix approach is to identify and weight categories of patients, defined by their diagnostic classification, in an attempt to associate costs with diagnostic-specific output, in other words to associate diagnostic characteristics with cost variations – not an unreasonable hypothesis. The catch is that it is difficult to aggregate up across the different categories of case-mix because it is unclear which categories are the heaviest users of hospital resources – i.e. the most costly – which makes it difficult to identify the relevant iso-cost curves. Early attempts to define output were based upon weighting case-mix by average costs or estimated marginal costs (Feldstein, 1967; Lave, Lave and Silverman, 1972). This is somewhat unsatisfactory, given that cost then appears on both sides of the equation. Later attempts have relied upon sophisticated statistical techniques, based upon linear dependency between variables or expected and outcome frequency distributions of case-mix across the hospital sector and may be related to the concentration and diversity measures used in industrial economics. (For further details see, Barer, 1982; Evans, 1971; Evans and Walker, 1972; Jenkins, 1980.)

While measurement problems remain it does appear that case-mix characteristics play a role in explaining the variations associated with cost. The explanatory power of such hospital cost equations increases even further if other patient characteristics, such as age and sex variables, are included. The exact role of such case-characteristic variables is difficult to determine as a number of studies do not pursue problems of econometric estimation. For example, testing for heteroscedasticity, which is likely to be present in cross-sectional data, has not been undertaken uniformly. Certainly this has presented problems for some data sets and has consequently reduced the explanatory power of specified cost functions (Barer, 1982). An outstanding difficulty associated with all such studies arises from the failure to measure case severity, which obviously has resource implications and should, therefore, be included in the cost function.

The normal rationale given for estimating cost functions is the search for evidence on economies of scale. Berki (1972, p. 115), in musing upon the evidence, sums it up as follows:

> the answer from the literature is clear: 'the exact general form of the function is unimportant' . . . but 'whatever its shape' . . . , and depending on the methodologies and definitions used, economies of scale exist, may exist, may not exist, or do not exist, but in any case, according to theory, they ought to exist.

In other words, given the different definitions of output, functional forms of cost function employed and varying data sets, it is not surprising to find a lack of consensus in the literature. Indeed if we remember that hospital production is only one aspect of the health care and social care process, then the empirical testing for scale economies becomes an even more difficult analytical problem.

Considerations of vertical integration means that the scale of the firm may be defined not merely with respect to its final output but also with regard to the degree of integration and the depth of production. An increase in the scale of hospital production, given its relation to the rest of the health care system and its heterogeneous output, may be reflected in an increase in the number of out-patient clinics, or even by an increase in smaller support hospitals within any given area. Therefore, particularly where the system is heavily integrated, such as in the UK, the search for scale economies may be something of a false trail.

It may be more important to concentrate upon other forms of efficiency. However, even here there are considerable difficulties. If, as argued in chapter 10, the atmosphere and the nature of the production process itself are important to consumer satisfaction, even this approach is dogged with difficulties. It is difficult enough to cope with a heterogeneous, yet in some sense tangible output. If costs are also associated with the atmosphere in which transactions are conducted, this adds a new dimension of complexity. To a large degree such considerations have been subsumed under the term quality, and remain to be resolved. Recognition that such intangibles are important has led some researchers to define efficiency with respect to the average cost functions as being behavioural in the sense of describing a particular pattern of resource usage at any particular point in time (Evans, 1971). Such conceptual conveniences are of course not strictly applicable to the definition of efficient cost curves. For this to be the case, the error terms of cost curves should be derived from a one-sided distribution. If this does not hold, then the estimated (average or behavioural) cost functions are only rough, first approximations to the question of efficiency which allow one to pinpoint the position of any individual hospital with respect to the relevant set of hospitals. The determination of hospital efficiency clearly requires further investigation.

A third policy orientated aspect stemming from the estimation of cost functions relates to marginal costs. The estimation of these falls easily out of the regression procedure, as they are simply the first derivatives (i.e. the slope estimates) of the total cost function. Given the problems noted above it is not surprising to learn that there is a wide variation in marginal cost estimates. All costs must be associated with an output and if that output is difficult to define and/or measure then the wide variance of estimated marginal cost may merely be a reflection of this.

Over and above all these specific problems we must deal with the usual problems in the estimation of cost function. For example, is accounting data adequate or should survey data be gained to arrive at appropriate costs? How should we deal with questions of historic cost and depreciation with regard to capital in the hospital sector? What happens if input costs differ across firms leading to different cost structures? Can we impute all costs?

Such difficulties are enhanced by considerations of hospital utilisation. Utilisation is a function of length of stay, occupancy rate and throughput. All are measures of the intensity of resource usage, although it is not always clear as to what is being measured. Thus Lave and Lave (1970) question the interpretation of length of stay as a definition of managerial efficiency suggesting that this variable may also be measuring case complexity and/or the health of the patient at the time of discharge. Length of stay may also be partly determined by the back-up social services available on release, i.e. by the degree of vertical integration. Indeed with specific reference to the Feldstein (1967) study, although the point does hold generally, Lave and Lave (op. cit., p. 298) argue that the analysis of case flow 'seems far too simple both from a theoretical viewpoint and from the way case flow enters the cost function'. Such difficulties in attaching a true meaning to case-flow variables will obviously affect interpretation of the cost curve.

The combined and aggregate effect of such practical problems has to be seen as complementary to the lack of association between the estimated cost functions and the behaviour of the agent under scrutiny – the hospital. To a great extent the literature has been devoted to problems of output measurement rather than explanation and the fact that there is little linkage of the theory of the hospital to the empirical literature merely emphasises this point. As a consequence we have no definition of the objective function to which we can attach the ambiguous notion of efficiency.

11.4 Hospital cost inflation

One area of the literature on the hospital which has at least attempted to emphasise explanation is that concerned with increasing costs over time. Given the fact that the cost increases in this sector have been substantial, the question dealt with is whether or not these increases are justifiable with regard to corresponding output increases and productivity gains or whether other factors, of an inflationary nature, are operating.

As the bulk of this literature is US-based, reflecting the structural conditions pertaining there, in most studies the hospital sector is generally held to be segmented and inherently competitive. At the simplest level inflationary tendencies are held to be derived from demand-pull factors. Rising demand, which is not inhibited by income constraints, given the insurance coverage of the population, is fuelled by moral hazard and is held to interact with an inelastic supply curve resulting in rising prices for health care. This mechanistic pressure is maintained as demand is also held to be inelastic (e.g. see Fuchs, 1972). This simple exposition, which relies upon the separation of demand and supply it will be noted, can be made more elaborate as indeed in Feldstein (1981).

Feldstein, while agreeing that hospital inflation is demand-pull initiated, criticises the simpler expositions of the mechanics of this on the grounds that the supply responses are naive. He argues that hospitals respond to an increase in demand by raising price, not because the supply of hospital care is inelastic but because of the institutional structure and the high demand elasticity associated with the quality of care. He argues that moral hazard leads to increased demand for hospital services. The supply response to an increase in demand is an increase in price; but this does not ration demand because of the third-party intervention of the insurance coverage. The price rises are then translated into cost increases by expanding the utilisation of volume inputs largely through improving the quality of hospital care. Thus hospital cost inflation is demand-pull initiated but is fanned by the institutional structure in such a way that the costs may be associated with unnecessary (defined in terms of medical outcome only) quality of care increases.

This is a crude exposition of the mechanics. The proposed solution is to ameliorate the inefficiencies and distortions in the health insurance market. However, in Feldstein's exposition there is little discussion of the objectives of the main agent: the hospital. There is acknowledgement of the agency relationship but little

223

consideration of supplier inducement and how this, rather than moral hazard, affects hospital costs. It is suggested, however, that hospitals may have philanthropic attitudes towards their employees. Thus the model is useful in analysing the mechanics of health insurance as it operates in a world of supply and demand. Its failure arises from the lack of an explicit model of hospital behaviour and from not dealing fully with institutional realities through an acknowledgement that the consumption of health care, as opposed to that of health care insurance, relies heavily upon suppliers' decisions. Such criticisms are all the more significant given the admitted importance of the supply-type responses.

An alternative view of hospital cost inflation emphasises autonomous supply-side influences. Ironically the increase in the quality of hospital care resulting from demand-pull inflationary tendencies, may be forwarded as a cost-push mechanism in its own right. Some studies have suggested that the utilisation of medical technology, for example, is the prime source of inflationary tendencies in that such technology increases neither output nor productivity. However, there is little discussion of the actual mechanisms involved or evidence on the direction and influence of costs partly due, no doubt, to the extended and vigorous discussion over the definition of technology itself which normally accompanies such analyses. Other explanations related to cost increases (rather than cost inflation *per se*) stress the changed composition of the labour force and the consequent rise in wage levels which accompanies an increase in skill characteristics (Feldstein, 1971; Fuchs, 1969). A large part of the literature on supply influences is concerned with the effects of convention or legislation upon labour costs. For example, it is suggested that unionisation and/or legislation on equal remuneration exerts considerable influence on costs. Monopolistic power and labour cartels are attributed with great strength in such studies, although once again there is little analysis of the employer's (i.e. the hospital's) behaviour. Furthermore, as Gray (1983, p. 100) states, such studies have normally been undertaken without prior detailed examination of hospital expenditure trends.

The difficulties in analysing hospital cost inflation are large and remain largely unresolved. It is a topic where behavioural motivations and the impact of the government, as well as the individual doctor, upon care have not been fully incorporated into the analysis. Nevertheless it is an area which has generated a considerable amount of empirical evidence.

However, whilst a lot of the literature is rigorous, unfortunately the data sources are less so. Definitional problems remain, with inputs and productivity being marginally less difficult to define than hospital output. Measurement problems are particularly hazardous with regard to *real* volume input. Not surprisingly, given the question addressed, the literature is overwhelmingly from the United States, and a general consequence is that the hospital sector tends to be viewed in isolation from the rest of the health care sector. Indeed analysis has tended to focus upon the hospital as an individual economic agent without adequate consideration being given to structural conditions. Where other aspects of the sector are acknowledged, for example, the significance of health care insurance in Feldstein's work, there is a tendency to rely upon the marked distortion of consumer sovereignty with regard to consumption decisions to explain the source of inflationary pressure, with little examination of the influence that the objectives and behaviour of various actors other than the consumer – e.g. doctors, hospitals, governments and insurers – have upon costs in this sector.

11.5 Conclusions

The analysis of the hospital as an economic agent has been pursued largely on an empirical basis. The questions addressed relate mainly to those of economic efficiency or explanations of inflationary trends. Both topics are concerned with a particular level of aggregation – the hospital is seen to be a decision-making unit – and both must be related to theories of hospital conduct. However, the theoretical analysis of hospitals has been developed largely in isolation from the empirical literature. As a result the significance of the structural setting has largely been ignored in the empirical studies. Analysis of the *modus operandi* of the system as a whole, given the importance of its integrated nature, should be a prerequisite to any solution of the controversy over hospital efficiency and inflation. However, the empirical literature has developed as a partial analysis, seemingly content to concentrate upon the problems of defining and measuring outputs, inputs and

225

productivity. Although these are important, it is difficult to see how the resolution of such problems will aid analysis if questions concerning the objectives of this particular agent, and its proper position within the health care system, remain. To some extent such problems are of a political nature and the contribution of economics to their resolution must necessarily be limited. Yet until they are resolved the empirical analysis of the hospital sector will remain severely constrained.

12

The organisation of health care

12.1 Introduction

In this last chapter, the major consideration is to examine what is happening by way of delivery of health care in different countries and some of the central issues involved in this, primarily at a pragmatic level. This is then discussed against the background of the economic framework built up in earlier chapters. Latterly, it is noted that while that economic framework appears relevant everywhere, the interpretation of how best to provide health care within that is subject to variation across the cultures and ideologies of different countries.

The chapter first sets out a brief background to recent trends in health care to allow a better understanding of why issues of organisation and financing often appear so important. Section 12.3 then describes four different health care systems – those of the United States, Canada, the United Kingdom and Australia. Apart from the importance of these countries in the English-speaking part of the world, they also help to exemplify the wide variation in systems that do exist. Thereafter, section 12.4 examines certain key economic issues in health services – cost-sharing, payment systems and competition. Section 12.5 ties these issues together with the ideological debate, before some brief conclusions are presented in section 12.6.

12.2 Recent trends in health care expenditure

In a major review of health care spending in OECD countries (OECD, 1985, p. 9) it is stated that through the 1960s and 1970s, 'expenditure on health has grown nearly twice as fast as GDP'. While there has been some general slowing down in recent years 'there are fears that health spending growth could again accelerate under the combined influence of ageing populations and rapid technical progress' (op. cit., p. 9).

The following tables, reproduced from that OECD report, provide evidence for the period from 1960 of the growth in health care expenditures, its pervasiveness in the countries presented and, additionally, the particularly rapid growth of public sector spending.

First, however, it is of interest to note the absolute differences in spending in different countries. These are indicated in Table 12.1.

Table 12.2 shows trends in expenditure on health both in total and in public spending in the period from 1960, in terms of proportions of GDP. Noteworthy here is the common rapid growth across different countries, although at often quite different rates, and the tendency for public spending to take up a larger and larger share of the total over time.

Table 12.3 shows the elasticities of health expenditures to GDP in constant prices, i.e. the percentage increase in health expenditures for a 1 per cent increase in GDP, in the period from 1960 to 1982.[1] There is a slight fall in the elasticity for total expenditure in the period from 1975 as compared with earlier. The fall in the elasticity for public expenditure is, however, more marked.

Possible explanations for these changes are several. The increased involvement of governments and with that, increased coverage rates have meant increased costs. For the OECD countries as a whole the public share of health care expenditure rose from 60 per cent to 75 per cent from 1960 to the early 1980s, coverage rates rising in the same period from 75 per cent to nearly 90 per cent.

Trends in prices have also been upward and generally much more so in health care than general inflation. This has been particularly true of hospital costs, although a partially offsetting factor has been the substantial fall in the relative price of

Table 12.1 1982 *per caput* expenditure on medical care in US$, 1982

	Measured at current exchange rates	Measured at current GDP purchasing power parity rates
Australia	828	796
Austria	664	684
Belgium	534	636
Canada	989	1,058
Denmark	746	736
Finland	692	629
France	931	996
Germany	874	883
Greece	187	256
Iceland	865	832
Ireland	436	532
Italy	441	607
Japan	602	673
Luxembourg	601	719
Netherlands	836	851
New Zealand	440	481
Norway	930	822
Portugal	132	248
Spain	302	417
Sweden	1,168	1,239
Switzerland	1,158	990
United Kingdom	508	539
United States	1,388	1,388

The second column reflects a broad order of magnitude of the resources allocated to medical care expressed in a common numerary.

Source: OECD (1985).

pharmaceuticals (of about 40 per cent over the 20 years to 1980).

The separate influence of changing utilisation rates is less clear but there is evidence to suggest that the process of population ageing will continue to add to the pressures on health services, largely as a result of higher utilisation rates by older age groups.

At the same time as indicating the generality of the cost escalation in so many different countries, the OECD report highlights the fact that the extent of such escalation varies quite markedly from country to country. For example, while Canada and the United States experienced broadly similar growth rates in

Table 12.2 The share of health expenditure in national expenditure, 1960–83

	% Of total (public) expenditure on health in GDP			
	1960	*1970*	*1980*	*1983*
Australia	5.1 (2.4)	5.7 (3.2)	7.4 (4.7)	7.5 (4.9)
Austria	4.4 (2.9)	5.3 (3.4)	7.0 (4.5)	7.3 (4.6)
Belgium	3.4 (2.1)	4.1 (3.5)	6.3 (5.5)	6.5 (6.0)
Canada	5.5 (2.4)	7.2 (5.1)	7.3 (5.4)	– (6.2)
Denmark	3.6 (3.2)	6.1 (5.2)	6.8 (5.8)	6.6 (5.6)
Finland	4.2 (2.3)	5.6 (4.1)	6.3 (5.0)	6.6 (5.2)
France	4.3 (2.5)	6.1 (4.3)	8.5 (6.1)	9.3 (6.6)
Germany	4.8 (3.2)	5.6 (4.2)	8.1 (6.5)	8.2 –
Greece	2.9 (1.7)	3.9 (2.2)	4.2 (3.5)	4.7 –
Iceland	5.9 (2.4)	8.7 (4.1)	7.7 (6.7)	– –
Ireland	4.0 (3.0)	5.6 (4.3)	8.7 (8.1)	– (7.5)
Italy	3.9 (3.2)	5.5 (4.8)	6.8 (6.0)	7.4 (6.2)
Japan	3.0 (1.8)	4.6 (3.0)	6.4 (4.6)	6.7 (5.0)
Luxembourg	– –	4.9 –	6.6 (6.6)	– –
Netherlands	3.9 (1.3)	6.0 (5.1)	8.3 (6.5)	8.8 (6.9)
New Zealand	4.4 (3.3)	4.5 (3.5)	5.7 (4.7)	– (5.3)
Norway	3.3 (2.6)	5.0 (4.6)	6.8 (6.7)	6.9 (6.2)
Portugal	– (0.9)	– (1.9)	6.1 (4.2)	– (3.9)
Spain	– –	4.1 (2.3)	5.9 (4.3)	– (4.4)
Sweden	4.7 (3.4)	7.2 (6.2)	9.5 (8.8)	9.6 (8.8)
Switzerland	3.3 –	5.2 –	7.2 (4.7)	– –
Turkey	– –	– (1.3)	– (1.1)	– (0.6)
United Kingdom	3.9 (3.4)	4.5 (3.9)	5.8 (5.2)	6.2 (5.5)
United States	5.3 (1.3)	7.6 (2.8)	9.5 (4.1)	10.8 (4.5)
OECD average	4.1 (2.5)	5.6 (4.0)	7.2 (5.3)	7.6 (5.8)

1. *All 1983 figures are provisional.*
2. *Nearest year where no figures available for the exact year before 1980.*
3. *Some of the underlying time series are discontinuous (e.g. Belgium from 1977).*
4. *The OECD average is a twenty-country average, excluding Luxembourg, Portugal, Switzerland and Turkey.*

Source: OECD (1985).

expenditure in the 1950s and 1960s, thereafter Canada's growth rate has been much lower (an issue we return to in section 12.4 below).

Underlying the growth in expenditure in health care are two key factors: one is the nature of the commodity health care *per se* (as

discussed in detail in chapter 3) and the other is the concept of
health care (or at least access to health care) as a right. Aaron
(1981, p. 30) has suggested: 'the recent continuing revolution in
the technology of medical care has inflated the cost of that right. If
all health care that provides benefit to the patient at zero price is
treated as a right, the scope for waste is large and getting larger'.
As Aaron continues: 'Until recently . . . the available technology
made it relatively inexpensive to regard health care as a right, not
as an ordinary economic commodity'. Such a statement presup-
poses that health care can ever be treated as an 'ordinary'
commodity. Earlier chapters have endeavoured to show that it
cannot be so treated and that that is the fundamental issue. It is

Table 12.3 Elasticities of health expenditure to GDP (constant prices)

	Total expenditure on health			Public expenditure on health		
	1960–75	*1975–82*	*1960–82*	*1960–75*	*1975–82*	*1960–82*
Australia	1.0	1.0	1.0	1.7	0.3	1.4
Austria	0.8	0.8	0.8	0.7	0.7	0.7
Belgium	1.5	2.3	1.6	1.9	2.8	2.1
Canada	1.7	1.6	1.7	2.5	1.4	2.3
Denmark	1.9	1.8	1.9	2.0	1.4	1.9
Finland	1.9	1.6	1.8	2.6	1.4	2.3
France	1.8	2.6	2.0	2.2	2.5	2.2
Germany	1.6	0.8	1.4	2.0	0.7	1.7
Greece	1.6	2.1	1.7	1.6	3.6	2.0
Ireland	2.3	1.0	1.9	2.4	1.5	2.1
Italy	0.9	0.8	0.9	0.9	0.7	0.9
Japan	1.5	1.4	1.5	1.7	1.5	1.6
Netherlands	1.5	0.7	1.4	2.9	1.1	2.6
Norway	1.6	1.2	1.5	2.0	1.2	1.8
Sweden	2.5	3.9	2.7	2.9	4.1	3.0
United Kingdom	2.3	1.2	2.1	2.5	0.9	2.2
United States	1.9	1.4	1.8	3.0	1.4	2.6
Average	1.7	1.5	1.6	2.1	1.6	2.0

The OECD average is a seventeen-country average.
*The measure of real health has been established with an implicit price deflator which is subject to
some caveats.*
*Different values are obtained when years other than 1975 or 1982 are selected but the differences
are generally not large.*

Source: OECD (1985).

that which creates the situation in which neither patient nor doctor seeks to or is indeed willing to act as 'rational economic man'. As Maynard (1982, p. 475) states:

health care systems encourage patients to maximise benefits regardless of costs, and producers (doctors) to maximise . . . benefits regardless of costs. Both demanders and suppliers have no incentives to compare and trade-off the costs and benefits of health care at the margin.

This then raises important questions regarding, *inter alia*, the legitimate distribution of property rights in deciding on the allocation of scarce health care resources. In this respect certain features of different health care systems need to be examined in greater depth. This is turned to in the next two sections.

12.3 Health care systems

In considering different systems, this section examines, albeit briefly, four countries: the United States, Canada, the United Kingdom and Australia. While there are other models of health care, these provide a sufficiently wide range of differences for the purposes of this chapter. The point is not to describe the health care systems in detail or at length but rather to point to some potentially interesting features, against the background of earlier discussions in this book.

12.3.1 The United States

The health care system in the US is more market-orientated than is the rule in most industrialised countries. While socialised medicine has never been popular in the United States, the extent of government intervention has been growing steadily. For example, federal, state and local governments now fund approximately 40 per cent of US health care. Direct charges to patients are relatively high compared with other countries and represent about a third of total health care expenditure. This proportion varies markedly with the type of care involved, e.g. 9.1 per cent for hospital care, 37.3 per cent for physicians' services, 82.7 per cent for drugs and 85.5 per cent for spectacles. The remaining sources of funds are private, for-profit, insurance organisations, not-for-profit organisations such as Blue Cross and Blue Shield, and Health Maintenance Organisations (HMOs).

A word of explanation about HMOs is appropriate. These are usually non-profit-making organisations which combine the supply of health care with insurance. They are pre-paid group practices where subscribers pay a capitation fee and receive in return fairly comprehensive health care, either zero or low priced at the point of consumption. Beyond that there are variations between HMOs, for example, in the extent to which they themselves employ doctors and/or own hospitals.

The most important change in recent years in US health care came in the 1960s with the introduction of Medicare and Medicaid. Medicare is run by the Federal Government and is a contributory social insurance scheme largely for the elderly. Medicaid is jointly organised by state and Federal Governments for poor people and is non-contributory. These two programmes represented a major shift in the balance of funding by government in the mid-1960s with some 16 per cent of total health care expenditures being spent on Medicare and 12 per cent on Medicaid.

Access to health care facilities is not universal. While estimates vary, it seems that some 10 per cent of Americans have no health insurance. Further, it appears that the quality of care tends to vary between the insured in the private sector and the uninsured under public care.

Hospitals have been paid largely on the basis of retrospective reimbursement. However, the current movement to prospective reimbursement under diagnostic related groups (DRGs) is leading to substantial changes in hospital management and financing. (More discussion of DRGs follows later.) Doctors are most frequently paid on the basis of fee-per-item of service.

Recently (see Feldstein, 1986) there have been moves towards increased competition in health care systems. Quite how this will develop is not yet clear, although we will come back to the issue in section 12.4 below.

12.3.2 Canada

Canada's health care system is one of national health insurance.

This was introduced in 1971 replacing a system which had been rather similar to that of the United States. It is largely based on the Provincial Governments and there are ten independent health care plans as a result. Federal and Provincial Governments contribute in approximately equal shares about three-quarters of total health care expenditure. The rest comes from private sources. The extent of cost-sharing by patients is small.

Coverage is universal of both people and services. Given the simplicity of the system as compared to that in the United States, it is administratively cheap: the administration of insurance in Canada is about 3 per cent of health care spending compared with about 15 per cent in the United States. Funding of hospitals is largely by prospective block budgets (based primarily on the previous year's allocation). Ownership of hospitals, however, remains largely in the independent, voluntary sector. Doctors are paid on a negotiated fee-for-item of service basis.

The system is thus 'a monopoly *insurance* system, not a *public* service, a monopoly maintained by legislative exclusion of private insurers. . . . There has been little intervention in the delivery system itself' (Evans, 1982, p. 376).

12.3.3 The United Kingdom

In the United Kingdom, there is a National Health Service (NHS) funded primarily by general taxation. Private health care does exist – and has been encouraged in various ways by central government in recent years – but it remains small (about 5 per cent of total expenditure).

Unlike Canada, in the United Kingdom both insurance and provision of health care were taken over by the state. National health care policies are determined by central government but, despite national funding, the service is decentralised to allow considerable autonomy at local level in determining the nature of local needs, the priority to be attached to meeting different needs and the deployment of the budget received.

The total budget for the NHS is determined in competition with other national spending programmes and then allocated out to the local areas on the basis of a needs formula (which takes account of population size, age and sex distribution and an index of health status). There is thus, as in Canada, prospective payment to health care facilities but in the case of the United Kingdom the facilities are owned by the state. Unlike Canada there is at least the potential for intervention in the delivery system itself.

There is little cost-sharing overall, although for certain items – prescriptions for medicine, teeth, spectacles – it has been growing in recent years. Thus overall direct payments account for 3 per cent of NHS funding but in the case of dentistry and ophthalmic services the figure rises to over 25 per cent.

All residents are entitled to receive care under the NHS and there is an explicit espousal of both geographical and social class equity.

All hospital staff are public sector employees. Primary care professionals on the other hand work for the NHS on a contractual basis. Doctors in hospital are salaried; general practitioners are paid largely through capitation payments but to a small extent on a fee-per-item of service basis. Doctors can and do work for both the NHS and the private sector. In the latter, remuneration is invariably fee-per-item of service.

Individuals cannot contract out of the NHS. Those who do use the private sector (about 7 per cent of the population are covered) are insured largely through group or company schemes. Most claims are for elective surgery.

12.3.4 Australia

Perhaps the most noteworthy aspect of the Australian health service in recent years is the extent to which it has undergone change. Largely this 'turbulence' as Andersen (1986, p. 199) describes it has arisen from the attempts by successive governments to pursue equity in the health insurance system.

The basic provision features of Australian health care are those of a private, fee-for-service system. Historically, those who were too poor to pay could obtain treatment at public hospitals.

Medibank, a compulsory health insurance system, was introduced in 1973. Under this at least 85 per cent and in some instances 100 per cent of fees were reimbursed to the patients.

The system was changed in various ways in the period from 1975 to 1983 when the Labour Party were out of government but in 1983 they brought in a compulsory health insurance scheme called Medicare, which is financed through a levy on income tax.

Under Medicare, 85 per cent and sometimes 100 per cent of fees paid are rebated to the patient. Outpatient attendance at the state financed hospitals is free as can be in-patient care. However, for the latter the patient can pay for 'private' care and can then choose their doctor – but at the expense of having to pay both the doctor and the hospital. The former are rebated through Medicare; the latter only through private insurance.

There are also private hospitals. While the more routine care dominates there is 'an increasing trend for private hospitals to develop facilities required to manage patients with complex medical problems' (Andersen, 1986, p. 201).

What emerges from the various changes in Australia remains somewhat obscure although Deeble (1982) casts some useful light on the effect of changes up until that time. He states:

> Those opposed to collective financing attribute virtually all of the cost expansion of the 1970s to the profligacy of public programmes and the weakening of incentives to cost minimization which they are supposed to produce. Those in favour point out that the realistic alternative is not a free market system but private insurance which may be restricted in its coverage, inequitable in its distribution of costs, indifferent to resource allocations, and even less effective in cost containment than its public counterpart.

He also adds, unfortunately, that 'the available material throws little light on these issues' (Deeble, op. cit., pp. 438–9).

These are but four systems: those of the United States, Canada, the United Kingdom and Australia. For a description of others see, for example, Griffiths (1982), McLachlan and Maynard (1982) and Olson (1981).

12.4 Key issues

12.4.1 Cost-sharing

Given its crucial importance in policy terms and the weight attached to it in the literature, the issue of cost sharing is discussed at some length. As stated in chapter 9, it can take various forms.

The arguments in favour of cost-sharing can be simply rehearsed.

By making the patient bear some of the financial cost at the point of consumption and assuming that there is an identifiable downward sloping demand curve, the quantity of health care demanded will be less than if it were zero money priced. The argument continues that the sovereign patient will, therefore, make more rational choices regarding health care consumption, will only consume those services at the margin on which he places a higher value than the marginal cost that he (the patient) bears, will, therefore, be closer to the point at which the socially efficient solution lies (i.e. marginal social cost equal to marginal social benefit) and will be correspondingly less subject to moral hazard.

If there is no (money) cost-sharing, some ill-health burdens may be borne by highly deserving cases, i.e. the willingness to pay features of a market clearing price fail to operate, inefficiency arises, queues are created and in terms of the allocative efficiency of, for example, doctors' time, more lower valued health care is provided (or provided earlier) at the expense of more highly valued health care (or perhaps its delay).

At a more sophisticated level the role of the supplier in specifying utilisation is recognised and it is then suggested that the increased cost consciousness created in the consumer by cost-sharing will in turn be conveyed to the doctor. For example, in the perfect agency relationship it has to be that the doctor is in a position to judge, *inter alia*, the costs involved in his decisions. Where the third-party insurers or the state are picking up the total payment, there are few incentives on the doctor to obtain information about relevant costs.

The argument is thus that cost-sharing provides something which may approximate to the price signals of a market, to both the consumer-patient and supplier-doctor. In so far as health care 'demand' and 'supply' prices assist efficient resource allocation then cost-sharing may help to promote efficiency.

Finally, cost-sharing means that some of the burden of payment is transferred directly to the patient. In other words, *ceteris paribus*, cost-sharing will cut the funding agency's total bill.

How justified are these arguments? For the patient to make more rational choices and weigh up marginal costs and benefits in determining his consumption patterns and levels requires sufficient knowledge and rationality to do so. It has already been argued in earlier chapters that the supply side of the health care market dominates to such an extent that there are limits to how far health care can usefully be viewed in such strictly conventional neoclassical terms.

The case for using cost-sharing to promote allocative efficiency again hinges on the extent to which patients are knowledgeable. For the argument to stand, it requires that the patients who fail to attend because of cost-sharing are those for whom the benefit of attending would be least. Given what has been said in chapters 7 and 8 about the problems underlying Grossman's model of the demand for health, it is apparent that the extent to which the consumer is able to judge the benefit of health care is severely constrained. Cost-sharing may in fact make social efficiency more rather than less elusive. Doctors cannot treat patients who might benefit from such treatment if those patients do not attend for care.

Cost-sharing will normally make the doctor more cost conscious. However, emphasising those aspects of cost borne by the patient will not necessarily lead to increased efficiency. Further if the goal is to increase cost awareness among doctors there are more direct ways of doing this.

Such cost consciousness may have some unintended results. For example, there is some evidence to show that in the United Kingdom when prescription charges to the patients for medicines have been raised, part of the supply response by doctors has been to increase the quantity of units of the medicine on the prescription in an attempt to protect the consumer from the full impact of the increased charge. It remains unclear whether such increased cost awareness has promoted or diminished efficiency.

Regarding revenue raising, it is likely that cost-sharing will result in decreased costs to the funding agency. Whether it will result in decreased total costs (i.e. those falling on both the funding agency and the patient) is however less clear. (Indeed in the instance quoted of UK prescription charges, it is possible that these could have *increased* revenue costs to the NHS not only as a result of the increase in the 'net ingredient cost' per prescription but also because it could have the effect of the price of drugs sold by the pharmaceutical industry to the NHS being raised to maintain profits.)

Barer *et al.* (1979, p. 29) suggest that for cost-sharing to reduce the cost of health care, four assumptions need to be met:

1. patients must be sensitive to prices in making decisions about health care use;
2. private insurance must not step into the gap left by the reduction in public funding;
3. providers of health care must not react to the new increase in such a manner as to offset the initial effect;
4. as a practical matter patients must in fact comply with the coinsurance requirements and pay their bills.

These assumptions are unlikely to hold, or at least not sufficiently, to justify cost-sharing on grounds of revenue raising alone.

There are, however, some possible disadvantages of cost-sharing not yet explicitly raised. First, knowledge by the doctor that the patient has to meet some direct charge, even if that charge does not directly affect the doctor's financial reward, may influence his decision on selection of the 'best' treatment. Now while it can be argued that doctors should take account of cost, (a) such charges are only part of the overall cost and (b) their influence has to be based on the doctor's (almost certainly ill-informed) perception of the ability of the patient to pay. Direct charges also alter the distribution of property rights still further in that in such a situation the doctor not only has influence over the health argument in the patient's utility function but also those related to the patient's financial holdings.

Second, there is the question of equity. Removal of direct charges by no means can ensure equity (see chapter 4); implementing direct charges does, however, run counter to the principle of equity, however it is defined.

Certainly there can be a conflict here between the individual non-paying patient and the individual taxpayer who has to meet the full costs irrespective of his own utilisation (Buchanan, 1965). That conflict is there under any system of financing health care which does not rely on 'pure' demand analysis. It is only the extent of it that varies with the extent of cost-sharing. At a more disaggregated level, Badgley and Smith (1979) in their international survey indicate that in general charging decreases utilisation and even more so for the poor. However, these same authors go on to suggest that under most national health insurance schemes while the levels of co-payment affect cost saving but little, they are important ideologically in indicating interest in value for money. Barer *et al.* (1979) suggest that while charges would be beneficial to many groups, this is unlikely to be true of the public as a whole.

However, this debate needs to be placed in the wider perspective of our discussion in earlier chapters of the lack of relevance of conventional demand analysis. Hurst (1985, p. 140) suggests that in looking at cost containment through cost-sharing it is important to know 'the elasticity of demand for medical care with respect to price, where price variations might occur, for example, through changes in deductibles and co-insurance'. One of the major difficulties here is obtaining measures of demand elasticities: as we have already noted most studies use utilisation measures and not measures of demand. For example, Hurst quotes results from a study by Phelps and Newhouse (1974) showing the following demand elasticities. The figures below are for 'the increase in quantity demanded for a decrease in the co-insurance rate from 25 per cent to zero' (Hurst, op. cit., p. 141).

	%
Physician house calls	108
Dental services	38
Physician office visits	33
Hospital expenses	17
Ambulatory ancillary services	15
Prescription drugs	15
Hospital admissions	8

Hurst then states (p. 141) that 'This suggests that consumers would cut back much more sharply on physician services and dental care than on hospital services.'

However, given the nature of 'demand' it does not appear legitimate to word this statement in these terms. It might be better and perhaps more apposite to suggest that, given the varying nature of the commodity in these different instances, the extent to which agents can influence utilisation elasticities will vary. It might also be possible to suggest that the variation will be a function of uncertainty, ignorance and attitude to risk-bearing by the consumer.

Another aspect that is relevant in this context is cross-elasticities of utilisation. Helms (1978) quotes evidence that increasing co-payment for physician office visits, while decreasing such visits by

8 per cent, increased hospital care by 17 per cent. Regarding insurance against cost-sharing, Hurst (op. cit., p. 44) reports that 'by 1976 nearly two-thirds of elderly patients covered by Medicare had taken out supplementary hospital insurance' most of which seemed to be for Medicare deductibles and coinsurance.

Thus in the context of Barer *et al.* (1979) four criteria for cost-sharing's succeeding in reducing the costs of health care, while the evidence tends to suggest that it does, it is not quantitatively in general a sizeable success and the mechanisms for its success are not as simple as those suggested by straightforward neoclassical analyses.

On cost-awareness and increases in such awareness leading to improved allocative efficiency, obtaining empirical evidence on this would clearly be difficult. However, one interesting aspect of this issue is highlighted by the figures quoted above on the differing elasticities across different services and the impact of cross-elasticities. Certainly both sets of figures suggest that cost-sharing would have an impact on resource allocation across different services. But it is not at all clear whether these changes would result in improved or reduced social efficiency. It may not be at all cynical to note that the costs that physicians are likely to be most aware of in any system of financing are those that directly and indirectly affect the income they receive. Consequently, cost sharing in general is unlikely to be welcomed by the medical profession if it adversely affects their income. It will be unwelcome more specifically in those situations where utilisation elasticities – or what might be termed demand elasticities after the supply response – are particularly high.

While there is, as reported above, growing evidence about the impact of cost-sharing, most of this has been aimed at assessing the outcome in terms of cost-containment, especially in North America. Other aspects – for example, and of particular importance but much more difficult, the impact on health – need further investigation, even in the wake of the RAND study results reported in chapter 9. Certainly, at the most basic level, one of the most disturbing aspects of Abel-Smith's review of cost-sharing measures in twelve European countries is that a vast range of measures have been introduced without, in the great majority of cases, any seemingly apposite evidence based on empirical evaluation on what the impacts of the measures were likely to be

(Abel-Smith, 1984). As we noted in chapter 9, even in the largest controlled experiment to date in this area, the RAND study, there was little consideration of the impact of cost-sharing on provider behaviour.

12.4.2 Payment systems

How different agents in the health care system are paid can have an impact on their behaviour regarding both efficiency and equity. In this section we will briefly consider payment mechanisms for hospitals and for doctors. Not that the evidence in practice suggests that efficiency or equity are primary objectives in determining such payment systems. More often, especially in hospital financing, it seems that administrative convenience dominates such determination.

The central economic problem with any payment system is attempting to devise it in such a way that it provides the right incentives (or disincentives) to promote (discourage) certain types of behaviour among different agents which will allow stated objectives (such as efficiency) to be pursued. In health care in this context, the major difficulty faced is that of measuring performance when that performance involves health status improvements as a major part of it.

Clinical freedom allows each individual doctor to do his best (in his judgement largely) for his patient(s). Certainly such freedom is bounded – particularly by ethical codes. But as was discussed in chapter 10, ethical codes provide guidelines for action rather than prescribing step-by-step protocols for conduct. There is consequently considerable scope for variance in behaviour by doctors within the constraints laid down by ethical codes. Add to that the problems of health status measurement (highlighted in chapter 2) and the difficulties of selecting the most efficient and effective payment systems become apparent.

The most common forms of payment of hospitals are by (i) global budgeting; (ii) *per diem* payment; and now, (iii) diagnostic related groups (DRG) reimbursement.

Under global budgeting, the hospital receives, normally in advance, or largely so, an allocation of funds out of which it has to meet all its expenses (with sometimes the exception of doctors' fees) for some set period (often a year). Such a budget then becomes in essence a financial plan within which the hospital management has to operate. There may of course be some form of contingency fund to which the hospital can apply for additional funds throughout the year, e.g. as a result of some epidemic unexpectedly breaking out. This is the way in which, for example, NHS hospitals in the UK are financed and is a good approximation to the funding mechanism of Canadian hospitals.

The extent of overspending permitted will of course influence how successful such a system is in controlling costs. In most circumstances, underspending of a budget in a particular period has to be returned to the funding agency. It is not surprising that such underspending is then a relatively rare occurrence.

How successful such a system of funding is will be dependent on a number of factors, not least being the mechanism or formula for determining the size of the budget in the first place. If in that determination it is possible to reward efficiency and penalise inefficiency then that has to be a benefit of the approach. In practice such rewarding and penalising are difficult. However, attempts have been made, for example in the UK, to build a series of 'performance indicators' to assist in the determination of the degree of efficiency exhibited by different agents, including hospitals. These however are almost exclusively concerned with intermediate outputs such as length of stay and cost per case (DHSS, 1983). It is clear that if performance indicators exclude health status explicitly then a hospital which performs 'well' on the criterion of, for example, low cost per case may be doing so by providing low quality care. There is a danger, if inadequately designed performance measures are adopted, that such prospective budgeting may create perverse incentives for efficiency.

Certainly such a system of prospective global budgeting can be used (and has been used in the UK) to assist in the pursuit of geographical equity. Thus under the 'RAWP' formula (see chapter 4) in the NHS (DHSS, 1976) the determination of a region's allocation for hospital expenditure was based on applying local demographic and health need indicators to *national* bed utilisation figures. (See chapter 4 for more detail.)

It is also important to note that if hospital financing is based on budgetary principles and considerations which are independent of the financing of other health and social services (for example, community nursing services and homes for the elderly) then there

243

are dangers that any attempts at improving efficiency in the hospital sector may simply increase inefficiency elsewhere. This is particularly the case where different health care sectors (e.g. hospitals and general practitioners) are funded separately. In the UK NHS, for example, where this is the case there is an incentive on the local health authorities, with financial responsibility for the hospitals but not for general practice, to push as many items of expenditure as possible on to the GPs.

A further common payment mechanism is '*per diem*' under which a hospital is reimbursed retrospectively on the basis of a fixed amount per patient day spent in the hospital. This amount can sometimes be varied depending on the nature of the diagnosis of the case or the type of hospital (e.g. acute or geriatric).

It is immediately obvious that again such a system can have perverse effects on efficiency. A hospital manager would quickly appreciate that half as many patients with, on average, double the length of stay will result in the same level of income – but, since it is the early days of stay which are generally the expensive ones, a lower level of cost. Further, if there is no, or only a crude, differentiation in amounts *per diem* for different categories of patients, then there may be incentives created for admitting or failing to admit particular types of patients on the grounds solely of the net revenue (positive or negative respectively) that will result. To improve on that position would of course mean very detailed costing procedures which might not be justified. (It has to be stated, however, particularly for those hospital systems which involve no billing, that for most industrialised countries and certainly developing countries, a much greater investment in hospital costing than is currently occurring would be almost always justified. The general standard of hospital accounting and costing is very poor indeed.)

It is possible to have a mixed system of a *per diem* charge for say basic hotel and perhaps nursing costs, and fees per item of service (such as drugs, laboratory tests, etc) thereafter. Such a process is in principle sound in that it could reflect fairly and accurately marginal cost pricing. However, it would involve a very detailed costing procedure in order to determine even what the approximate marginal cost was in each hospital for each item.

An alternative is to reimburse on the basis of the average marginal cost across all the hospitals being funded. Since marginal cost is a function of the level of output there would be some difficulty in assessing what the average marginal cost was, is or would be (depending on the extent of prospective or retrospective reimbursement). It would also mean that those hospitals with a marginal cost below the average marginal cost would tend to expand that service beyond its technically efficient level and/or use its surplus on that item to allow it to maintain, through cross subsidy, another item at a level above its efficient level of operation.

However, such a system, of what amounts to the best approximation to marginal cost pricing, does have considerable appeal in principle. It is in the practical difficulties, especially in the finer ss and detail of the cost required, that the disadvantages lie.

In part to overcome these disadvantages in the United States, the system of reimbursement based upon diagnostic related groups (DRGs) has been introduced. This system funds hospitals on the basis of their case mix where a particular type of case (a diagnostic related group) has a particular fee attached to it, irrespective of what happens to that particular case in that particular hospital. (In practice some other factors such as patient age and procedures undertaken are taken into account.)

Certainly such a system has some advantages – provided that the extent of 'legitimate' variance across different patients can be allowed for in terms of, for example, degree of severity, home conditions on discharge, etc. However, there has to be some doubt about the extent to which all these relevant variations can in practice be taken into account.

What does the empirical evidence show? Perhaps the best example of the impact of prospective block budgeting is provided by Canada. Hospitals there are primarily independent voluntary institutions but are financed largely by prospective block budgets from the provincial governments. (It should also be noted that cost-sharing is low.)

Comparing the US with Canada, in the 1960s when the health care systems in the two countries were broadly similar, the proportions of GNP spent on health care were also similar. Since 1971, when the health care services have taken different directions with the introduction at that time of Canada's national health insurance programme; while US expenditure has continued to rise to 10.8 per cent of GNP, Canada's share of GNP going to health care has stabilised at a little over 7 per cent.

What has happened in Canada? It seems that as a result of the changes in the organisation of health care in 1971, it has proved possible to exercise greater control over health care spending. Utilisation rates (e.g. bed days per head of population) have stabilised whereas previously they were increasing; relative earnings of health service staff increased before 1971, continued to increase to 1976 but thereafter levelled off; and the growth of intensity (as measured by an index of hospital services per patient day) has slowed markedly post 1971 (Evans, 1984). Whether this has led to greater or less efficiency, 'underfunding' or other 'good' or 'bad' changes, is too early to identify. However, the concern with cost escalation in the United States, the lack of such concern in Canada, response of the Canadian Medical Association and the general popularity of the system among the Canadian people (see Hall, 1980) all suggest that the Canadians have been more successful on these fronts than the US.

The most significant feature of the Canadian system is the prospective block budgeting for hospitals. It is a feature shared with the NHS in the United Kingdom. Not only does it appear to help to keep costs down but it can, if used properly, promote greater technical and allocative efficiency together with delegation of decision-making. As we have argued previously, the question of the legitimate distribution of property rights in health service decision-making is crucial. Whatever the overall level of spending on health care, delegation of decision-making to those who appropriately can make the decisions is an important feature of any system. It also allows the enhancement of clinical freedom if the prospective budgeting system is used in allocative efficiency decision-making down to the level of clinical or specialty budgeting – and clinical freedom then operates largely within that constrained environment. It would seem that it is largely because of concern with rising costs, but also the relative envy of Americans who cast their eyes northward, that DRGs have become so popular in the US. As discussed earlier in this chapter, these however have problems of their own making.

Perhaps this is all best summed up by two Canadians. First of all Hall (1980) suggests that Canadians are generally agreed that their health care system is one of the great achievements of Canadian society. Or more pithily Evans (1980) has remarked that Canadians visiting the USA and feeling ill might be tempted to head to the airport rather than the hospital.

What is surprising in most of the discussions about hospital financing is two things: first, the fact that the developments on this front have not linked up more with developments on medical audit and peer review. At least part of the concern at cost escalation stems from the fact that doctors' behaviour is so variable. Reduce that variability in the right way and costs may be reduced and/or the quality of care on average increased. Second, there has been relatively little discussion about the relationship between hospital financing and doctor remuneration. Let us turn to that.

There are primarily three ways of paying doctors: by fee-per-item of service, by per capitation fees and by salary. Under fee-for-service remuneration, the doctor receives a fee for each type of service provided which may be paid directly by the patient or through the third-party funding agency. This fee can be set in different ways. For example in the United States under private health insurance it is set according to what is called 'customary, prevailing and reasonable reimbursement'. However, most countries operating fee-for-service remuneration do so on the basis of a prospectively determined fee schedule which is set after negotiation between the funders (normally insurance companies) and the providers (the medical association acting on behalf of the doctors).

Capitation fees are paid for being available to treat rather than for treatment *per se*. Thus for example a sizeable proportion of general practitioners' remuneration in the UK NHS is paid on the basis of a fixed amount *per caput* of the population covered in the practice. (As of 1987 this was £7.05 for patients under 65, £9.15 for patients aged 65–74, and £11.25 for patients over 75.) The fee is paid whether or not the patient makes use of the general practitioner and is not affected by frequency of visits. A similar system of remuneration is common to Health Maintenance Organisations (HMOs) in the United States where doctors agree to provide certain types of care, if these should prove necessary, for a fixed per capitation fee.

The final mechanism is salary whereby doctors are paid on the basis of providing a certain amount of their time to perform some broadly defined role rather than a set of detailed tasks. The amount of remuneration is again likely to be determined in negotiation between the medical association and the funding agency. It will frequently vary depending on the age, experience and responsibilities of the individual doctor.

Some types of activities lend themselves more to one form of remuneration than another. For example, dentists are frequently paid on a fee-for-service basis even in public health care systems, at least in part because outputs are more easily quantified in dentistry than in many other medical activities. Recent moves to alter UK dentists' remuneration to either salaries or *per caput* fees are in part a reflection of the move towards preventive dentistry as caries is reduced and the consequent desire of dentists to prop up steadily falling incomes. Indeed, generally, hospital doctors are more likely to be salaried or paid on a fee-per-item of service basis than general practitioners who are more frequently paid on a capitation fee basis. Community medicine specialists are more commonly salaried.

Does it matter how doctors are paid? The answer is likely to be yes. On the margin, *ceteris paribus*, a general practitioner is more likely to treat a patient with a particular condition himself than refer him to hospital if he is paid on a fee-per-item of service basis than if he is salaried or paid on a per capitation basis. This will be true whether it is assumed that doctors are income maximisers or utility maximisers since in the latter case the fee influences the trade-off with whatever in addition to income is assumed to be in the utility function. (However, the effects of variations in fee level from a policy stance are likely to be different depending on what it is that the doctor is maximising.)

There is also likely to be the appearance of highly inelastic demand or, what may be a more accurate description of what appears to be the same phenomenon, lack of relevance of the concept of demand as a constraint on supply. It follows that the doctor in such circumstances is well placed to be a price-setter, especially as frequently it is deemed unethical for doctors to publish information about their fees.

Given the weakness of the conventional notion of demand, the exent to which the doctor can influence the arguments in the patient's utility function and the resultant ability of the doctor to be a price-setter, these are strong arguments for not paying doctors on a fee-for-service basis, especially where the fees are set by the doctor himself. However, at least part of that argument hinges on whether the 'extra' treatment then provided leads to greater or less efficient resource use in health care. As discussed in chapter 8, supplier-induced demand does not necessarily lead to greater inefficiencies, nor is it necessarily unethical. Lacking other information – about treatment effectiveness and the relevant opportunity costs – we simply cannot tell.

Capitation payments and salaries suffer from an apparent lack of incentives to treat. If doctors can pass patients to elsewhere in the system without loss of income, *ceteris paribus*, they will then be more inclined to do so whatever the other constraints on their behaviour. A hospital doctor on a salary may choose, with a given bed availability, to have a longer average length of stay than a faster throughput when the former involves less work and no less income.

Which remuneration system is optimal is not clear. Certainly there is plenty of evidence on differing utilisation rates under different systems, especially showing that fee-per-item of service payments tend to have higher utilisation rates (see for example Gaus *et al.*, 1976). However, the evidence which combines utilisation data with information on health status is less readily available. It is here that the analyses supported by the RAND Corporation are particularly important. For example Ware *et al.* (1986) compared the health outcomes and costs for a group of individuals randomly allocated to an HMO and a fee-for-service system. There were substantially lower costs in the HMO. On health status, those on higher incomes appeared to do better under the HMO while those on lower incomes better under the fee-for-service system. How generalisable these results are is, however, not clear.

12.4.3 Competition

One feature of health economics which is particularly noteworthy is the emphasis on neoclassical economics. This is particularly dominant in the United States literature and since that dominates health economics generally so neoclassical analysis is pervasive in the health care literature; but not all pervasive. In particular the Canadians seem to have been most successful in thinking through what the 'market' for health care is really like rather than trying to fit it into what sometimes seems a potentially empty, but at the same time recognised, economic box.

It is worth quoting a few relevant comments in this context as these provide some indication that economists do not always enter the health care field ideologically neutral. For example, Kahn (1981, p. 495), the then Adviser to the (US) President on inflation, at a conference on the economics of health care stated: 'If we accept competition as the ultimate goal [and it is clear that he does] we then have to confront the question of its locus'.

Again Starr (1981, p. 128) suggests that:

Consumers have an interest in preserving the sense of moral responsibility that professionalism helps to cultivate, and there is a real danger that a corporate state would remove the locus of control and responsibility to a distant tier of management. I think a takeover of medical care by national corporations is the antithesis of what either professionals or patients would like to see.

Indeed it is easy to see how competition and with it neoclassical economics can become themselves goals of health care rather than means to ends. This is an aspect that Evans (1982, p. 379) is keenly aware of. He writes on the subject of price rationing (PR) and non-price-rationing (NPR):

The superiority of PR . . . rests on its conforming with *a priori* ethical principles defined over allocation processes, whatever results these achieve must be the best available, and actual outcome data are irrelevant. . . . If one accepts the faith, then PR is always to be preferred to NPR, and further discussion is pointless.

It is worth noting this competition proclivity of the economics profession in examining recent changes in the US health care system. On the one hand, the existing situation there is described by Guest (1985, p. 1000) as follows:

Government provision for the needy is inadequate and attempts to control costs have so far failed. Government policies of fiscal restraint and the encouragement of free competition appear doomed to failure. Public sectors face extinction as the for-profit sector erodes their economic base. The trend is towards increasing numbers of people being without access to health care forming an unacceptable cost burden on the economy. It is clearly up to government, not the private sector, to respond constructively to these pressing problems.

On the other hand it is argued that competition is improving the efficiency of the US health care system. Thus Feldstein (1986) suggests that 'the public now has greater choice of delivery systems . . . as more parents want to give birth in their own homes and/or use nurse midwives, hospitals have responded with "birthing rooms", to simulate home conditions'. He further suggests that 'Increased concern by business over employee health costs and premium competition among insurers is resulting in greater efficiency in the provision of medical services.' Yet it is difficult to know what Feldstein means by 'greater efficiency' in this context since he goes on to say that 'it is too early to document the effect of market competition on quality'.

Clearly this question of defining efficiency is crucial. Certainly consumers can choose between delivery systems but whether such choice reflects demand for health *care* is less than clear (as the example of 'birthing rooms' quoted above from Feldstein perhaps demonstrates). More cynically one might argue that suppliers will tend to introduce additional aspects of process utility into the patients' 'demand' function. In other words it is far from clear that competition will be about the quality of health care in terms of its impact on health status.

What is clear and admitted by Feldstein is that equity suffers under competition in the sense that the poor may receive inadequate care. He writes (op. cit.) however: 'If a state is unwilling to spend sufficient funds for the care of its poor, then a competitive system will not provide that care.' And he adds: 'The problem is not with the competitive system but with the state.' Yet as Guest (1985) states, private hospitals have been 'dumping' high cost uninsured patients for years. 'Federal, state, and local pressure on the mainly not-for-profit community hospitals to contain costs is incompatible with expecting those hospitals to care for an increasing proportion of high cost, poor and uninsured patients.'

On competition it is of interest to note Enthoven's analysis of the need for competition in the NHS (Enthoven, 1985). Essentially his main recommendation is to convert the NHS into a series of HMOs, which in some respects it already is. He writes: 'When all of the alternatives have been considered, it becomes apparent that there is nothing like a competitive market to motivate quality and economy of services.' Unfortunately, and it is a crucial omission, it is not at all clear what evidence he has to support this statement.

In the debate over competition it becomes apparent that it may well be resolved differently in different cultures because of the different value systems and indeed arguments in the relevant welfare functions. Consequently of particular relevance here is our earlier discussion of the various characteristics of the commodity health care. It is to these issues that the next section turns.

12.5 Which system?

One of the interesting characteristics of health care organisations, as exemplified by the brief outline of four systems in the early part of this chapter, is just how diverse they are. That then raises the question: since they can't all be 'right', which is best? Much of course depends on what is meant by 'right' and 'best'. Clearly 'right' will have something to do with efficiency and equity and 'best' will then be concerned with devising some economic organisation to allow an optimal solution to the use of scarce resources for health care.

In chapter 3, we discussed at some length the nature of the commodity health care and its various characteristics. This suggested that conventional neoclassical markets for health care are likely to fail. What then needs to be discussed is 'what succeeds'? A number of answers are possible but they sit on a spectrum which is encompassed in the phrase 'the market *vs.* the state'. If markets fail can the solution for health care best be found by propping up and regulating the market or by replacing it by the public ownership of health services?

The question of what is 'best' is best left to the reader to answer. In forming a judgement about this however a number of factors are relevant.[2] In particular, against the background of what has been said in earlier chapters, it is important to accept that there may be legitimate differences in the health care utility function of a patient/citizen in Birmingham, Alabama as compared with that of his counterpart in Birmingham, England. The arguments, and the weights attached to them, in the utility function of a pregnant woman may differ in Perth, Australia from Perth, Scotland.

In other words the key issue is not whether the health care system of Australia is more efficient than that of the UK or whether equity is more prevalent in the Canadian system than in that of the US. Rather the question is: given the objectives of the health service in, say, Canada how well is that system performing?

One of the great difficulties here is establishing what the objectives of health care systems are, at least at a level where it becomes possible to assess the extent to which these objectives are being met. It is, for example, one of the problems in the UK NHS initiative on 'performance indicators' (DHSS, 1983) that the indicators being used (for example, cost per specialty bed day) have been devised largely without much thought apparently being given to what objectives are being monitored. Clearly this is difficult; it is also clear that it is necessary.

To give more thought to the objectives of health care is a necessary but not sufficient condition for assessing different systems. Collecting the appropriate data to allow such assessment is also necessary. Thus, despite the enormous potential for assessing the various changes in financing and organisation in Australia in recent years, this was largely not achieved because, as Deeble (1982, p. 439) indicates, 'the collection of policy-relevant data was not a major operational priority'.

Again the recent movement to increased competition in the US is more difficult to assess than need be the case if the objectives of US health care were explicitly stated. For example, as quoted above, Feldstein's defence of competition on the grounds of greater efficiency would be more tenable if his definitions of efficiency embraced some concept of quality or, essentially, health status. Placing responsibilities for inadequate care of the poor on the state rather than on the competitive system is clearly only acceptable if the goal of equity is excluded from those of the competitive system.

This point about different systems having different objectives is made in a particularly cogent way by Culyer, Maynard and Williams (1981, p. 134). It is worth quoting them at some length. They suggest that it is possible to picture two idealised viewpoints on health care. The first:

has as its guiding principle consumer sovereignty in a decentralised market, in which access to health care is selective according to willingness and the ability to pay. It seeks to achieve this sovereignty by private insurance; it allows insured services to be available partially free at time of consumption; it allows private ownership of the means of production and has minimal state control over budgets and resource distribution; and it allows the rewards of suppliers to be determined by the market.

The second:

has as its guiding principle the improvement of health for the population at large; it allows selective access according to the effectiveness of health care in improving health ('need'). It seeks to improve the health of the population at large through a tax-financed system free at the point of service. It allows public ownership of the means of production subject to central control of budgets; it allows some physical direction of resources; and it allows the use of countervailing monopsony power to influence the rewards of suppliers.

They further suggest, following Donabedian (1971), that it is possible to distinguish sharply between two rival ethical bases, on each of which a system of health care can be constructed and justified. The first considers access to health care to be essentially similar to access to all the other good things in society (food, shelter, leisure pursuits); that is, it is part of society's reward system. The second regards access to health care as a citizen's right, like access to the ballot box or the courts of justice, which should not depend in any way on an individual's income and wealth.

That is potentially a useful way to view health care systems and the debate surrounding them. However, we would rather consider the issue more specifically in terms of the arguments in the utility function as discussed earlier, for example in chapter 3 – essentially health status, equity and risk bearing in decision-making. All of these, we would submit, are potentially relevant to the choice of systems even if in some systems it may be the case that a zero weight is attached to one or more argument. For example, much of the US literature tends to be based on a neoclassical view of the world which, à la Hahn (1982) as quoted in chapter 3, includes freedom of choice of health care *system* (as distinct perhaps from health care) as an argument in the utility function. That issue might attract a zero weighting among commentators discussing the merits of the UK NHS.

Let us take each of the arguments of health status, equity and risk-bearing in decision-making in turn. On health status, the question presumably is: how do different health care systems perform in terms of their effectiveness? This apparently simple question turns out to be difficult to answer largely because it is a complicated matter to determine the contribution of health care to health status when so many other variables are also at work. (See chapter 2.)

One question which is more readily capable of being answered is what different health care systems *do* in terms of their use of resources. For example, are some systems more hospital orientated, others more community based? Are some more geared to prevention, others to high technology rescue?

Aaron and Schwartz (1984) made a bold attempt to try to answer some of these questions in their comparison of US and UK health care. The budget limits of the NHS they suggest result in curtailment of particular types of services – those dependent on highly specialised staff and equipment; those where the need is not clearly evident to patients (an example they quote being computerised tomographic scans); services for the elderly; treatments involving large shares of the total budget; and services where the quality of life is low after treatment.

Perhaps of particular relevance here is the discussion in chapter 3 of what constitutes 'effectiveness'. This may itself be culturally dependent. As one British oncologist quoted by Aaron and Schwartz (op. cit., p. 49) stated: 'The main difference between American and British practice (in cancer therapy) is that Americans tend to assume that treatment will do people good and we tend to assume that for many solid tumors it will not do so.' In the specific context of what constitutes effectiveness another is quoted as saying that US doctors 'confuse activity with progress'.

Patients in the UK are perhaps less knowledgeable than their US counterparts and as a result less ready to press for some intervention they have read or heard about. Consequently what may be termed the 'expressed demand' for particular forms of care/treatment is less in the UK.

What is more difficult to judge than this question of (strictly) medical effectiveness in terms of impact on health status is the extent to which there is a difference among patients in different countries regarding the utility of intervention as a separate argument from any subsequent change in health status. This form of process utility may be more important in some cultures than others.

Beyond this question of effectiveness, what about equity?

255

Certainly equity is a much more explicit goal in the UK NHS than it is in the US health care system, although as indicated in chapter 4 it is not absent in the US. There is, as the quotes from Culyer, Maynard and Williams (1981) above imply, a much greater weight attached to equity in health care in the British citizen's utility function than his US counterpart.

It is also the case that while clinical freedom is present in both systems, it perhaps has a wider role in the UK (as indicated in chapter 10) as the doctor is forced to take on the role of gatekeeper and form judgements not only about the effectiveness of care but also the equitable distribution of such limited care over a group of patients not all of whom can receive the medically optimal amount. Whether vesting property rights in clinicians in decision-making over this aspect of equity is appropriate is something that merits more debate (but is not pursued in this book).

Finally on the question of risk-bearing in decision-making, again the degree of importance and success of this is likely to vary across different systems. Given the predominance of fee for service in US medicine it might be argued that this might 'bias' decision-making away from that which would be chosen on straight 'medical need' criteria, which is closer to the UK system. The utility to the patient might then be lessened. At the same time the separation of the US physician from the hospital (of which he is not an employee) and the separate billing of the patient by the physician and the hospital may mean that the US physician can divorce himself much more from economic considerations than his UK counterpart. If true, then the utility to the patient of being able to pass difficult decisions to the clinician may be greater in the US.

12.6 Conclusions

Largely this chapter has been concerned with description – of different systems of health care and some key attributes of these systems. Also the chapter has looked at the trends in health care, particularly relevant being expenditure in recent years.

At the same time, however, much of the economic framework developed earlier has been used in examining systems and the features of cost-sharing, payment schemes and competition.

Conclusions are difficult largely because they involve important value judgements of what the health care utility function 'should' look like, what arguments 'ought' to be contained within it and what weight 'should' be attached to these arguments.

However, the features of the framework we have developed suggest to us (and we believe may persuade others) that health systems which attempt to endorse the principles of neoclassical economics are likely to result in inequity, possibly less effective care, possibly attempts to include largely irrelevant characteristics in the commodity health care and may be less likely to provide the optimal level of utility to patients associated with the decision-making process itself. At the same time we have suggested that these arguments and the relative weights to be attached to them are at least partially culturally and ideologically determined. Perhaps our cultural and ideological biases are all too apparent to the reader.

Notes

Chapter 2 Health and health care

1 The Hawthorne Effect (Last, 1983): The effect (usually positive or beneficial) of being under study upon the person being studied; their knowledge of the study often influences their behaviour. The name derives from work studies by Whitehead, Dickson, Roethlisberger and others, in the Western Electric Plant, Hawthorne, Illinois, reported by Elton Mayo in *The Social Problems of an Industrial Civilisation* (London, Routledge & Kegan Paul, 1949).

Chapter 3 Health care as an economic commodity

1 Strictly speaking there is a distinction between risk and uncertainty (see Knight, 1933). Risk is where the individual feels able to attach probabilities to the states of the world. This point is made in section 5.2.5 and in chapter 7. Also see Hey (1979).

2 Other approaches are of course possible. For example, in the Bayesian approach people can assimilate information as it comes in and thereby alter their preferences. Further, prospect theory may provide an opportunity to take account of process utility more generally. (See Kahneman and Tversky, 1979 and Schoemaker, 1982.)

Chapter 5 The cost-benefit approach in theory

1 Ways of overcoming this problem have been suggested such as the Clarke-Groves tax (see, for example, Ng, 1983). The advantage of this tax is that the individual's utility maximising strategy is to state his or her true

258

CV rather than to exaggerate in an attempt to influence the outcome.
2 Note that Tables 5.2 and 5.3 give values in $US at 1983 prices while
those in the text are in £ sterling and reported in prices pertaining during
various years.
3 In the UK the discount rate for public sector appraisals has been set at
5 per cent by the Treasury based, apparently, upon the SOC (Heald,
1980).

Chapter 7 The demand for health – a household production theory approach

1 For a fuller discussion and critique see Blaug (1980). Also see Deaton
and Muellbauer (1980).
2 See Lancaster (1966) and Rosen (1974).
3 Grossman (1972a) does in fact discuss joint production. However, the
discussion is brief and does not affect his main results in any significant
manner. Indeed the discussion is formulated in terms of a check on the
consistency of the consumption and investment models.
4 See Wagstaff (1986a) for a discussion of the relationship between
structural and reduced-form equations.
5 On the issue of health insurance and the Grossman model see Phelps
(1973).

Chapter 8 Is there a demand for health care?

1 A substantial part of the classic 1963 article by Arrow is devoted to a
discussion of this role.
2 See chapters 3 and 4, and Tobin (1970) and Weitzman (1977).
3 For example see Banks *et al.* (1975), or Dunnell and Cartwright
(1972).
4 Although see Langlois (1986).
5 The target income hypothesis is based on the proposition that doctors
seek to attain a predetermined level of income.

Chapter 9 The utilisation of health care

1 Stoddart and Barer acknowledge the influence of Feldstein (1966) who
pointed out that consumers 'demand' combinations of services (i.e.
treatments) rather than specific services (e.g. an office visit) in the health
care sector.

2   See Pauly (1986) for a full review of this literature.

3   See van de Ven (1983) for a full discussion.

4   See Newhouse, Phelps and Marquis (1980) and Newhouse (1981) for further discussion.

5   Pauly (1986) reviews these studies.

Chapter 10 The supply of health care

1   This agency role should be contrasted with that discussed in chapter 8.

2   See the discussion on forms of coinsurance in chapter 9.

3   This may be an oversimplification given that, in the literature on the economics of regulation, emphasis is upon the extraction of rent by interested groups and not on the maximisation of social welfare. In this context regulation may thus be seen as a mechanism which helps to ensure that full return is gained from the utilisation of medical services.

4   Although our discussion is couched in terms of ethical conduct we are not so concerned with normative aspects of conduct as much as we are with professional standards. We believe ethical conduct defines the boundaries of professional behaviour and is important in this (constraining) sense. Certainly the use of professional practice as a substitute for medical ethics does not, we think, materially affect our arguments.

5   On 'quality' the articles by Donabedian (1985) and Donabedian, Wheeler and Wyszewianski (1982) are useful. For a direct economic analysis see Feldstein (1977).

6   Although see Usher (1977) and Weitzman (1974) and (1977).

Chapter 12 The organisation of health care

1   This then leads into a debate about whether health care should be considered as a luxury good or not. For more discussion see Parkin, McGuire and Yule (1987).

2   Weitzman (1977) and Usher (1977) have both formalised the question. They both stress that, *ceteris paribus*, the effect of distributional objectives and tastes will be fundamental to whether a commodity is optimally provided publicly or privately. Thus, for example, both use standard maximisation techniques to show that whether welfare is maximised by public provision of a commodity (say health care) is partly a function of the variance of consumers' tastes, as revealed in their demand curves for that commodity. Note that this is far removed from the Grossman type of approach (see chapter 7) which attempts to abstract completely from the effect of consumers' tastes.

Bibliography

Aaron, H. (1981), 'Economic aspects of the role of government in health care', in van der Gaag, J. and Perlman, M. (eds), *Health, Economics and Health Economics*, Amsterdam, North Holland.

Aaron, H. J. and Schwartz, W. B. (1984), *The Painful Prescription*, Washington, The Brookings Institute.

Abel-Smith, B. (1984), *Cost Containment in Health Care*, Occasional Papers on Social Administration, No. 73, London, Bedford Square Press.

Acton, J. P. (1973), *Evaluating Public Programs to Save Lives: The Case of Heart Attacks*, Research Report R-73-02, Santa Monica, RAND Corporation.

Acton, J. P. (1975), 'Nonmonetary factors in the demand for medical services: some empirical evidence', *Journal of Political Economy*, vol. 83, pp. 595–614.

Adamsen, L. and Alban, A. (1984), *Consequences of Medical Treatment: Breast Cancer*, Notat 015, Copenhagen, Danish Hospital Institute.

Akerlof, G. A. and Dickens, W. T. (1982), 'The economic consequences of cognitive dissonance', *American Economic Review*, vol. 72, pp. 307–319.

Alderson, M. (1983), *An Introduction to Epidemiology* (2nd edition), London, Macmillan.

Altman, S. H. (1970), 'The structure of nursing education and its impact on supply', in Klarman, H. E. (ed.), *Empirical Studies in Health Economics*, Baltimore, Johns Hopkins Press.

Andersen, N. A. (1986), 'Primary care in Australia', *International Journal of Health Services*, vol. 16, pp. 199–212.

Andersen, R. O. and Benham, L. (1970), 'Factors affecting the relationship between family income and medical care consumption', in

Bibliography

Klarman, H. E. (ed.), *Empirical Studies in Health Economics*, Baltimore, Johns Hopkins Press.

Arrow, K. J. (1963), 'Uncertainty and the welfare economics of medical care', *American Economic Review*, vol. 53, pp. 941–73, reprinted in Cooper, M. H. and Culyer, A. J. (eds) (1983), *Health Economics, Selected Readings*, Harmondsworth, Penguin.

Arrow, K. J. (1969), 'The Organisation of Economic Activity', in *The Analysis and Evaluation of Public Expenditure: The PPB System*, Washington, Joint Economic Committee of US Congress.

Arrow, K. J. (1974a), 'Gifts and exchanges', *Philosophy and Public Affairs*, vol. 1, pp. 343–62.

Arrow, K. J. (1974b), 'Government decision-making and the preciousness of life', in Tancredi, L. R. (ed.), *Ethics of Health Care*, Washington, National Academy of Sciences.

Arrow, K. J. and Hahn, F. (1971), *General Competitive Analysis*, Edinburgh, Oliver & Boyd.

Artells, J. J. (1981), 'Effectiveness and decision making in health planning context: the case of outpatient ante-natal care', unpublished M.Litt. thesis, Oxford, University of Oxford.

Ashford, J. R., Butts, M. S. and Bailey, T. C. (1981), 'Is there still a place for independent research into issues of public policy in England and Wales in the 1980s? A case study from the field of health care: modelling hospital costs', *Journal of the Operational Research Society*, vol. 32, pp. 851–64.

Auster, R., Levenson, R. and Sarachek, D. (1969), 'The production of health: an exploratory study', *Journal of Human Resources*, vol. 4, pp. 441–36.

Auster, R. D. and Oaxaca, R. L. (1981), 'Identification of supplier induced demand in the health care sector', *Journal of Human Resources*, vol. 16, pp. 325–42.

Badgley, J. and Smith, R. D. (1979), *User Charges for Health Services*, Ontario, Ontario Council of Health.

Banks, M., Beresford, S., Morrell, D., Waller, J. and Watkins, C. (1975), 'Factors influencing demand for primary medical care in women aged 20–44: a preliminary report', *International Journal of Epidemiology*, vol. 4, pp. 189–95.

Barer, M. L. (1982), 'Case-mix adjustment in hospital cost analysis: information theory revisited', *Journal of Health Economics*, vol. 1, pp. 53–80.

Barer, M. L., Evans, R. G. and Stoddart, G. L. (1979), *Controlling Health Care Costs by Direct Charges to Patients: Snare or Delusion?*, Ontario, Ontario Economic Council.

Beck, R. G. (1974), 'The effects of co-payment on the poor', *Journal of Human Resources*, vol. 19, pp. 124–42.

Becker, G. (1965), 'A theory of the allocation of time', *Economic Journal*, vol. 65, pp. 493–517.

Berki, S. (1972), *Hospital Economics*, Lexington, Lexington Books.

Berry, R. E. (1970), 'Product heterogeneity and hospital cost analysis', *Inquiry*, vol. 7, pp. 67–75.

Berwick, D. M. and Weinstein, M. C. (1985), 'What do patients value? Willingness to pay for ultrasound in normal pregnancy', *Medical Care*, 23, pp. 881–93.

Beveridge, Sir W. (1942), *Social Insurance and Allied Services*, London, HMSO, cmd. 6404.

Blades, C. A., Culyer, A. J., Wiseman, J. and Walker, A. (1986), *International Bibliography of Health Economics*, parts 1 and 2, Brighton, Harvester.

Blaug, M. (1980), *The Methodology of Economics: Or How Economists Explain*, Cambridge, Cambridge University Press.

Blomquist, G. (1979), 'Value of life saving: implications of consumption activity', *Journal of Political Economy*, vol. 87, pp. 157–64.

Boulding, K. E. (1966), 'The concept of need for health services', *Milbank Memorial Fund Quarterly*, part 2, pp. 202–21.

Brook, R. H. *et al.* (1984), *'The effect of coinsurance on the health of adults: results from the RAND Health Insurance experiment'*, Report No. R–3055–HHS, Santa Monica, RAND Corporation.

Broome, J. (1978), 'Trying to value a life', *Journal of Public Economics*, vol. 9, pp. 91–100.

Broyles, R. W. *et al.* (1983), 'The use of physician services under a national health insurance scheme', *Medical Care*, vol. 21, pp. 1037–54.

Buchanan, J. M. (1965), *The Inconsistencies of the National Health Service*, Institute of Economic Affairs, Occasional paper 7, November.

Buchanan, J. M. and Faith, R. L. (1979), 'Trying again to value a life', *Journal of Public Economics*, vol. 10, pp. 245–8.

Buchanan, J. and Lindsay, C. (1970), 'Financing health care in the United States', in *Health Service Financing*, British Medical Association, London.

Bunker, J. P. and Brown, B. (1974), 'The physician-patient as an informed consumer of surgical services', *New England Journal of Medicine*, vol. 290, pp. 1051–5.

Bush, J. W., Chen, M. M. and Patrick, D. L. (1973), 'Health status index in cost effectiveness: analysis of PKU program', in Berg, R. L. (ed.), *Health Status Indexes*, Chicago, Hospital Research and Education Trust, pp. 172–94.

Buxton, M. J. and West, R. R. (1975), 'Cost-benefit analysis of long-term haemodialysis for chronic renal failure', *British Medical Journal*, vol. ii, pp. 376–9.

Carr, W. J. and Feldstein, P. J. (1967), 'The relationship of cost to hospital size', *Inquiry*, vol. 4, pp. 45–65.

Carrin, G. and van Dael, J. (1984), 'An empirical model of the demand for health care in Belgium', *Applied Economics*, vol. 16, pp. 317–34.

Clarkson, K. (1972), 'Some implications of property rights in hospital management', *Journal of Law and Economics*, vol. 15, pp. 363–84.

Cochrane, A. L. (1972), *Effectiveness and Efficiency: Random Reflections on Health Services*, London, Nuffield Provincial Hospitals Trust.

Coffey, R. M. (1983), 'The effect of time prices on the demand for medical services', *Journal of Human Resources*, vol. 18, pp. 407–24.

Collard, D. (1978), *Altruism and Economy: A Study in Non-Selfish Economics*, Oxford, Martin Robertson.

Colle, A. D. and Grossman, M. (1978), 'Determinants of pediatric care utilisation', *Journal of Human Resources*, vol. 13 (supplement), pp. 115–58.

Collins, E. and Klein, R. (1980), 'Equity and the NHS: self-reported morbidity, access and primary care', *British Medical Journal*, vol. 281, pp. 1111–15.

Corman, H. and Grossman, M. (1985), 'Determinants of neonatal mortality rates in the US: a reduced form model', *Journal of Health Economics*, vol. 4, pp. 213–36.

Cretin, S. (1977), 'Cost-benefit analysis of treatment and prevention of myocardial infarction', *Health Services Research*, vol. 12, pp. 174–89.

Cropper, M. L. (1977), 'Health, investment in health and occupational choice', *Journal of Political Economy*, vol. 85, pp. 1273–94.

Culyer, A. J. (1976), *Need and the National Health Service*, Oxford, Martin Robertson.

Culyer, A. J. (1979), *Expenditure on Real Services: Health*, Milton Keynes, The Open University, D323, Block 3, Unit 9.

Culyer, A. J. (1980), *The Political Economy of Social Policy*, Oxford, Martin Robertson.

Culyer, A. J., Maynard, A. K. and Williams, A. (1981), 'Alternative systems of health care provision: an essay on motes and beams', in Olson, M. (ed.), *A New Approach to the Economics of Health Care*, Washington, American Enterprise Institute.

Dahlgren, G. and Diderichsen, F. (1985), 'Strategies for equity in health and health services in Sweden – some experiences and suggestions', Paper presented at the WHO meeting on Social Justice and Health, Leeds, July, 1985.

Daniels, N. (1985), *Just Health Care*, Cambridge, Cambridge University Press.

Dasgupta, A. and Pearce, D. W. (1972), *Cost-Benefit Analysis – Theory and Practice*, London, Macmillan.

Dasgupta, P., Marglin, S. and Sen, A. K. (1972), *Guidelines for Project Evaluation*, New York, UNIDO.

Davis, K. and Russell, L. B. (1972), 'The substitution of hospital outpatient care for inpatient care', *Review of Economics and Statistics*, vol. 54, pp. 109–20.

Deaton, A. and Muellbauer, J. (1980), *Economics and Consumer Behavior*, Cambridge, Cambridge University Press.

Deeble, J. S. (1982), 'Unscrambling the omelet: public and private health care financing in Australia', in McLachlan, G. and Maynard, A. K. (eds), *The Public/Private Mix for Health: The Relevance and Effects of Change*, London, Nuffield Provincial Hospitals Trust.

DHSS (1976), *Sharing Resources for Health in England: Report of the Resource Allocation Working Party*, London, HMSO ('The RAWP Report').

DHSS (1980), *Report of a Research Working Group on Inequalities in Health*, London, DHSS ('The Black Report').

DHSS (1983), *Performance Indicators: National Summary for 1981*, London, DHSS.

Donabedian, A. (1971), 'Social responsibility for personal health services: an examination of basic values', *Inquiry*, vol. 8, pp. 3–19.

Donabedian, A. (1983), 'The quality of care in a health maintenance organisation: a personal view', *Inquiry*, vol. 20, pp. 218–22.

Donabedian, A. (1985), 'The epidemiology of quality', *Inquiry*, vol. 22, pp. 282–92.

Donabedian, A., Wheeler, J. C. and Wyszewianski, L. (1982), 'Quality, cost and health: an integrative model', *Medical Care*, vol. 20, pp. 975–92.

Dowie, J. (1975), 'The portfolio approach to health behaviour', *Social Science and Medicine*, vol. 9, pp. 619–31.

Dreze, J. H. (1962), 'L'utilité sociale d'une vie humaine', *Revue Français de Recherche Operationnelle*, vol. 22, pp. 139–55.

Dreze, J. and Stern, N. (1985), *The Theory of Cost-Benefit Analysis*, Coventry, University of Warwick, Department of Economics, Discussion Paper No. 59.

Drummond, M. F. (1980), *Principles of Economic Appraisal in Health Care*, Oxford, Oxford University Press.

Drummond, M. F. (1981), *Studies in Economic Appraisal in Health Care*, Oxford, Oxford University Press.

Drummond, M. F., Ludbrook, A., Lowson, K. and Steele, A. (1986), *Studies in Economic Appraisal in Health Care Vol. 2*, Oxford, Oxford University Press.

Dunnell, K. and Cartwright, A. (1972), *Medicine-Takers, Prescribers and Hoarders*, London, Routledge & Kegan Paul.

Bibliography

Edgeworth, F. Y. (1881), *Mathematical Psychics*, London, London School of Economics.

Elwood, P. C., Waters, W. E., Green, W. J. and Wood, M. M. (1967), 'Evaluation of a screening survey for anaemia in adult non-pregnant women', *British Medical Journal*, vol. 4, pp. 714–17.

Enthoven, A. (1978), 'Consumer choice health plan, parts I and II', *New England Journal of Medicine*, vol. 298, pp. 650–8, 709–20.

Enthoven, A. (1981), 'The behavior of health care agents: provider behavior', in van der Gaag, J. and Perlman, M. (eds), *Health, Economics and Health Economics*, Amsterdam, North Holland.

Enthoven, A. C. (1985), *Reflections on the Management of the NHS*, Occasional Paper No. 5, London, Nuffield Provincial Hospitals Trust.

Evans, R. G. (1971), 'Behavioural cost functions', *Canadian Journal of Economics*, vol. 4, pp. 198–215.

Evans, R. G. (1974), 'Supplier-induced demand: some empirical evidence and implications', in Perlman, M. (ed.), *The Economics of Health and Medical Care*, New York, John Wiley; London, Macmillan.

Evans, R. G. (1980), 'Is health care better in Canada than in the US?', Paper presented at the University Consortium for Research on North America Seminar, Cambridge, Mass.

Evans, R. G. (1981), 'Incomplete vertical integration: the distinctive structure of the health-care industry', in van der Gaag, J. and Perlman, M. (eds), *Health, Economics and Health Economics*, Amsterdam, North Holland.

Evans, R. G. (1982), 'Health care in Canada: patterns of funding and regulation', in McLachlan, G. and Maynard, A. K. (eds), *The Public/Private Mix for Health: The Relevance and Effects of Change*, London, Nuffield Provincial Hospitals Trust.

Evans, R. G. (1984), *Strained Mercy: The Economics of Canadian Health Care*, Toronto, Butterworths.

Evans, R. G. and Walker, H. D. (1972), 'Information theory and the analysis of hospital cost structure', *Canadian Journal of Economics*, vol. 5, pp. 398–418.

Evans, R. G., Parish, E. M. A. and Sully, F. (1973), 'Medical productivity, scale effects, and demand generation', *Canadian Journal of Economics*, vol. 6, pp. 376–93.

Evans, R. G. and Wolfson, A. D. (1980), *Faith, Hope and Charity: Health Care in the Utility Function*, Department of Economics, Discussion Paper No. 80–46, Vancouver, University of British Columbia.

Feldstein, M. S. (1967), *Economic Analysis for Health Service Efficiency*, Amsterdam, North Holland.

Feldstein, M. S. (1971), 'Hospital cost inflation: a study of non profit price dynamics', *American Economic Review*, vol. 61, pp. 853–72.

Feldstein, M. S. (1974), 'Econometric studies in health economics' in

Intriligator, M. D. and Kendrick, D. A. (eds), *Frontiers of Quantitative Economics*, Amsterdam, North Holland.

Feldstein, M. S. (1977), 'Quality change and the demand for hospital care', *Econometrica*, vol. 45, pp. 1681–702.

Feldstein, M. S. (1981), *Hospital Costs and Health Insurance*, Boston, Harvard University Press.

Feldstein, M. S., Piot, M. A. and Sundaresan, K. J. (1973), 'Resource allocation model for public health planning: a case study of tuberculosis control', Geneva, WHO (supplement to vol. 48 of the *Bulletin of the World Health Organisation*).

Feldstein, P. J. (1966), 'Research on the demand for health services', *Milbank Memorial Fund Quarterly*, vol. 44, pp. 128–62.

Feldstein, P. J. (1986), 'The emergence of market competition in the US health care system: its causes, likely structure and implications', *Health Policy*, vol. 6, pp. 1–20.

Francisco, E. W. (1970), 'Analysis of cost variations amongst short-term general hospitals', in H. E. Klarman (ed.), *Empirical Studies in Health Economics*, Baltimore, Johns Hopkins Press.

Fuchs, V. R. (1969), *Production and Productivity in the Service Industries*, NBER Studies in Income and Wealth No. 34, New York, Columbia University Press.

Fuchs, V. R. (1970), Comment on 'Price elasticity of demand for short-term general hospital services' by G. Rosenthal in H. E. Klarman (ed.), *Empirical Studies in Health Economics*, Baltimore, Johns Hopkins Press.

Fuchs, V. R. (1972), 'The basic forces influencing the costs of medical care', in Fuchs, V. R., (ed.), *Essays in the Economics of Health and Medical Care*, New York, National Bureau of Economic Research.

Fuchs, V. R. (1978), 'The supply of surgeons and the demand for operations', *Journal of Human Resources*, vol. 13 (supplement), pp. 35–56.

Fuchs, V. R. (1979), 'Economics, health and post-industrial society', *Milbank Memorial Fund Quarterly*, vol. 57, pp. 153–82.

Fuchs, V. R. and Kramer, M. J. (1972), *Determinants of expenditures for physician's services in the United States, 1948–1968*, NBER Occasional Paper no. 17, New York, National Bureau of Economic Research.

Furubotn, E. and Pejovich, S. (1972), 'Property rights and economic theory: a survey of recent literature', *Journal of Economic Literature*, vol. 10, pp. 1137–62.

Gaus, C., Cooper, B. and Hirschman, C. (1976), 'Contrast in HMO and fee-for-service performance', *Social Security Bulletin*, vol. 39, pp. 3–14.

Geiser, E. E. and Menz, F. C. (1976), 'The effectiveness of public dental care programs', *Medical Care*, vol. 14, pp. 189–98.

Ghosh, D., Lees, D. and Seal, W. (1975), 'Optimal motorway speed and some valuations of time and life', *Manchester School*, vol. 433, pp. 134–43.

Glass, N. (1979), 'Evaluation of health service developments', in Lee, K. (ed.), *Economics and Health Planning*, London, Croom Helm, pp. 100–117.

Le Grand, J. (1978), 'The distribution of public expenditure and the case of health care', *Economica*, vol. 45, pp. 125–42.

Le Grand, J. and Rabin, M. (1986), 'Trends in British health inequality, 1931 to 1983', in Culyer, A. and Johnsonn, B. (eds), *Public and Private Health Services: Complementarities and Conflicts*, Oxford, Basil Blackwell.

Gravelle, H. S. E., Simpson, P. R. and Chamberlain, J. (1982), 'Breast cancer screening and health service costs', *Journal of Health Economics*, vol. 1, pp. 185–207.

Gray, A. M. (1983), The Rising Cost of Scottish Hospitals; 1951–1981, Unpublished PhD Thesis, Aberdeen, University of Aberdeen.

Griffiths, A. (1982), 'Health economics and financing of health services', in *Health Services in Europe*, Copenhagen, WHO Regional Office for Europe.

Grossman, M. (1972a), *The Demand for Health: A Theoretical and Empirical Investigation*, New York, National Bureau of Economic Research.

Grossman, M. (1972b), 'On the concept of health capital and the demand for health', *Journal of Political Economy*, vol. 80, pp. 223–55.

Grossman, M. (1975), 'The correlation between health and schooling', in Terleckyj, N. E. (ed.), *Household Production and Consumption*, New York, National Bureau of Economic Research.

Guest, D. B. (1985), 'Health care policies in the United States: can the "American Way" succeed?', *Lancet*, November, pp. 997–1000.

Hahn, F. (1982), 'On some difficulties of the utilitarian economist', in Sen, A. and Williams, B. (eds), *Utilitarianism and Beyond*, Cambridge, Cambridge University Press.

Hall, E. M. (1980), *Canada's National-Provincial Health Program for the 1980s*, Ottowa, Health and Welfare Canada.

Hampton, J. R. (1983), 'The end of clinical freedom', *British Medical Journal*, vol. 287, pp. 1237–8, (leading article).

Harris, J. E. (1977), 'The internal organisation of hospitals: some economic implications', *The Bell Journal of Economics*, vol. 8, pp. 467–82.

Harrison, A. J. (1974), *The Economics of Transport Appraisal*, New York, John Wiley.

Harsanyi, J. C. (1982), 'Morality and the theory of rational behaviour', in Sen, A. and Williams, B. (eds), *Utilitarianism and Beyond*, Cambridge, Cambridge University Press.

Hay, J. and Leahy, M. J. (1982), 'Physician-induced demand: an empirical analysis of the consumer information gap', *Journal of Health Economics*, vol. 1, pp. 217–309.

Heald, D. (1980), 'The economic and fundamental control of UK nationalised industries', *Economic Journal*, vol. 90, pp. 243–65.

Helms, R. B. (1978), 'Contemporary health policy: dealing with the cost of care', in Fellner, W. (ed.), *Contemporary Economic Problems*, Washington, American Enterprise Institute.

Henderson, J. B., Beattie, C. P., Hale, E. G. and Wright, T. (1984), 'The evaluation of new services: possibilities for preventing congenital toxoplasmosis', *International Journal of Epidemiology*, vol. 13, pp. 65–71.

Henderson, J. B., McGuire, A. and Parkin, D. (1984a), *Acute Hospital Beds for Fife – I Appraisal of Options*, Health Economics Research Unit, SOAP 3, Aberdeen, University of Aberdeen.

Henderson, J. B., McGuire, A. and Parkin, D. (1984b), *Acute Hospital Beds for Fife – II Using Economics in Health Service Planning*, Health Economics Research Unit, SOAP 5, Aberdeen, University of Aberdeen.

Henderson, P. D. (1968), 'Investment criteria for public enterprises' in Turvey, R. (ed.), *Public Enterprise*, Harmondsworth, Penguin.

Hershey, J. C., Luft, H. S. and Gianaris, J. M. (1975), 'Making sense out of utilisation data', *Medical Care*, vol. 13, pp. 838–54.

Hershey, J. C., Kunreuther, H., Schwartz, S. and Williams, S. (1984), 'Health insurance and competition: would people choose what is expected?', *Inquiry*, vol. 21, pp. 349–60.

Hey, J. D. (1979), *Uncertainty in Microeconomics*, Oxford, Martin Robertson.

Hey, J. D. (1982), 'Whither uncertainty?' *Economic Journal*, vol. 92, supplement, pp. 130–9.

Hume, D. (1736), *Treatise on Human Nature*: reprinted in Selby-Bigge, L. A. (1897), *British Moralists*, Oxford, Oxford University Press.

Hurst, J. M. (1985), *Financing Health Services in the United States, Canada and Britain*, London, King Edward's Hospital Fund.

Illsley, R. and Svensson, P. G. (1986), *The Health Burden of Social Inequities*, Copenhagen, WHO Regional Office for Europe.

Jenkins, A. W. (1980), 'Multiproduct cost analysis: service and case-type cost equations for Ontario hospitals', *Applied Economics*, vol. 12, pp. 103–13.

Jones, I. G. and Cameron, D. (1984), 'Social class analysis – an embarrassment to epidemiology', *Community Medicine*, vol. 6, pp. 37–46.

Jones-Lee, M. W. (1976), *The Value of Life: An Economic Analysis*, London, Martin Robertson.

Jones-Lee, M. W. (1979), 'Trying to value a life – why Broome does not sweep clean', *Journal of Public Economics*, vol. 10, pp. 249–56.

Jones-Lee, M. W. (1980), Review of Collard, op. cit., *Economica*, pp. 204–5.

Jones-Lee, M. W. (1985), 'The value of life and safety: a survey of recent developments', *The Geneva Papers on Risk and Insurance*, vol. 10, pp. 141–73.

Jones-Lee, M. W., Hammerton, M. and Philips, P. R. (1985), 'The value of safety: results of a national sample survey', *The Economic Journal*, vol. 95, pp. 49–72.

Kahn, A. E. (1981), 'Health care economics: paths to structural reform', in Olson, M. (ed.), *A New Approach to the Economics of Health Care*, Washington, American Enterprise Institute.

Kahneman, D. and Tversky, A. (1979), 'Prospect theory: an analysis of decision under risk', *Econometrica*, vol. 47, pp. 263–91.

Keeler, E. B. *et al.* (1985), *How free care reduced hypertension of participants in the RAND health insurance experiment*, Report No. R–3326–HNS, Santa Monica, RAND Corporation.

Keeney, R. L. (1982), 'Evaluating mortality risks from an organisation perspective', in Jones-Lee, M. W. (ed.), *The Value of Life and Safety*, Amsterdam, North Holland.

Kind, P., Rosser, R. and Williams, A. (1982), 'Valuation of quality of life: some psychometric evidence', in Jones-Lee, M. W. (ed.), *The Value of Life and Safety*, Amsterdam, North Holland.

Knight, F. H. (1933), *Risk, Uncertainty and Profit*, Boston, Houghton Mifflin.

Kuhn, T. S. (1962), *The Structure of Scientific Revolutions*, Chicago, University of Chicago Press.

Lancaster, K. (1966), 'A new approach to consumer theory', *Journal of Political Economy*, vol. 74, pp. 132–57.

Langlois, R. N. (ed.) (1986), *Economics as Process: Essays in the New Institutional Economics*, Cambridge, Cambridge University Press.

Last, J. M. (ed.) (1983), *A Dictionary of Epidemiology*, Oxford, Oxford University Press, for the International Epidemiology Association.

Lave, J. R. and Lave, L. B. (1970), 'Hospital cost functions', *American Economic Review*, vol. 60, pp. 379–95.

Lave, J. R. and Lave, L. B. (1971), 'The extent of role differentiation among hospitals', *Health Services Research*, vol. 16, pp. 15–38.

Lave, J. R., Lave, L. B. and Silverman, L. P. (1972), 'Hospital cost estimation controlling for case-mix', *Applied Economics*, vol. 4, pp. 165–80.

Layard, R. (1972) (ed.), *Cost-Benefit Analysis: Selected Readings*, Harmondsworth, Penguin.

Lee, M. L. (1971), 'A conspicuous production theory of hospital behavior', *Southern Economic Journal*, vol. 38, pp. 48–58.

Lees, D. S. (1962), 'The logic of the British National Health Service', *Journal of Law and Economics*, vol. 5, pp. 111–18.

Lindsay, C. M. (1969), 'Medical care and the economics of sharing', *Economica*, pp. 531–7. Reprinted in Cooper, M. H. and Culyer, A. J. (eds), *Health Economics* (1973), Harmondsworth, Penguin.

Lindsay, C. M. and Buchanan, J. M. (1970), 'The organisation and financing of medical care in the United States', in *Health Service Financing*, A report commissioned by the British Medical Association, London, BMA.

Linnerooth, J. (1982), 'Murdering statistical lives?' in Jones-Lee, M. W. (ed.), *The Value of Life and Safety*, Amsterdam, North Holland.

Logan, R. F. L., Klein, R. E. and Ashley, J. S. A. (1971), 'Effective management of health', *British Medical Journal*, vol. ii, pp. 519–21.

Ludbrook, A. (1986), *Identifying Options: Community Services in Bromley*, Health Economics Research Unit, SOAP 9, Aberdeen, University of Aberdeen.

McCarthy, M. (1982), *Epidemiology and Policies for Health Planning*, London, King Edward's Hospital Fund.

McGuire, A. J. (1986), 'Ethics and resource allocation: an economist's view', *Social Science and Medicine*, vol. 22, pp. 1167–74.

McGuire, A. and Mooney, G. H. (1985), *Back to Life: Resurrecting the Value of Life Debate*, Discussion paper 05/85, Health Economics Research Unit, Aberdeen, University of Aberdeen.

McKeown, T. (1976), *The Role of Medicine: Dream, Mirage or Nemesis?*, London, Nuffield Provincial Hospitals Trust.

McKeown, T. (1979), *The Role of Medicine: Dream, Mirage or Nemesis?* (2nd edition), Oxford, Basil Blackwell.

McLachlan, G. and Maynard, A. K. (eds) (1982), *The Public/Private Mix for Health: The Relevance and Effects of Change*, London, Nuffield Provincial Hospitals Trust.

Manning, W. G. *et al.* (1981), 'A two part model of the demand for medical care: preliminary results from the Health Insurance Study', in van der Gaag, J. and Perlman, M. (eds), *Health, Economics and Health Economics*, Amsterdam, North Holland.

Manning, W. G. *et al.* (1984), 'A controlled trial of the effect of a prepaid group practice on use of services', *New England Journal of Medicine*, vol. 310, pp. 1505–10.

Margolis, H. (1982), *Selfishness, Altruism and Rationality*, Cambridge, Cambridge University Press.

Marin, A. (1983), 'Your money or your life', *Three Banks Review*, vol. 138, pp. 20–37.

Marin, A. and Psacharopoulos, G. (1982), 'The reward for risk in the labor market: evidence from the UK and a reconciliation with other studies', *Journal of Political Economy*, vol. 90, pp. 827–53.

Marshall, A. (1890), *Principles of Economics*, London, Macmillan.

Mather, H. G., Pearson, W. G., Read, K. L. *et al.* (1971), 'Acute myocardial infarction: home and hospital treatment', *British Medical Journal*, vol. iii, pp. 334–8.

Maynard, A. K. (1982), 'The regulation of public and private health care markets', in McLachlan, G. and Maynard, A. K. (eds) (1982), *The Public/Private Mix for Health: The Relevance and Effects of Change*, London, Nuffield Provincial Hospitals Trust.

Maynard, A. K. and Ludbrook, A. (1981), 'Thirty years of fruitless endeavour?: an analysis of government intervention in the health care market', in van der Gaag, J. and Perlman, M. (eds), *Health, Economics and Health Economics*, Amsterdam, North Holland.

Melinek, S. J. (1974), 'A method of evaluating human life for economic purposes', *Accident Analysis and Prevention*, vol. 6, pp. 103–14.

Melinek, S. J., Woolley, S. K. D. and Baldwin, R. (1973), *Analysis of a Questionnaire on Attitudes to Risk*, Borehamwood, Joint Fire Research Organisation, Fire Research Note 962.

Mill, J. S. (1909), *Principles of Political Economy*, London, Longman, Green & Co.

Mishan, E. J. (1971), *Cost Benefit Analysis*, London, Allen & Unwin.

Mishan, E. J. (1974), 'Flexibility and consistency in project evaluation', *Economica*, vol. 41, pp. 81–96.

Mishan, E. J. (1975), *Cost Benefit Analysis* (2nd edition), London, Allen & Unwin.

MMWR (1986), 'Premature mortality due to malignant neoplasms – United States, 1983', *Journal of the American Medical Association*, vol. 256, pp. 821–8.

Mooney, G. H. (1977), *The Valuation of Human Life*, London, Macmillan.

Mooney, G. H. (1982), 'Breast cancer screening: a study in cost-effectiveness analysis', *Social Science and Medicine*, vol. 14, pp. 1277–1283.

Mooney, G. H. (1983), 'Equity in health care: confronting the confusion', *Effective Health Care*, vol. 1, pp. 179–85.

Mulligan, P. J. (1977), *Willingness to pay for decreased risk from nuclear plant accidents*, Working Paper No. 3, Energy Extension Programs, Pennsylvania State University.

Muurinen, J. M. (1982), 'Demand for health: a generalised Grossman model', *Journal of Health Economics*, vol. 1, pp. 5–28.

Nash, C. A., Pearce, D. W. and Stanley, J. K. (1975), 'An evaluation of cost-benefit analysis criteria', *Scottish Journal of Political Economy*, vol. 22, pp. 121–34.

National Center for Health Statistics (1983), *Health, United States, 1983*,

DHHS Pub. No. (PHS) 84–1232, Public Health Service, Washington, US Government Printing Office.

Needleman, L. (1980), 'The valuation of changes in the risk of death by those at risk', *Manchester School*, vol. 48, pp. 229–54.

Nelson, W. and Swint, J. M. (1976), 'Cost-benefit analysis of fluoridation in Houston, Texas', *Journal of Public Health Dentistry*, vol. 36, pp. 88–95.

Neumann, J. von and Morgenstern, O. (1944), *Theory of Games and Economic Behavior*, Princeton, Princeton University Press.

New English Bible (1970), Oxford, Oxford University Press; Cambridge, Cambridge University Press.

Newhouse, J. P. (1970), 'Toward a theory of non-profit institutions: an economic model of the hospital', *American Economic Review*, vol. 60, pp. 64–74.

Newhouse, J. P. (1977), *American Economic Review*, vol. 60, pp. 64–74.

Newhouse, J. P. (1974), 'A design for a health insurance experiment', *Inquiry*, vol. 11, pp. 5–27.

Newhouse, J. P. (1981), 'The demand for medical care services: a retrospective and perspective', in van der Gaag, J. and Perlman, M. (eds), *Health, Economics and Health Economics*, Amsterdam, North Holland.

Newhouse, J. P. and Phelps, C. E. (1974), 'Price and income elasticities for medical care services', in Perlman, M. (ed.), *The Economics of Health and Medical Care*, London, Macmillan.

Newhouse, J. P. and Phelps, C. E. (1976), 'New estimates of price and income elasticities of medical services', in Rossette, R. N. (ed.), *The Role of Health Insurance in Health Services Sector*, New York, National Bureau of Economic Research.

Newhouse, J. P., Phelps, C. E. and Marquis, S. E. (1980), 'On having your cake and eating it too', *Journal of Econometrics*, vol. 13, pp. 365–90.

Newhouse, J. P. *et al.* (1981), 'Some interim results from a controlled trial of cost sharing in health insurance', *New England Journal of Medicine*, vol. 30, pp. 1501–7.

Newhouse, J. P. and Marquis, S. E. (1978), 'The norms hypothesis and the demand for medical care', *Journal of Human Resources*, vol. 13 (supplement), pp. 159–82.

Ng, Y.-K. (1983), *Welfare Economics: Introduction and Development of Basic Concepts* (2nd edition), London, Macmillan.

OECD (1985), *Measuring Health Care 1960–1983: Expenditure, Costs and Performance*, Paris, OECD.

Olson, M. (ed.) (1981), *A New Approach to the Economics of Health Care*, Washington, American Enterprise Institute.

OPCS (1978a), *General Household Survey 1975*, London, HMSO.

Bibliography

OPCS (1978b), *Occupational Mortality 1970–72*, OPCS Series DS No. 1, London, HMSO.

OPCS (1985), *Hospital In-Patient Enquiry 1983: Main Tables*, OPCS Series MB4, no. 23, London, HMSO.

OPCS (1986), *Mortality Statistics 1984*, OPCS Series DH1, no. 16, London, HMSO.

OPCS/RCGP/DHSS (1986), *Third National Study of Morbidity Statistics From General Practice, 1981–2*, OPCS Series MB5, London, HMSO.

Parkin, D. W. and Henderson, J. B. (1985), *Estimating the Costs of Patients' and Visitors' Travel to Hospital*, Health Economics Research Unit, SOAP 6, Aberdeen, University of Aberdeen.

Parkin, D. W., McGuire, A. and Yule, B. F. (1987), 'Aggregate health care expenditures and national income: is health care a luxury good?', *Journal of Health Economics*, vol. 6.

Parkin, D. W. and Yule, B. F. (1984), *Economic Interpretations of Supplier Inducement*, Health Economics Research Unit, Discussion Paper No. 03/84, Aberdeen, University of Aberdeen.

Pauker, S. P. and Pauker, S. G. (1977), 'Prenatal diagnosis: a directive approach using decision analysis', *The Yale Journal of Biology and Medicine*, vol. 50, pp. 275–89.

Pauly, M. V. (1968), 'The economics of moral hazard: a comment', *American Economic Review*, vol. 57, pp. 231–7.

Pauly, M. V. (1978), 'Is medical care different?', in Greenberg, W. (ed.), *Competition in the Health Care Sector*, Proceedings of a conference sponsored by Bureau of Economics, Federal Trade Commission, Germanstown, Aspen Systems.

Pauly, M. V. (1980), *Doctors and Their Workshops: Economic Models of Physician Behavior*, NBER monograph, Chicago, University of Chicago Press.

Pauly, M. V. (1986), 'Taxation, health insurance, and market failure in the medical economy', *Journal of Economic Literature*, vol. 24, pp. 629–75.

Pauly, M. and Redisch, M. (1973), 'The not-for-profit hospital as a physician's co-operative', *American Economic Review*, vol. 63, pp. 87–100.

Pearce, D. W. and Nash, C. A. (1981), *The Social Appraisal of Projects: A Text in Cost-Benefit Analysis*, London, Macmillan.

Petch, M. C. (1983), 'Active management of myocardial infarction', *British Medical Journal*, vol. 286, pp. 1841–2.

Phelps, C. E. (1973), *Demand for Health Insurance: A Theoretical and Empirical Investigation*, Santa Monica, RAND Corporation.

Phelps, C. E. (1983), *Taxing Health Insurance: How Much Is Enough?*, Report P–6915, Santa Monica, RAND Corporation.

Phelps, C. E. and Newhouse, J. P. (1972), 'Effects of coinsurance: a multivariate analysis', *Social Security Bulletin*, vol. 35, pp. 20–9.

Phelps, C. E. and Newhouse, J. P. (1974), 'Co-insurance and the demand for medical services', Santa Monica, RAND Corporation.

Phillips, S. J., Zeff, R. H., Kongtahworn, C., *et al.* (1982), 'Surgery for evolving myocardial infarction', *Journal of the American Medical Association*, vol. 248, pp. 1325–8.

Rawls, J. (1972), *A Theory of Justice*, Oxford, Oxford University Press.

Reder, M. W. (1965), 'Some problems in the economics of the hospital', *American Economic Review*, vol. 55, pp. 472–80.

Reindhardt, U. (1978), 'Comment on Frank A. Sloan and Roger Feldman', in Greenberg, W. (ed.), *Competition in the Health Care Sector*, Proceedings of a conference sponsored by Bureau of Economics, Federal Trade Commission, Germanstown, Aspen Systems.

Rice, R. (1966), 'An analysis of the hospital as an economic organisation', *The Modern Hospital*, vol. 106, pp. 87–91.

Rich, G., Glass, N. J. and Selkon, J. B. (1976), 'Cost-effectiveness of two methods of screening for asymptomatic bacteriuria', *British Journal of Preventive and Social Medicine*, vol. 30, pp. 54–9.

Richardson, J. (1981), 'The inducement hypothesis: that doctors generate demand for their own services', in van der Gaag, J. and Perlman, M. (eds), *Health, Economics and Health Economics*, Amsterdam, North Holland.

Roemer, R. and Shain, M. (1959), 'Hospital costs relate to the supply of beds', *The Modern Hospital*, vol. 92, pp. 71–3.

Romeder, J.-M. and McWhinnie, J. R. (1977), 'Potential years of life lost between ages 1 and 70: an indicator of premature mortality for health planning', *International Journal of Epidemiology*, vol. 6, pp. 143–51.

Rosen, S. (1974), 'Hedonic prices and implicit markets: product differentiation in price competition', *Journal of Political Economy*, vol. 82, pp. 34–55.

Rosenthal, G. (1970), 'Price elasticity of demand for short-term hospitals', in Klarman, H. E. (ed.), *Empirical Studies in Health Economics*, Baltimore, Johns Hopkins Press.

Rossett, R. N. and Huang, L. F. (1973), 'The effect of health insurance on the demand for medical care', *Journal of Political Economy*, vol. 18, pp. 281–305.

Russell, I. T., Devlin, B., Fell, M., Glass, N. J. and Newell, D. J. (1977), 'Day-case surgery for hernias and haemorrhoids: a clinical, social and economic evaluation', *The Lancet*, vol. 1, pp. 844–7.

Russell, L. B. (1986), *Is Prevention Better Than Cure?*, Washington, The Brookings Institution.

Sackett, D. L. and Torrance, G. W. (1978), 'The utility of different health states as perceived by the general public', *Journal of Chronic Disease*, vol. 31, pp. 697–704.

Schelling, T. C. (1968), 'The life you save may be your own', in Chase, S. B. (ed.), *Problems in Public Expenditure Analysis*, Washington, The Brookings Institution.

Schoemaker, P. J. H. (1982), 'The expected utility model: its variants, purposes, evidence and limitations', *Journal of Economic Literature*, vol. 20, pp. 529–63.

Schweitzer, S. O. (1974), 'Cost-effectiveness of early detection of disease', *Health Services Research*, vol. 9, pp. 22–32.

Schweitzer, S. and Rafferty, J. (1976), 'Variations in hospital product: a comparison of proprietary and voluntary hospitals', *Inquiry*, vol. 13, pp. 158–66.

Scitovsky, A. A. and McCall, N. (1977), 'Coinsurance and the demand for physician services: four years later', *Social Security Bulletin*, vol. 40, pp. 19–27.

SHHD (1977), *Scottish. Health Authorities Revenue Equalisation (SHARE)*, Edinburgh, HMSO.

Sen, A. (1970), *Collective Choice and Social Welfare*, Edinburgh, Oliver & Boyd.

Sen, A. (1977), 'Rational fools: a critique of the behavioural foundations of economic theory', *Philosophy and Public Affairs*, 6, pp. 317–44. Reprinted in Hahn, F. and Hollis, M. (eds) (1979), *Philosophy and Economic Theory*, Oxford, Oxford University Press.

Sen, A. (1982), *Choice, Welfare and Measurement*, Oxford, Basil Blackwell.

Shakotoko, R. A., Edwards, L. N. and Grossman, M. (1981), 'An exploration of the dynamic and cognitive development in adolescence', in van der Gaag, J. and Perlman, M. (eds), *Health, Economics and Health Economics*, Amsterdam, North Holland.

Simon, H. A. (1957), *Models of Man*, New York, John Wiley.

Simon, H. A. (1959), 'Theories of decision-making in economics and behavioural science', *American Economic Review*, vol. 49, pp. 797–825.

Simon, H. A. (1961), *Administrative Behavior*, New York, Macmillan.

Singer, C. and Underwood, E. A. (1962), *A Short History of Medicine* (2nd edition), Oxford, Oxford University Press.

Singer, P. (1973), 'Altruism and commerce: a defence of Titmuss and against Arrow', *Philosophy and Public Affairs*, vol. 2, pp. 314–20.

Sloan, F. (1979), 'The internal organisation of hospitals: a descriptive study', *Health Services Research*, vol. 14, pp. 203–30.

Sloan, F. A. and Feldman, R. (1978), 'Competition among physicians', in Greenberg, W. (ed.), *Competition in the Health Care Sector*, Proceedings of a conference sponsored by Bureau of Economics, Federal Trade Commission, Germanstown, Aspen Systems.

Smith, A. (1776), *An Inquiry into the Nature and Causes of the Wealth of Nations*, E. Cannan (ed.), London, Methuen, 904.

Stahl, I. (1981), 'Can equity and efficiency be combined?: the experience of the planned Swedish health care system', in Olson, M. (ed.), *A New Approach to the Economics of Health Care*, Washington, American Enterprise Institute.

Starr, P. (1981), 'Commentary on Zeckhauser and Zook', in Olson, M. (ed.), *A New Approach to the Economics of Health Care*, Washington, American Enterprise Institute.

Steinwald, B. and Sloan, F. A. (1974), 'Determinants of physician's fees', *Journal of Business*, vol. 47, pp. 493–511.

Stoddart, G. L. and Barer, M. L. (1981), 'Analysis of demand and utilisation through episodes of medical services', in van der Gaag, J. and Perlman, M. (eds), *Health, Economics and Health Economics*, Amsterdam, North Holland.

Stoddart, G. L. and Drummond, M. F. (1984), 'How to read clinical journals: VII To understand an economic evaluation (part B)', *Canadian Medical Association Journal*, vol. 130, pp. 1542–9.

Stoddart, G. L. and Labelle, R. J. (1985), *Privatization in the Canadian Health Care System: Assertions, Evidence, Ideology and Options*, Ottawa, Health and Welfare Canada.

Strull, W. M., Lo, C. and Charles, G. (1984), 'Do patients want to participate in medical decision making?', *Journal of the American Medical Association*, vol. 252, pp. 2990–4.

Sugden, R. (1981), *The Political Economy of Public Choice: An Introduction to Welfare Economics*, Oxford, Martin Robertson.

Sugden, R. (1986), 'New developments in the theory of choice under uncertainty', *Bulletin of Economic Research*, vol. 38, pp. 1–24.

Sugden, R. and Williams, A. (1978), *The Principles of Practical Cost-Benefit Analysis*, Oxford, Oxford University Press.

Tatchell, M. (1983), 'Measuring hospital output: a review of the service-mix and case-mix approaches', *Social Science and Medicine*, vol. 13, pp. 871–31.

Thaler, R. and Rosen, S. (1973), 'The value of saving a life: evidence from the labor market', in Terleckyj, N. E. (1976) (ed.), *Household Production and Consumption*, New York, National Bureau of Economic Research.

Thompson, M. S. (1986), 'Willingness to pay and accept risks to cure chronic disease', *American Journal of Public Health*, vol. 76, pp. 392–6.

Titmuss, R. M. (1970), *The Gift Relationship*, London, Allen & Unwin.

Tobin, J. (1970), 'On limiting the domain of inequality', *Journal of Law and Economics*, vol. 13, pp. 263–77.

Bibliography

Torrance, G. W. (1986), 'Measurement of health state utilities for economic appraisal', *Journal of Health Economics*, vol. 5, pp. 1–30.

Trussell, J. T. (1974), 'Cost versus effectiveness of different birth control methods', *Population Studies*, vol. 28, pp. 85–106.

Tversky, A. and Kahneman, D. (1981), 'The framing of decisions and the psychology of choice', *Science*, vol. 211, pp. 453–8.

Ulph, A. (1982), 'The role of *ex ante* and *ex post* decisions in the valuation of life', *Journal of Public Economics*, vol. 18, pp. 265–76.

Usher, D. (1975), 'Comments on "The correlation between health and schooling"', in Terleckyj, N. E. (1976) (ed.), *Household Production and Consumption*, New York, National Bureau of Economic Research.

Usher, D. (1977), 'The welfare economics of the socialization of commodities', *Journal of Public Economics*, vol. 8, pp. 151–68.

US President's Commission for the Study of Ethical Problems in Medicine and Biomedical and Behavioral Research (1983), *Securing Access to Health Care*, Washington, US Government Printing Office.

Veatch, R. M. (1981), *A Theory of Medical Ethics*, New York, Basic Books.

Veljanovski, C. (1978), 'The economics of job safety regulation: theory and evidence: part I – the market and common law', mimeo, Oxford, Centre for Socio-Legal Studies.

van de Ven, W. P. M. M. (1983), 'Effects of cost-sharing in health care', *Effective Health Care*, vol. 1, pp. 47–8.

Viscusi, W. K. (1978), 'Labor market valuations of life and limb: empirical evidence and policy implications', *Public Policy*, vol. 26, pp. 359–86.

Wadsworth, M., Butterfield, W. and Blaney, R. (1971), *Health and Sickness: The Choice of Treatment*, London, Tavistock.

Wagstaff, A. (1986a), 'The demand for health: some new empirical evidence', *Journal of Health Economics*, vol. 5, pp. 195–233.

Wagstaff, A. (1986b), 'The demand for health: a simplified Grossman model', *Journal of Epidemiology and Community Health*, vol. 40, pp. 1–11.

Ware, J. E., Brook, R. H., Rogers, W. H. *et al.* (1986), 'Comparison of health outcomes at a Health Maintenance Organisation with those of fee-for-service care', *Lancet*, May, pp. 1017–22.

Warner, K. E. and Luce, B. R. (1982), *Cost-Benefit and Cost-Effectiveness Analysis in Health Care*, Ann Arbor, Health Administration Press.

Waters, W. E. (1970), 'Controlled clinical trial of ergotamine tartrate', *British Medical Journal*, vol. ii, pp. 325–7.

Weale, A. (1983), *Political Theory and Social Policy*, London, Macmillan.

Weisbrod, B. A. (1978), 'Comment on M. V. Pauly', in Greenberg, W. (ed.), *Competition in the Health Care Sector*, Proceedings of a conference sponsored by Bureau of Economics, Federal Trade Commission, Germanstown, Aspen Systems.

Weitzman, M. L. (1974), 'Prices vs. Quantities', *Review of Economic Studies*, vol. 41, pp. 477–91.

Weitzman, M. L. (1977), 'Is the price system or rationing more effective in getting a commodity to those who need it most?', *Bell Journal of Economics*, vol. 8, pp. 517–24.

West, P. (1981), 'Theoretical and practical equity in the National Health Service in England', *Social Science and Medicine*, vol. 15C, pp. 117–22.

WHO (1961), *Constitution of the World Health Organisation: Basic Documents* (15th edition), Geneva, WHO.

Wilensky, G. R. and Rossiter, L. F. (1981), 'The magnitude and determination of physician-initiated visits in the US', in van der Gaag, J. and Perlman, M. (eds.), *Health, Economics and Health Economics*, Amsterdam, North Holland.

Wilensky, G. R. and Rossiter, L. F. (1983), 'The relative importance of physician-induced demand in the demand for medical care', *Milbank Memorial Fund Quarterly*, vol. 61, pp. 252–77.

Williams, A. (1977), 'Health service planning', in Artis, M. J. and Nobay, A. R. (eds), *Studies in Modern Economic Analysis*, Oxford, Basil Blackwell.

Williams, A. (1978), 'Need – an economic exegesis', in Culyer, A. J. and Wright, K. G. (eds), *Economic Aspects of Health Services*, Oxford, Martin Robertson.

Williams, A. (1985), 'Economics of coronary artery bypass grafting', *British Medical Journal*, vol. 291, pp. 326–9.

Williamson, O. E. (1973), 'Markets and hierarchies: some elementary considerations', *American Economic Review*, vol. 63, pp. 316–25.

Williamson, O. E. (1975), *Markets and Hierarchies: Analysis and Anti-Trust Implications*, New York, Free Press.

Winch, D. M. (1971), *Analytical Welfare Economics*, Harmondsworth, Penguin.

Yett, D. E. (1970), 'The chronic shortage of nurses: a public policy dilemma', in Klarman, H. E. (ed.), *Empirical Studies in Health Economics*, Baltimore, Johns Hopkins Press.

Index

Index